FICTIONAL TRANSFIGURATIONS
OF JESUS

FICTIONAL TRANSFIGURATIONS OF JESUS

Theodore Ziolkowski

PRINCETON, NEW JERSEY

PRINCETON UNIVERSITY PRESS

Library of Congress Catalogue card number 70-39794
ISBN 0-691-01346-2 (paperback edition)
ISBN 0-691-06235-8 (hardcover edition)

This book has been composed in Linotype Caledonia

Printed in the United States of America
by Princeton University Press, Princeton, New Jersey

First PRINCETON PAPERBACK printing, 1978

For Gretchi, Jan, and Eric

Uns überfüllts. Wir ordnens. Es zerfällt.
Wir ordnens wieder und zerfallen selbst.

Rilke, *Duineser Elegien*

Preface

A NY WORK OF ART can be regarded in one sense as a point at which innovation intersects convention or, to borrow a different image, as a moment of tension between the forces of what T. S. Eliot called "Tradition and the Individual Talent." This is not to say that a work cannot be apprehended or appreciated as an autonomous entity without reference to such extrinsic criteria as genre or theme. Yet the critic of Rilke's *Duino Elegies* who neglects to attribute any weight to the specific generic conventions of the German elegy misses as much as the reader who fails to realize that the thematic pattern of the *Odyssey* underlies Joyce's *Ulysses*. Obviously, to point out these elements in a work does not amount to an interpretation. At the same time, I believe that any valid understanding and evaluation of the work must begin by taking into account the shaping forces of convention and tradition. Scholarship that contents itself with the mere cataloguing of these factors often descends to pedantry; but criticism that purports to evaluate the work in ignorance of them rapidly reaches the other extreme of sheer impressionism. The most fruitful labor of the scholar-critic often goes on in the sensitive border area where we can observe the individual talent attempting to assert itself within or against the limitations imposed by tradition and convention.

This conviction has prompted me to bring together some twenty novels of the past century that, for all the differences among them, turn out to share a basic theme and its accompanying set of conventions: they all pattern their modern action on the life of Jesus. Chapter One proposes a provisional definition of the category that I call "fictional transfiguration," distinguishing it rigorously from other kinds of fiction involving or inspired by Jesus. Chapter Two outlines the background of intellectual history against which, in the course of the nineteenth century, this new form was first able to emerge. Chapters Three through Seven take up the twenty novels according to five groups into which, both chronologically and thematically, they seem to fall. In these central chapters it becomes clear that the traditions of theme and the conventions of form must often be radically modified to accommodate the innovations demanded by successive generations of new talents with new concerns. These chapters not only constitute a capsule history of the rise and fall of a specific literary genre; they also reflect the vagaries of society's image of the culture-hero Jesus over the past hundred years.

In Chapter Eight, which subjects the material produced by the chronological survey to a systematic analysis, I have drawn some conclusions about inherent conventions of the "fictional transfiguration of Jesus" and about the usefulness of the category for the understanding and critical evalua-tion of individual texts. I have made no attempt to deal fully and originally with each of the novels; indeed, I have grate-fully consulted the available criticism whenever possible. But it is my argument that none of these works can be seen in the proper perspective if the shaping force of the fic-tional transfiguration is ignored or misunderstood. I would like to think that this book might provide a useful model of at least one possibility for bringing the study of convention and innovation—that is, literary history and criticism—to-gether in a methodologically consistent manner.

Any reader with the patience to follow my argument to its conclusion will discover that this book itself is ultimately adduced as symptomatic of a generation that, having no strong religious ties, has come to regard the figure of Jesus with an aesthetic detachment bound by few preconceptions of doctrine or denomination. Like the writers discussed in Chapter Seven, I became acquainted with the Bible, and specifically with the Gospel story, as a cultural possession rather than as an item of faith. Even in our secularized so-ciety, of course, one does not grow up wholly innocent of the principal Bible stories: Cecil B. De Mille has seen to that. But it is the rare individual under fifty who can claim to be *bibelfest* in the sense of earlier generations. It is characteristic that our schools today, while they often teach classical mythology or the ceremonial rites of primitive tribes, rarely deal in any systematic fashion with that pervasive Judaeo-Christian *matière* that constituted until recently the core of most Western culture. In any case, I was permitted to get through school and college with an irresponsibly casual acquaintance with the Bible; and my conversations with students and colleagues have not persuaded me that my own experience was in any way unique.

Similarly, I was familiar with the postfigurative technique of *Ulysses* and *Doctor Faustus* long before my study of Hesse's *Demian* first made it clear to me that the life of Jesus could also be used as the model for a modern novel and that the Gospels, therefore, deserved the same kind of critical attention that we readily give to Greek myth, Germanic legend, Jungian archetypes, or—most recently—anthropological "structures." After *Demian*, the first "fictional transfiguration" that I consciously identified as such, I happened to read Hauptmann's *Emanuel Quint* and Faulkner's *A Fable* in quick succession. At that point it began to dawn on me that these "fictional transfigurations" might be far more than the isolated cases as which they have usually been treated in scholarship and criticism—that they might, in fact, constitute a literary genre that had never been adequately defined.

For several years I read casually, collecting random fictional examples as I stumbled across them, studying the Bible carefully for the first time, and exposing myself to some of the more important New Testament scholarship of the past century. In the spring of 1970, about a year after I had begun to perceive certain patterns in my material, I had the opportunity of systematizing and refining my ideas when I used them as the basis for a Senior Seminar that I devoted to this topic at Princeton. If the book has achieved any lucidity of exposition or any plausibility of argument, then I am indebted in no small measure to the bright and critical young men and women who forced me to explain myself and my categories and who encouraged me with their own enthusiasm.

It would be futile to aspire to bibliographical completeness in any undertaking of this sort. Two relevant novels appeared in the fall of 1970, just as I was trying to complete my manuscript; and a new one may be published next week. (For that reason I have chosen 1970 as an arbitrary cut-off date.) And there are no doubt other fictional transfigurations that neither luck, systematic bibliographical combing, nor the suggestions of friends have brought to my attention. But I hope that my examples are extensive enough to lay claim to a certain representative validity. It has been my intention to define a literary category that has not been adequately recognized before; to account for its appearance; and to outline its history. If the category is viable, then other works should easily fit into the general pattern that I have suggested.

Many friends, colleagues, and students have heard me out with patience and responded with generous suggestions. I am specifically grateful to my colleague Albert Sonnenfeld for calling my attention to Carlo Coccioli, to my brother-in-law Robert Bonfield for urging me to read *491*, and to Professor Peter Bien for his bibliographical assistance in connection with Kazantzakis. It is a pleasure to express my thanks again to my friend Miriam Brokaw of Princeton University Press for her continuing interest in my work. George Robinson's enthusiasm and, above all, his knowledgeability regarding my topic enabled him to handle both author and text with supreme editorial tact. Finally, I am indebted as always to Yetta for never permitting uxorial partiality to interfere with her frankness or her critical sensibilities.

THEODORE ZIOLKOWSKI

Princeton, New Jersey
September 1971

Contents

FICTIONAL TRANSFIGURATIONS
OF JESUS

1. Fictional Transfiguration
A Working Definition

ROUGHLY three quarters of the way through Thomas Mann's *The Magic Mountain* (1924), Clawdia Chauchat reappears at the International Sanatorium Berghof in the company of the Dutch plantation-owner Pieter Peeperkorn. Three or four weeks after their arrival Hans Castorp is formally introduced to Mynheer Peeperkorn, who takes an immediate liking to the young hero and decides to celebrate the occasion with an impromptu party. Hans Castorp is dispatched to round up some of the other patients for a few hands of cards—hence the chapter heading "Vingt et un." After several hours of wine and games the wealthy old gentleman orders food for the group: first a generous cold buffet, which he promptly dismisses as "frippery" and "garbage"; then a more substantial *omelette aux fines herbes*, consumed along with glasses of Dutch gin, a beverage that Peeperkorn half-jocularly eulogizes as "bread." At this point Peeperkorn engages Hans Castorp in their first real conversation, if we can call it a conversation when one participant utters cryptically profound incoherencies that the other merely recapitulates in nicely articulated, tidy little sentences. This conversation begins with praise of the simple pleasures of life—food, drink, sex—and gradually crescendos into an astonishing revelation of the aging Dutchman's despair at the subsiding of his life forces. When Madame Chauchat interrupts their *tête-à-tête* to point out that the other guests are bored, Peeperkorn rouses himself out of his gloom to send for another round of refreshments, this time champagne and sweets, topped off with coffee and liqueurs. Finally, at two o'clock in the morning, the gathering, which by now has sunk into a drunken stupor after some six hours of revelry, breaks up at the rumor that the director of the sanatorium is wrathfully approaching.

This brilliant scene is memorable largely because here, for the first time, the reader is exposed directly to the bacchantic force of Peeperkorn's majestic personality. Despite all his incoherent ramblings, the formidable old man is revealed as a presence capable of dominating any group. With a single compelling gesture he is able to put far more eloquent figures in the shadow. Yet various clues alert us to another dimension of the nocturnal spree. For Peeperkorn is more than a stumbling Bacchus who must be helped to his room by his solicitous companions; he is more than a parodistic conglomerate of features borrowed from Gerhart Hauptmann. He turns out also to be Jesus at the Last Supper.

We first become aware of the parallels when we calculate that twelve people sit down at the huge table. If we include the dwarfish servant girl who runs in and out with food and drink—and include her we must, for she will be the Judas who circulates the rumor of the director's approach—we find a precise numerical correspondence to Jesus and the twelve disciples. (Hans Castorp—Johannes—is of course "the disciple whom Jesus loved.") Then we note other traits that, taken separately, seem innocuous enough but, collectively, contribute to the composite image. Five times in the course of the evening Peeperkorn admonishes the gathering with the raised index finger that is familiar as an iconographic motif in scores of paintings of the Teaching Jesus or, particularly, the seated Christ in Majesty. His great head is encircled with a fiery nimbus of white hair. And when Peeperkorn orates on such secular matters as food and sex, he reverts to a vocabulary that is conspicuously reminiscent of the Bible. Thus, regarding himself as "God's own wedding organ," he calls the diminution of his sexual powers *Weltuntergang* ("Judgment Day"), a term that the startled Hans Castorp cannot recall having ever heard uttered outside of his catechism classes in school. It occurs to Hans Castorp, in fact, that Peeperkorn displays true "biblical grandeur," and, appropriately enough, within minutes

4

the old reprobate is quoting the Gospels. When Peeperkorn attempts to stir his guests from their lethargy, he cites Jesus' words to his sleeping disciples. "The flesh, ladies and gentlemen, is simply—never mind! No, permit me: 'weak.' Thus it is written in the Scriptures." And he concludes his reproval with a moving paraphrase of the scene in Gethsemane. It is this "appalling example of Peter and his brethren" that shames the group into a last burst of frenetic gaiety. When the party finally breaks up, "betrayed" by the weary servant girl who wants only to get to bed, Peeperkorn's last words are "Judgment Day—Gethsemane."

What we see here goes far beyond a humorous pairing of Jesus and Dionysos for the delectation of readers with a taste for subtle blasphemy. The entire scene, which revolves around the poignant disclosure of Peeperkorn's anxiety of death, is based closely on the passages in the New Testament in which Jesus, after sharing the Last Supper with his disciples, suffers agonies of fear while his followers slumber in the garden of Gethsemane. The Passion of Jesus, in other words, is invoked to add structure as well as an ironic dimension of meaning to a single specific episode in the novel. Our pleasure of recognition is heightened when we recall other details that fit the same pattern. Peeperkorn arrives at the sanatorium shortly after the beginning of Advent; Hans Castorp first meets him and pays tribute to him around Christmas; and the old man dies not long after Easter. Peeperkorn's final appearance in the novel—the picnic at the waterfall—is described in terms that clearly recall the agony on the cross: he is specifically called "an image of the Man of Sorrows" (*Schmerzensmann* is a technical term, in art history and elsewhere, for the suffering Jesus); and his last recorded word is *erledigt*, which, though not precisely the biblical phrase *Es ist vollbracht*, unmistakably means "It is finished." The scene in Peeperkorn's bedroom just after his suicide, moreover, evokes unmistakable associations with a conventional Lamentation tableau.

Thomas Mann's chapter provides us, for purposes of initial discrimination, with a representative example of what this book means by "fictional transfiguration." It is a fictional narrative in which the characters and the action, irrespective of meaning or theme, are prefigured to a noticeable extent by figures and events popularly associated with the life of Jesus as it is known from the Gospels. That is, in this instance we recognize Peeperkorn as a "Jesus figure" not because of what he says or any doctrine that he preaches; in fact, he is virtually inarticulate—his most impressive "sermon" consists of a rhetoric of gestures before a thundering waterfall—and his beliefs are more Dionysian than Christlike. But the action, the imagery, and the organization of the scene identify him beyond any doubt as a "transfigured" Jesus: the supper of "bread" and wine, his "halo" and gestures, his agony in the midst of dozing disciples, his "betrayal," and so forth.

In the following chapters it will be our purpose to inquire whether or not the fictional transfiguration, as we have tentatively defined it, constitutes a useful literary category. Our procedure is dictated to a great extent by the paradox of the hermeneutic circle. With our provisional definition in hand we shall ransack modern literature in the hope of finding other works it fits. We shall use these works, in turn, to test and modify our definition. As we proceed, we might keep certain basic questions in mind. It will be useful to find out, first of all, whether this category can be clearly distinguished from other fictional treatments of Jesus with which, in criticism, it has hitherto been jumbled together. We will want to determine, in addition, whether the category has a history. Did it arise as the response to a specific set of circumstances? Has it undergone discernible transformations? Finally, if it is indeed a viable category, what are the common features and techniques that characterize it?

Many readers will already have noted that what I have provisionally called the "fictional transfiguration" constitutes a specific branch of a larger category of novels that can be defined quite precisely as "postfigurative" since their action is "prefigured" in a familiar mythic pattern. The term "transfiguration" is useful and suggestive inasmuch as it is etymologically recognizable as a cognate of "postfiguration" and, at the same time, culturally associated specifically with Jesus.

Twentieth-century literature abounds with postfigurative novels.[1] The most famous example and the one most often cited as a model is unquestionably James Joyce's *Ulysses* (1922), in which a modern Odysseus is set adrift in the Dublin of 1904, where he re-enacts the adventures of the Homeric epic. But many other authors have exploited the same general technique and even the same particular myth. Hans-Erich Nossack, for instance, sends his Odyssean wanderer into an underworld that resembles the bombed-out Hamburg after the holocaust of World War II (*Nekyia: Bericht eines Überlebenden*, 1947). Thomas Mann's Faustian composer, Adrian Leverkühn, acts out the life of the Reformation hero in Weimar Germany (*Doktor Faustus*, 1947), while John Hersey's undergraduate Faust—John Fist—goes through the same classic paces in an Ivy League college of the sixties (*Too Far to Walk*, 1966). In *The Centaur* (1962), John Updike updates the myth of Chiron in the unlikely setting of a contemporary American high school. Alfred Döblin chose postwar England as the scene for his modern *Hamlet* (*Hamlet, oder die lange Nacht nimmt ein Ende*, 1956). Paul Schallück has reincarnated Cervantes' hidalgo—this time on a bicycle—in the Federal Republic of Germany (*Don Quichotte in Köln*, 1967). And Sheila MacLeod, in *The Snow-White Soliloquies* (1970), has transposed the familiar old fairy tale into a contemporary European setting. These are but a representative few of the numerous postfigurations of Don Juan, Prometheus,

---

[1] John J. White, "Myths and Patterns in the Modern Novel," *Mosaic*, 2 (1969), 42-55. See also White's *Mythology in the Modern Novel: A Study of Prefigurative Techniques* (Princeton, N.J.: Princeton Univ. Press, 1972).

7

Perceval, Orpheus, and other mythic heroes who drift through modern fiction—not to mention modern poetry, drama, and cinema. Every reader will recall his own favorite examples.[2]

In *The Magic Mountain* Thomas Mann has done with Jesus precisely what Joyce did with Odysseus: viewing Jesus' life as a pattern of action that can be divorced or abstracted from any meaning it may once have embodied, he has taken this pattern as the basis for an entirely modern plot. In all these cases—the transfigurations of Jesus as well as the postfigurations of other myths—the structure of action establishes the parallel between the original source and the modern counterpart: the meaning can range from a serious reinterpretation to the most blatant parody. It is the similarity, indeed, the identity of their common prefigurative pattern, that permits us to put into a single category a group of twentieth-century novels as diverse in quality and substance as Gerhart Hauptmann's *The Fool in Christ Emanuel Quint* and John Steinbeck's *The Grapes of Wrath*, Hermann Hesse's *Demian* and Ignazio Silone's *Bread and Wine*, Nikos Kazantzakis' *The Greek Passion* and William Faulkner's *A Fable*, or Gore Vidal's *Messiah* and Günter Grass's *Cat and Mouse*. In some of them the pattern is so obtrusive as to be tediously allegorical; in others it is subtle to the point of being overlooked by the casual reader. But all of these novels, along with others that will be discussed, are based to a determining degree on the events of the Gospels.

It cannot be stressed enough that the parallels are essentially formal, not ideological. The modern hero whose life

[2] E.g., W. B. Stanford, *The Ulysses Theme: A Study in the Adaptability of a Traditional Hero* (Oxford: Blackwell, 1954); André Dabezies, *Visages de Faust au XXe siècle: Littérature, Idéologie, et Mythes* (Paris: Presses universitaires de France, 1967); Leo Weinstein, *The Metamorphoses of Don Juan* (Stanford, Cal.: Stanford Univ. Press, 1959). Elisabeth Frenzel, *Stoffe der Weltliteratur*, 2nd ed. (Stuttgart: Kröner, 1963), provides a comprehensive bibliography of thematological studies.

is prefigured by the life of Jesus may occasionally be a good or even Christlike man; but, as we shall see, he may also be an obsessed paranoid, a Nietzschean élitist, an atheistic Party functionary, or a scheming opportunist. The distinction has occasionally been noted: "The Christ figure of modern literature in his moral actions often does not reflect Christ at all. The writer is free, of course, to make whatever he wishes of the Christ figure, but the writer's beliefs will determine the significance of his imagery and symbolism."[3] But all too often the distinction is overlooked by critics, who tend to speak loosely of "christological" themes in literature when they actually mean that a work is transfigurative in form, or to refer interchangeably to Jesus-figures and Christ-figures.

We are concerned primarily with the pattern of events that characterizes the life of Jesus as recorded in its most familiar source, and only secondarily with the *kerygma*—the meaning conventionally attributed to those events by Christian faith. I do not wish to suggest that these novels were written in a spiritual vacuum. Very often they are inspired with a strong sense of Christian mission; and even when the author is prompted by hostility toward institutionalized Christianity, the motivating impulse might be called generally "religious." But understanding of the kerygmatic Christ is qualified very much by historical circumstances, while the life of Jesus—at least the record of that life in the Gospels—remains constant. As a result, we shall find that "meaning" is useful mainly for establishing differences—that is, for distinguishing between various groups of novels. But to the extent that we want to define a useful literary category, it will be necessary to focus our attention primarily on the common denominator that transcends the historical shifts in meaning and that is accessible of aesthetic analysis: their form. In other words, our

---

[3] Vincent Ferrer Blehl, S.J., "Literature and Religious Belief," in *Mansions of the Spirit: Essays in Literature and Religion*, ed. George A. Panichas (New York: Hawthorn Books, 1967), p. 111.

9

criteria are furnished by Jesus in his capacity as the mythic figure or culture-hero whose life consisted of a series of traditionally associated motifs or mythologems: baptism, temptation, gathering of disciples, performing of various "miracles," proclaiming a new way of life, a last supper, lonely agony, betrayal, trial, and crucifixion. (The resurrection, of course, intrudes into the realm of Christian faith: the historical Jesus was crucified, but only the kerygmatic Christ of faith was resurrected.)

That recognizable aesthetic shapes exist quite independently of any "meaning" with which they are burdened may be easier to accept, perhaps, in such ostensibly "value-free" media as music and painting than in literature. The process that we have been discussing is familiar to musicologists under the label *contrafactum*. Music from the thirteenth to the seventeenth century is filled with secular songs—medieval courtly poetry or folksongs—that were appropriated by the Church for religious purposes; a song in praise of one's earthly beloved was adapted, quite simply, into a hymn to the Virgin. This process, whereby the original form is invested with a totally new sense, has a counterpart in the phenomenon known to art historians as iconotropy: an iconographic motif is detached from the thematic values that it customarily embodies and is used in a wholly new context. Just as the musician-poet converted secular music to churchly ends, the medieval illustrator adapted classical motifs to Christian themes: for instance, the classic pose of Hercules dragging Cerberus out of Hades provided the model for paintings of Jesus pulling Adam out of Limbo.[4]

During the later Middle Ages and the Renaissance the direction of this movement was, for the most part, from the secular to the religious. Toward the end of the eighteenth

[4] Erwin Panofsky, "Iconography and Iconology: An Introduction to the Study of Renaissance Art," in *Meaning in the Visual Arts*, by Erwin Panofsky (Garden City, N. Y.: Doubleday-Anchor, 1955), pp. 26-54.

century the trend was reversed as painters began to exploit the emotive connotations associated with various conventional Christian poses in order to enhance their wholly secular subjects. Benjamin West counted on the fact that any viewer looking at *The Death of General Wolfe* (1770) would instantly recognize, in the disposition of the figures, the underlying pattern of the Lamentation over the dead Jesus, a motif familiar from scores of paintings. Similarly *The Death of Nelson*, as painted by West and others, arouses equally clear associations with the Deposition of the body of Jesus.[5] David's *The Death of Socrates* (1787) depicts a remarkably Jesus-like Socrates, with index-finger raised, preparing to drink his last cup in the midst of precisely twelve disciples. And Delacroix's *The Death of Lara* (1847) employs the classic pose of the *pietà* to lend additional pathos to a theme taken from Byron. In all these cases the painter achieves two goals by using conventional iconographic motifs: the classic pose supplies the basic spatial organization for the painting (e.g., the number and disposition of the figures), and the associations aroused by the pattern expand the implications of the painting from its specific historical subject to a more universal validity. Precisely the same process took place in music, of course: jazz, for instance, was created in part through a secularization of spiritual hymns.

By analogy, we are concerned here with novels in which the life of Jesus has been wholly secularized: it prefigures the life of a fictional character to such a pronounced extent that it determines the structure of entire episodes (as in *The Magic Mountain*) or, indeed, of entire novels. This pattern is not always obvious; in fact, from the end of the nineteenth to the middle of the twentieth century the pattern, in fiction, becomes increasingly subtle and less overt. But

[5] Charles Mitchell, "Benjamin West's *Death of Nelson*," in *Essays in the History of Art Presented to Rudolf Wittkower*, ed. Douglas Frazer, Howard Hibbard, and Milton J. Lewine (London: Phaidon, 1967), pp. 265-73.

the reader who recognizes the pattern—like the viewer of a painting or the hearer of the music—is vouchsafed an additional aesthetic pleasure as well as an often unexpected dimension of meaning that ranges from premonitions of tragedy to the titillations of blasphemy.

Now some thoughtful critics have argued that such fictional transfigurations of Jesus are doomed to failure by their very nature: the action is prescribed at the outset; the tragic outcome is inevitable; the imitation must necessarily fall short of the original.[6] It is easy to understand these objections, for they have been voiced primarily by critics writing from an acquaintance with the generally rather depressing catalogue of transfigurational works in English. In principle, however, we cannot accept the argument, for it amounts—if we press it to its logical conclusion—to a denial of the possibility of postfigurative fiction altogether, and that is of course nonsense. If Thomas Mann had been discouraged by the prescriptive limitations of the plot, he would never have begun *Doctor Faustus*. If Joyce had accepted the contention that the modern version must fall short of the original, he would never have undertaken *Ulysses*. And the claim that the outcome is inevitably tragic fails to take into account the broad spectrum of possible variations, ranging from the tragic through the critical to the comical, that make this category potentially fascinating. In addition, we should recognize the fact that some writers, just as they willingly submit themselves to the discipline of such strict poetic forms as the sonnet, are stimulated by the challenge of being original within the framework of the

---

[6] Alan Paton and Liston Pope, "The Novelist and Christ," *Saturday Review of Literature*, December 4, 1954, pp. 15-16 and 56-59; John Killinger, *The Failure of Theology in Modern Literature* (New York-Nashville: Abingdon, 1963), p. 48; R.W.B. Lewis, *The Picaresque Saint: Representative Figures in Contemporary Fiction* (1959; rpt. New York: Lippincott-Keystone, 1961), p. 215. Lewis expresses his reservations in connection with Faulkner's *A Fable*; when he discusses Silone's *Bread and Wine* and Graham Greene's *The Power and the Glory* he seems implicitly to credit the form with more viability.

most familiar story in Western culture. But before we turn to our primary task of analyzing works within the category, we should first attempt systematically to distinguish the "transfigurations" of Jesus from four other categories of fiction with which they are often confused: the fictionalizing biography; *Jesus redivivus*; the *imitatio Christi*; and "pseudonyms" of Christ.[7]

The often sensationally successful fictionalizing biographies can be divided into two principal groups, but they both have one thing in common that sets them apart from the transfigurations: their subject is the historical Jesus, not a modern hero whose life is merely prefigured by Jesus. The "modern apocrypha," first of all, take in a middle ground between scholarship, fiction, and literary forgery: they purport to be original documents, newly discovered, that cast fresh light on the life of Jesus—notably on the so-called Silent Years from twelve to thirty, about which the Gospels say nothing.[8] One of the most influential of these apocrypha was the "Unknown Life" (*La vie inconnue de Jésus Christ*) that Nicolas Notovitch published in 1894. Notovitch, a Russian war correspondent who visited India and Tibet in 1887, claimed to have discovered in a Himalayan monastery an ancient "Life of Saint Issa, Best of the Sons of Men." According to the fourteen chapters of this work, Issa (Jesus) as a teenager journeyed to India, where he studied the teachings of Buddha; on his way back to Jerusalem he stopped in Persia to preach to the Zoroastrians. Notovitch's book was merely the most successful of a genre that followed generally the same pattern. Levi H. Dowling's *Aquarian Gospel of Jesus the Christ* (1908), which still finds avid readers in theosophical circles, is nothing but an

[7] I have intentionally omitted the category defined by Horton Davies, *A Mirror of the Ministry in Modern Novels* (New York: Oxford, 1959). Davies is concerned solely with heroes who are in fact clergymen, and his examples only rarely overlap with the fictional transfiguration.

[8] Edgar J. Goodspeed, *Modern Apocrypha* (Boston: Beacon, 1956).

elaboration of the same basic formula. Here, following his years among the Buddhists, Jesus goes to Tibet, where he meets the sage Meng-ste. After visiting the Magi in Persia, he passes through Assyria and Babylonia on his way to Greece, where he preaches to the Athenians and consults the Delphic oracle. He is ordained by the Seven Sages of Alexandria before he finally returns to Jerusalem to carry out his mission. According to still another of these apocrypha, published by Ernst von der Planitz—the spurious letter allegedly written by Benan, a priest at Memphis (*Der Benan-Brief*, 1910)—Jesus won his reputation as a great healer while studying medicine in Egypt. This activity brought him in touch with the Therapeutae, a group of Essenes who practiced healing. It was the High Priest of the Jewish temple in Egypt who ultimately confirmed Jesus in his mission, sending him to teach and heal his people in Jerusalem.

Apart from these more exotic fantasies, every generation produces lives of Jesus adapted to the circumstances and tastes of the times. Around A.D. 300, for instance, the Spanish priest Juvencus cast the life of Jesus into the form of a classical epic poem of three thousand verses (*Historiae evangelicae libri quattuor*). A few centuries later the author of the Old Saxon *Heliand* (c. A.D. 830) sought in some six thousand alliterating lines to make the figure of Jesus comprehensible to a Low German audience emerging from paganism. Incidents not in keeping with the Germanic concept of honor and dignity were simply omitted; Jesus appears as the warrior-hero of a heroic epic, surrounded by his loyal vassals. Many modern fictionalizing lives which simply retell the Gospel story in contemporary terms are motivated by precisely the same spirit. In his *Story of Christ* (*Storia di Cristo*, 1921), which was enormously popular in a dozen languages, Giovanni Papini frankly set out to write "a book by a layman for laymen." Basing his work on the four Gospels, he produced a no-nonsense biography in ninety-six impressionistic scenes, of which the first is typical: "Jesus was born in a stall. A stall. A real stall, and not the dainty portico that Christian painters have constructed for the Son of David." In his introduction "To the Reader" Papini concedes that no life of Jesus can be more beautiful and perfect than the Gospels. "But who, today, reads the Evangelists?" Since each generation has its own concerns, he argues, it is necessary to retranslate the Gospels into their terms. This approach to the New Testament differs in quality, but not in kind, from the fictionalizing reportage of such writers as Jim Bishop, who sets out to describe *The Day Christ Died* (1957) just as a contemporary journalist might have reported the day's news from Jerusalem. In a pretense at journalistic accuracy Bishop deals hour by hour with the period between Jesus' arrival in Jerusalem (6:00 P.M. on Thursday) and his deposition from the cross (4:00 P.M. the following afternoon). He claims to have added nothing to the facts: "The fundamental research was done a long time ago by four fine journalists: Matthew, Mark, Luke and John" (p. 9). But from the very first sentence he moves beyond objectivity into the fictional recreation of events: "They came through the pass slowly, like men reluctant to finish a journey."

The whole thrust of these works is to produce a Poor Man's Jesus, as it were, a Gospel reduced to the lowest common denominator of the times and put into terms that require no effort of the imagination. In his preachy novel *Holyland* (*Hilligenlei*, 1905) Gustav Frenssen interpolated a lengthy account of the life of Jesus in which he equated Jerusalem geographically with Schleswig-Holstein (both are heath countries with a long sea coast and a great city in the South) and portrayed Jesus' mission in terms of the political strife of Wilhelmine Germany. From Frenssen, Papini, and Bishop it is but a short step to those fictionalizing biographies that have added nothing to the Gospel account but the author's own modernizing psychology or point of view: Emil Ludwig's *The Son of Man* (*Der Menschensohn: Geschichte eines Propheten*, 1928), John

15

Erskine's *The Human Life of Jesus* (1945), Frank G. Slaughter's *The Crown and the Cross* (1959), Robert Payne's *The Shepherd* (1959), and countless others in many languages.

The two most brilliant fictionalizing biographies of the last twenty-five years have emerged, respectively, from the modern apocrypha and the "lives for laymen," but they transcend the average by the radicality of their approach and method: Robert Graves's *King Jesus* (1946) and Nikos Kazantzakis' *The Last Temptation of Christ* (1953). Graves's Jesus turns out to be the legitimate pretender to the throne of Jerusalem because he is the child of a secret wedding of Mary and Antipater before Mary was betrothed to the carpenter Joseph. In his "Historical Commentary" Graves assures the reader that "every important element in the story is based on some tradition, however tenuous" and that he has taken "more than ordinary pains to verify the historical background." The book aspires, in fact, to be a new scholarly interpretation of the life of Jesus. But it is turned into fiction by Graves's "analeptic method," which puts the story into the words of a Hellenist historian writing around A.D. 93. Kazantzakis' novel takes a different approach. Making no use of unusual scholarly evidence, the author achieves a bold new vision through the originality of his view. "That part of Christ's nature which was profoundly human," Kazantzakis notes in his prologue, "helps us to understand him and love him and to pursue his Passion as though it were our own." Through the sheer power of imagination Kazantzakis reconstructs, as the last temptation that he suffered, Jesus' vision of a parallel life to the one recounted in the Gospels—a life in which he falls in love, marries, has children, and lives to a ripe old age. It is this vision that Jesus must repudiate when he decides to die on the cross: "Every moment of Christ's life is a conflict and a victory. He conquered the invincible enchantment of simple human pleasures. . . ."

One of the great difficulties encountered by the authors

of fictionalizing biographies stems from the paucity of incident supplied by the Gospel narrative. Graves met this difficulty with a mass of recondite historical detail and Kazantzakis with the creative power of imagination and psychological understanding. For the most part, however, the fictionalizing biographies have not been works of literary distinction. Generally speaking, they have been more interesting as fiction when the figure of Jesus is not presented directly by the author, but is seen only indirectly or peripherally through the eyes of another character: Lew Wallace's *Ben-Hur: A Tale of the Christ* (1880), George Moore's *The Brook Kerith: A Syrian Story* (1916), Shalom Asch's *The Nazarene* (1939), Lloyd C. Douglas's *The Big Fisherman* (1948), Pär Lagerkvist's *Barabbas* (1950), Gertrud von le Fort's *The Wife of Pilate* (*Die Frau des Pilatus*, 1955), or Taylor Caldwell's *Great Lion of God* (1970).

As we move from the fictionalizing biographies toward the fictional transfigurations, we encounter that curious category that might be called *Jesus redivivus*: stories set in modern times, in which—miraculously—the historical Jesus appears.[9] In Balzac's tale of "Jesus Christ in Flanders" ("Jésus-Christ en Flandre," 1831) a mysterious stranger saves the passengers from a ferry foundering off Ostend: the faithful are able to follow him across the waters, while the skeptics go down with the ship.

A more elaborate example was written fifteen years later by Alphonse Louis Constant (1810-75), who later became famous under the pseudonym Eliphas Lévi as the author of a celebrated *History of Magic* (1860). Before his turn to occultism, Constant was an advocate of the semi-mystical socialism of Charles Fourier, and he wrote *The Last Incarnation* (*La Dernière Incarnation*, 1846) in order to ad-

[9] Frank P. Bowman, "On the Definition of Jesus in Modern Fiction," *Anales Galdosianos*, 2 (1967), 53-66, refers briefly to this category under the heading "Jesus revived."

17

vance his notions on such topics as profit sharing and women's rights, including an attack on the corruption of the modern Church. "We have now to offer these legends to all our brothers who labor with us upon the social edifice," he announced in the Epilogue.[10] "We have not had the intention of writing a new gospel, but we have endeavored to apply to the diseases of modern society the always powerful virtue of the ancient gospel spirit, by making the Christ speak as we think he would speak, should he again come among us." The book consists of nineteen "legends" in which Jesus, in order to instruct men, assumes the appearance of childhood, of weakness, of suffering. "I shall go through all the phases of life in my appearances," he tells the Virgin Mary, "and will transfigure myself as my doctrine must be transfigured" (p. 26). Following roughly the sequence of the Gospels, this *Jesus redivivus* witnesses "The Martyrdom of the Innocents" in the "horrible industrial purgatory" of the nineteenth century. Taking a job as an apprentice carpenter in a shipyard, he outlines his theory of socialism to the other workers. He defends "The Daughters of Magdalen" and advocates the emancipation of women in "The New Adulterous Woman." In "The Heirs of Pilate" he chastises a virtuous merchant who, while serving on a jury, acquiesces in a false verdict. And in his "Sermon on the Plains" he urges the workers to be strong, intelligent, just and—above all—to unite.

The most famous example of this type occurs in the Fifth Book of Dostoevsky's *The Brothers Karamazov* (1880), where Ivan shares with a startled Alyosha his account of "The Grand Inquisitor." Here Christ returns to earth in Seville during the Inquisition. Greeted enthusiastically by the people, he performs various miracles and expounds his teaching. Soon, however, he is imprisoned by the Grand Inquisitor who, in a renowned colloquy, points out to Christ

[10] I have not seen the original; I refer to the "3rd American edition" (no translator mentioned) with a Preface by Charles H. Kohlmann (Boston: Gorham, 1914).

the fundamental error of his teaching and its inadequacy for the present: men do not wish the freedom of choice offered by Christ; they seek rather the peace of mind and security vouchsafed by an authoritarian Church.

Toward the end of the nineteenth century the theme of *Jesus redivivus* showed up all over Europe in a variety of forms. In Gerhart Hauptmann's dramatic tear-jerker *The Assumption of Hannele* (*Hanneles Himmelfahrt*, 1895) a village schoolmaster is apotheosized into an image of Jesus in the eyes of the dying heroine. During these same years (1896-98) Rilke wrote the eleven poems of a cycle entitled *Visions of Christ* (*Christus: Elf Visionen*), in which Jesus appears to comfort a child mourning over the grave of its mother ("The Orphan"), strolls through the arcades of a modern city ("Venice"), and berates an artist for depicting him as a weak pauper rather than in regal glory ("The Painter").

Rilke was inspired by the paintings of Fritz von Uhde (1848-1911), who executed a well-known series depicting the historical Jesus in various contemporary settings (e.g., *Let the Children Come Unto Me*; *The Last Supper*). In one of his most popular paintings, *Come, Lord Jesus, Be Thou Our Guest* (1885), Jesus, with flowing locks and gown, enters a worker's home that could be a stage setting for one of Hauptmann's naturalistic dramas or, even more aptly, a scene from Max Kretzer's sensational novel *The Vision of Christ* (*Das Gesicht Christi*, 1897), which places Jesus in the tenement districts of Berlin in the nineties. Kretzer's story deals with the family of the unemployed worker Andorf. Circumstances bring Andorf repeatedly close to despair and atheism—his family is starving, one of his children dies, his daughter is almost violated by her employer, and so forth. But always in the nick of time Jesus turns up, and Andorf's faith is restored. Kretzer wrote his book in such a way that the events can be explained as a case of mass hallucination: from Easter Eve until Easter Monday people all over Berlin see Jesus walking around the city in his traditional garb, performing good deeds and punishing scoffers. But the basic impulse of the book reflects the mysticism that was fashionable around the turn of the century.

The *Jesus redivivus* is by no means an exclusively European phenomenon. Archibald McCowan's novel *Christ, the Socialist* (1894) includes an interpolated story in which Jesus, appearing on the steps of the New York City Hall, berates the scribes and pharisees of modern society: "And ye corporations, which fatten at the expense of the whole people! Ye make slaves of your brethren, yet ye begrudge payment of their honest wages" (p. 351). A curious analogy to McCowan's novel can be seen in the muckraking report *If Christ Came to Chicago* (1894) by the English journalist and social reformer, William T. Stead. Stead's book was published with a cover-illustration depicting Jesus driving the money-changers from the Temple; but the merchants' faces were easily recognizable as those of Chicago business and political leaders. Today it is difficult to judge whether the seventy thousand copies sold on the day of publication were bought by indignant Christians or by those who simply wanted to obtain the closely annotated "Black List of Property Used for Immoral Purposes" appended to Stead's volume. The following year Edward Everett Hale published a semi-fictional response to Stead entitled *If Jesus Came to Boston* (1895). Reasoning that Jesus could have seen whorehouses and saloons in Jerusalem, Hale leads him around Boston and introduces him to the heads of the various charitable organizations.

This odd sub-genre has survived from the mid-nineteenth century right down to the present. The best known version in English was undoubtedly J. K. Jerome's play *The Passing of the Third Floor Back* (1908)—based on Jerome's own short story—in which Jesus takes a room in a London boarding house and works miraculous changes in the lives of all the tenants. In 1911 Betty Winter wrote a novel (*Unser Heiland ist arm geblieben*) to show what would happen if Jesus should be introduced into the aristocratic circles of a Strauss-waltz Vienna.

Upton Sinclair's "Tale of the Second Coming," *They Call Me Carpenter* (1922), goes into more allegorical detail than most of these works. The narrator, coming out of a performance of *The Cabinet of Dr. Caligari*, is beaten up by a mob picketing the "Hun" film and retreats to a nearby church, where he falls unconscious; the bulk of the novel, in which Jesus returns to earth in an American city bearing a strong resemblance to Hollywood, is presumably his vision or dream. The figure of Jesus steps down from the stained glass window of the church and enters the affairs of Western City for a few days. Calling himself Mr. Carpenter, Jesus begins by supporting the local tailors' union in a strike. In the course of his activities he is joined by a group of characters including Matthew Everett, the secretary of a movie mogul; Mark Abell, the secretary of the local socialist party; Luka Korwsky, the secretary of the Tailors' Union; and John Colver, a poet and Wobbly agitator. The cast is rounded out by such figures as Mary Magna, the film diva. Because of his growing notoriety as "the Bolsheviki Prophet," Carpenter runs afoul of the Ku Klux Klan and the American Legion. Eventually arrested for disturbing the peace—he is betrayed by a secret agent of the American Legion posing as one of his disciples—he is scheduled to be tried in Judge Ponty's court. But weary by this time of modern civilization, the harassed Jesus rushes back to the church and climbs back up into the sanctuary of his stained glass window.

The effect of this genre depends in large measure upon the intentional anachronism, the glaring incongruity between past and present. For this reason the device has also been popular with artists. During the expressionist period, for instance, Georg Grosz painted his well-known *Christ with a Gasmask*. And in 1970 the Information Service of the Cuban government distributed in Latin American countries

a painting of Jesus with a carbine slung over his shoulder—
a symbol of the revolutionary Church. Similar anachro-
nisms are conspicuous in the picaresque novel by Richard
Voss, *The Redemption* (*Die Erlösung*, 1918), in which
Jesus takes part in World War I, then descends into the
Hell of the Sicilian sulphur mines and works as a rickshaw
man in Ceylon before he is murdered by a Russian priest.
In Alexander Blok's poem *The Twelve* (1918) Jesus appears as the leader of the St. Petersburg revolution, and his
apostles are twelve members of the Red Guard. (Blok's
poem, by the way, antagonized Communists and Christians
alike.) In conclusion, we might note A. J. Langguth's playful fiction *Jesus Christs* (1968). Not really a novel, Langguth's book consists of a series of witty, often blasphemous,
scenes organized much like Virginia Woolf's *Orlando*: the
central figure is always Jesus, but the times and circumstances change around him as he moves from ancient Jerusalem to contemporary hippie settings, which are often
suggested by New Testament sayings or parables. In his
"futuristic novel" entitled *Jesus in Osaka* (1970), Günter
Herburger shifts the time forward: his Jesus rides in jets,
goes skiing, participates in television interviews with a progressive theologian, and experiences a variety of situations
designed to expose the ambivalent nature—utopia or technological nightmare?—of a socialized and wholly technolo-
gized Bavaria and Japan around the year 2000. Thus, the
Jesus redivivus sometimes, as in Constant's *The Last Incarnation* or Sinclair's *They Call Me Carpenter*, loosely follows the sequence of the Gospels. But more often the incidents have no basis in the New Testament; the figure of
Jesus is invoked purely as an ideal that contrasts dramatically with contemporary reality.

Thomas à Kempis's *The Imitation of Christ* enjoyed a remarkable revival around the end of the nineteenth century,
when it was often reprinted, widely read, and frequently

cited in the literature of the *fin de siècle*.[11] This vogue is
symptomatic of the genre that might be called the *imitatio
Christi*: novels in which the hero makes up his mind to live
consistently as Jesus would have lived had he been born
into our world. Here we are dealing not with the resurrected historical Jesus, but with modern heroes who act out
their own conception of Christ.

"To reconceive the Christ!" (p. 496) is the goal announced programmatically by Mrs. Humphry Ward in
Robert Elsmere (1888).[12] This work, possibly the most controversial novel of its decade, was an instant best-seller and
sold half a million copies in its first year. Widely praised by
such critics as Walter Pater, Henry James, and Oliver Wen-
dell Holmes, who appreciated both its literary qualities and
its liberal tendencies, it was vigorously attacked by Glad-
stone and the orthodox establishment. Mrs. Ward, who
grew up in the Oxford of the sixties, was exposed to liberal
theology primarily through her uncle, Matthew Arnold, and
her work was intended as a thesis novel. In the words of the
introduction, she "wanted to show how a man of sensitive
and noble character, born for religion, comes to throw off
the orthodoxies of his day and moment, and to go out into
the wilderness where all is experiment, and spiritual life begins again." Set in Oxford, Surrey, and London of the

[11] Hans Hinterhäuser, "Die Christusgestalt im Roman des 'Fin de
Siècle'," *Archiv für das Studium der neueren Sprachen und Litera-
turen*, 198 (1961), 1-21. For the popularity of generally christological
works around the turn of the century see also Heinrich Spiero, *Die
Heilandsgestalt in der neueren deutschen Dichtung* (Berlin: Eckart,
1926); Karl Röttger, ed. *Die moderne Jesusdichtung: Eine Anthologie*.
Mit einer religiösen und literarischen Einleitung (München und
Leipzig: Piper [1907]); Gustav Pfannmüller, *Jesus im Urteil der
Jahrhunderte* (Leipzig und Berlin: Teubner, 1908); Jennie Alma
Whitten, "The Christlike Figure in the Modern German Novel,"
Diss. Univ. of Wisconsin, 1934; Adolf Heuser, *Die Erlösergestalt in
der belletristischen Literatur seit 1890 als Deuterin der Zeit* (Bonn:
Hanstein, 1936).

[12] *Robert Elsmere, by Mrs. Humphry Ward*, ed. Clyde de L. Ryals
(Lincoln, Neb.: Univ. of Nebraska Press, 1967).

eighties, the novel traces the career of Robert Elsmere, who is unable to reconcile his theological studies, based as they are on German liberal theology, with his activities as vicar of a comfortable country parish. Because he can no longer accept the creed of the English Church he resigns his orders and goes among the workingmen of London to form what he calls the New Brotherhood. "If we turn away from the true Jesus of Nazareth because he has been disfigured and misrepresented by the Churches, we turn away from that in which our weak wills and desponding souls are meant to find their most obvious and natural help and inspiration—from that symbol of the Divine, which, of necessity, means most to us. No! Give him back your hearts—be ashamed that you have ever forgotten your debt to him! Let combination and brotherhood do for the newer and simpler faith what they did once for the old—let them give it a practical shape, a practical grip on human life" (p. 499). Mrs. Ward's novel established the pattern for many inspirational novels to come, but few of them can match *Robert Elsmere* in interest, intelligence, or quality.

The most famous of the *imitations* is beyond any doubt Charles M. Sheldon's Bible Belt classic, *In His Steps* (1896). The action begins when the Reverend Henry Maxwell, pastor of a prosperous Congregational Church in the Middle West (presumably Sheldon's own parish in Topeka, Kansas) has his Christian assumptions shaken by the queries of a jobless tramp. Realizing that they have been living according to dogma and not the example of Christ, he approaches his congregation with the following proposal: "I want volunteers from the First Church who will pledge themselves, earnestly and honestly, for an entire year, not to do anything without first asking the question, 'What would Jesus do?' And after asking that question, each one will follow Jesus as exactly as he knows how, no matter what the result may be" (p. 15). This "Christian discipleship" produces a remarkable series of events in the town:

24

the local newspaper owner loses circulation because he refuses to print the fight results; a society girl forgoes her promising career as a concert soloist to sing at revival meetings in the slums; a businessman, inspired by Christian love, introduces profit-sharing among his employees. At the end of the predictable turmoils and successes produced by Reverend Maxwell's challenge, so-called "Endeavor Societies" are beginning to spring up all over the Midwest, even in that godless city Chicago.

For millions of fundamentalists, in America and all over the world, *In His Steps* long represented the culminating model of inspirational fiction. Translated into over twenty languages, it was more widely circulated during the thirties than any book besides the Bible. The spiritual need suggested by this spectacular success undoubtedly prompted Glenn Clark to write a sequel entitled *What Would Jesus Do?* (1950): "Wherein a new generation undertakes to walk in His Steps." Clark assures his readers that he obtained Sheldon's "permission and blessing" before undertaking his novel, in which the chief characters turn out to be the children and grandchildren of the figures in the original. This time the story begins on a Sunday in August, 1945, when the Reverend Charles S. Maxwell preaches a Victory Sermon to his congregation: again, the minister's faith is shaken when a "Japanese gentleman" commits suicide in his church after the service. The Reverend realizes that he has lost sight of Christ's human charity. Accordingly, Maxwell digs out his grandfather's exhortation and reads it to his own congregation, whereupon the wheels of plot begin to grind once more. But this time the action is transposed into the mood of the forties: the newspaper owner pledges to carry no ads for liquor and tobacco; the leading problems are war and communism. The novel ends on a positive note when Maxwell is appointed "spiritual advisor and ambassador" of the newly elected governor and sets out "to clean up the nation." The author concludes with the hope that yet

25

a third book in the series will be written some fifty years hence.

The *imitatio Christi*, in its literary as well as its subliterary forms, is clearly quite different from the fictional transfiguration. Here we find few hints of any parallels between the life of the modern hero and the life of Jesus; all we have is a decision and commitment to live and act as the authors imagine that Christ would have acted under similar circumstances. Not the Jesus of history, but the Christ of faith provides the model for the action. At its best the type amounts to little more than a tendentious *roman à thèse*, and at worst it descends into the lugubrious bathos of the Sunday school lesson.

We come, finally, to the category that seems to be most often confused with the fictional transfiguration: the form that has been designated as "pseudonyms of Christ."[13] The fictional transfiguration can be delimited quite precisely: it is restricted to those works in which, all questions of meaning aside, the events as set down immutably in the Gospels prefigure the action of the plot. The "pseudonyms of Christ," in contrast, constitute a much broader and vaguer category which includes any novel in which the hero is felt to be somehow "Christlike."

But whereas prefigured plot is a specific criterion, based as it is on events recorded in a specific textual source, the pseudonym of Christ is highly relative, depending as it does upon the author's understanding and interpretation of Christianity. Thus F. W. Dillistone, in his study of *The Novelist and the Passion Story*, considers several of the novels that we take to be transfigurations, but his criterion is theme rather than structure: "In each of the novels with which I shall be concerned the 'theme' in general terms is the power of redemptive suffering. There is always a cen-

[13] Edwin M. Moseley, *Pseudonyms of Christ in the Modern Novel: Motifs and Methods* (Pittsburgh: Univ. of Pittsburgh Press, 1962).

tral character who is ready to accept suffering and even
death in the service of a transcendent value, a worthy
end."[14] In some cases, of course, there can be a coincidence
of theme and structure; but Dillistone would be compelled
to exclude many works that we consider transfigurations because, for all their Gospel structure, they reveal no redemptive suffering. Similarly John Killinger, appropriating Dillistone's definition, concludes that fiction, "when it attempts
to present the figure of Christ, is limited to the presentation
of a kind of spiritually scented humanism. . . ."[15] For Robert Detweiler, also, the Christ-figure must have a redemptive role, even though it may be transferred to the secular
realm.[16] His hero is a good and moral man who suffers, a
misguided idealist in a materialistic world, a servant of
humanity. Ursula Brumm argues that "in a secular age
Christ becomes a literary symbol for the man who suffers
innocently for his brethren."[17] In his study of the crisis of
faith in literature Ludwig W. Kahn discusses the literary
Christ-figures, especially those of Melville and Faulkner, in
a chapter entitled "The Metaphysics of Suffering": the
meaning of Christ is reduced to his unique and inimitable
act of suffering.[18] W. H. Auden, finally, subsumes all of
these criteria in his discussion of the Christlike figure: he
must be a man innocent of sin and yet subject to temptation;
his beliefs cause him to collide with the law of the world;

[14] F. W. Dillistone, *The Novelist and the Passion Story* (New
York: Sheed & Ward, 1960), p. 22. Dillistone discusses François
Mauriac's *The Lamb*, Melville's *Billy Budd*, Kazantzakis' *The Greek
Passion*, and Faulkner's *A Fable*.

[15] Killinger, p. 48.

[16] Robert Detweiler, "Christ and the Christ Figure in American
Fiction," *The Christian Scholar*, 47 (1964), 111-24.

[17] Ursula Brumm, *Die religiöse Typologie im amerikanischen Denken: Ihre Bedeutung für die amerikanische Literatur und Geistes-
geschichte* (Leiden: Brill, 1963), p. 174. See also Miss Brumm's
article, "The Figure of Christ in American Literature," *Partisan
Review*, 24 (1957), 403-13.

[18] Ludwig W. Kahn, *Literatur und Glaubenskrise* (Stuttgart: Kohl-
hammer, 1964), pp. 148-72.

and his suffering must be, in part, willed so that it will not strike us as merely pathetic.[19]

All of these discussions of the "pseudonyms" of Christ, in short, have as their common denominator not the figure of Jesus as specified by the New Testament narrative, but rather the archetypal figure of the redeemer; Detweiler speaks of "an archetypal figure representing some verity or recurring action of life."

Of course, the archetype of redemptive death is most familiar to Western man in its embodiment in the figure of Jesus.[20] But since the general archetype of the redeemer is not necessarily limited by details of plot and organization as known from the New Testament, the definition of these "pseudonyms" of Christ has often been expanded to include so many different works that, as a literary category, it has become virtually meaningless. Dostoevsky's *The Idiot* as well as *Crime and Punishment*, Joseph Conrad's *Lord Jim*, Camus's *The Stranger*, Faulkner's *The Bear*, and Nathanael West's *Miss Lonelyhearts* are a few of the works cited by various critics as being "christological" in this broad sense. Christ has been resurrected in the person of Seymour Glass in the stories of J. D. Salinger and Yossarian in Joseph Heller's *Catch-22*. No character who lies down or dies with his arms outstretched—like the heroes of Hemingway's *The Old Man and the Sea* and Kafka's *The Trial*—is safe from the critical cross. Whether the category of pseudonyms and archetypes and motifs is useful or not, it should be rigorously distinguished from the more sharply definable category of fictional transfigurations of Jesus.

It would seem that the distinctions between these various

[19] W. H. Auden, *The Enchafèd Flood, or The Romantic Iconography of the Sea* (1950; rpt. New York: Random House-Vintage, 1967), pp. 141-42. Auden defines his category with sole reference to *Don Quixote* and *Billy Budd*.

[20] This distinction between general archetype and particular embodiment has become a commonplace in thematological studies. See Raymond Trousson, *Un problème de littérature comparée: les études de thèmes; essai de méthodologie* (Paris: Minard, 1965), p. 13; and John J. White, *Mythology in the Modern Novel*, pp. 45-51.

categories, once spelled out, would be sufficiently clear to obviate any confusion. I stress these differences here only because all of these types—the fictionalizing biography, the *Jesus redivivus*, the *imitatio Christi*, and the pseudonyms of Christ—are, in critical practice, very often blurred together with the very specific form that we have labeled the fictional transfiguration.[21] There can be overlappings, of course: a novel written as a transfiguration may be related in its generally Christian theme to the *imitatio Christi* or to the pseudonyms of Christ. As categories, however, they are quite distinct. To cite an analogy: one can have a love sonnet, but the sonnet and love poetry, seen respectively as form and content, are wholly different categories.

Let us insist, then, on the differences in order to isolate and define what may turn out to be a useful literary category. The fictional transfiguration, in sum, differs from the fictionalizing biography and *Jesus redivivus* to the extent that it introduces a modern hero and not the historical Jesus himself. And it is distinguished from the *imitatio Christi* and the "pseudonyms of Christ" to the extent that its action is specifically based on the life of the historical Jesus as depicted in the Gospels, and not loosely inspired by the conception of the kerygmatic Christ as it has evolved in Christian faith. These considerations bring us directly to the topic of the following chapter. For before such a distinction between Jesus and Christ became possible—between history and faith, action and meaning, form and content—it was necessary for nineteenth-century theology to conceive and pursue the quest of the historical Jesus.

[21] Heinrich Schirmbeck, "Der moderne Jesus-Roman: Die Wiederkehr des Teufels," in *Christliche Dichter der Gegenwart*, ed. Hermann Friedmann and Otto Mann (Heidelberg: Rothe, 1955), pp. 436-55; Wilhelm Grenzmann, "Christus-Thematik in der heutigen Literatur," *Stimmen der Zeit*, 164 (May 1959), 97-113; and the lengthy but undiscriminating discussion of works in G. Stanley Hall, *Jesus, the Christ, in the Light of Psychology* (Garden City, N. Y.: Doubleday-Page, 1917), I, 39-156: "Jesus in Literature." Notable beginnings toward discrimination have been made, on the other hand, by Bowman and Detweiler in the articles cited above (Notes 9 and 16).

2. The De-Christianizing
of Jesus

OUR MODERN OBSESSION with biography in every form—from the driest scholarly researches to the most indiscreet journalistic probings—makes it easy, at least for a non-theologian, to forget that man's interest in the person of the historical Jesus is a phenomenon of notably recent origin. St. Paul initiated the trend toward indifference when he turned away from the man Jesus, whom after all he could not claim to have known, in favor of the disembodied *kerygma* of the resurrected Christ. And the Gospels, as any comparison with such classical lives as those by Plutarch reveals, are essentially inspirational discourses that aspire to no biographical accuracy or thoroughness, even by the standards of antiquity. In fact, the frequent disparities among the Gospels, which drove nineteenth-century scholars to distraction, suggest that the authors and the communities for which these accounts were composed were more interested in a spiritual relationship to the Christ than any human record of the recently deceased Jesus.

In the course of many centuries with no historical consciousness and times that looked forward to the millennium rather than backward to the pre-crucifixion era there was simply no reason to think about the person of Jesus. The medieval churchman might be tempted to while away the hours by speculating on an imaginative variety of sophisticated theological problems, but it never occurred to him to seek information about the Redeemer beyond that provided in the New Testament. Until the end of the eighteenth century most Christians felt that the Gospels furnished as full and reliable an account of the life of Jesus as any reasonable man might wish. Even theologians—Martin Luther, for instance—did not waste a thought on seeming discrepancies among the versions of Matthew, Mark, Luke, and John. For readers with a greater need for order, Tatian's second-century *Diatessaron* provided a model for all subsequent harmonies—the more elaborate antecedents of the harmonies found at the back of most modern editions of the Bible—that simply arranged the events of the four Gospels into a unilinear narrative. Some of these, combining an absolute respect for Scripture with a well-nigh fiendish consistency, reasoned that if a saying or action was reported in more than one of the Gospels, then it must have occurred or been uttered on several occasions. As a result, in certain harmonies we find Jesus, with a remarkable proclivity for self-quotation, cleansing the Temple as many as three times. On no occasion were the supernatural happenings called into doubt.

It was only in the later eighteenth century that a more detached attitude toward religion and the Bible produced a new view of Jesus in the occasional remarks of such rationalists as Voltaire and Thomas Paine, who regarded him as a great ethical teacher rather than the divine Son of God; and this attitude gradually made possible a more critical appraisal of the reliability of the Gospels.[1] The first systematic criticism was the work of a professor of Oriental languages, Hermann Samuel Reimarus (1694-1768), who portrayed Jesus as a Jewish nationalist whose political execution was only subsequently reinterpreted by his fol-

[1] This fascinating story—one of the most exciting chapters of nineteenth-century intellectual history—has been written many times, notably by Albert Schweitzer in his *Geschichte der Leben-Jesu-Forschung* (1906; 2nd rev. ed. 1913). I have referred to *The Quest of the Historical Jesus*, trans. from 1st ed. by W. Montgomery (1910; rpt. New York: Macmillan, 1968). For additional information I have also consulted Heinrich Weinel and Alban G. Widgery, *Jesus in the Nineteenth Century and After* (Edinburgh: T. & T. Clark, 1914); Maurice Goguel, *The Life of Jesus*, trans. Olive Wyon (New York: Macmillan, 1933); James M. Robinson, *A New Quest of the Historical Jesus* (London: SCM Press, 1959); James Peter, *Finding the Historical Jesus: A Statement of the Principles Involved* (London: Collins, 1965); Wolfgang Trilling, *Fragen zur Geschichtlichkeit Jesu* (Düsseldorf: Patmos, 1966); Charles C. Anderson, *Critical Quests of Jesus* (Grand Rapids, Michigan: W. B. Eerdmans, 1969).

lowers as an act of spiritual self-sacrifice. Despite—or rather because of—their great originality, Reimarus' ideas were too daring to have any impact on the conservative theology of his day, which still depended more heavily upon faith than reason. For years, in fact, Reimarus was known less as a theologian than as the catalytic agent in one of the fiercest intellectual controversies in the history of German culture: Lessing's continuing battle with that rabid defender of the faith, Pastor Goeze of Hamburg, was signaled when Lessing published seven chapters of Reimarus' study under the title *Anonymous Fragments from Wolfenbüttel* (*Fragmente des Wolffenbüttelschen Ungenannten*, 1774-78).

An amusing offshoot of rationalism can be seen in the imaginative biographies—forerunners of the modern apocrypha as well as the fictional biographies of today—by Karl Friedrich Bahrdt and Karl Heinrich Venturini, who were concerned above all with filling in the Silent Years in the life of Jesus. These works, which are heavily indebted to the Gothic romances of the late eighteenth century, present Jesus as a member of a secret society, not unlike the Freemasons or Rosicrucians or Illuminati, that trains him and aids him in his mission. Bahrdt (1741-92) began his career as a professor of sacred philology at Leipzig, but after his dismissal for scandalous conduct he moved steadily down the social ladder and ended his years as an innkeeper. The eleven volumes of "Letters to Truth-Seeking Readers" that he published under the title *Explanation of the Plan and Aim of Jesus* (*Ausführung des Plans und Zwecks Jesu*, 1784-92) introduce Jesus as a member of the secret order of the Essenes. The Passion and crucifixion are presented as a plot to provide the Jews with a Messiah who would die and rise again according to their ancient prophecies. The Essene physicians gave Jesus special drugs, which permitted him to survive the scourging and the crucifixion. Afterwards he was removed from the cross and nursed back to health. Jesus lived in secrecy for years to come, appearing publicly from time to time to a few disciples as well as to Paul on the road to Damascus and directing the affairs of the Essene community.

Venturini's explicitly non-supernatural account of Jesus in four volumes (*Natürliche Geschichte des grossen Propheten von Nazareth*, 1800-1802) also portrays the Essenes as a secret brotherhood. This time, however, the crucifixion is not a plot planned in advance. It was only after Joseph of Arimathea removed the body from the cross that it occurred to the Essenes to attempt to revive their companion by means of herbs and medicines. Two points should be noted in connection with these works. First, although they are largely fictional, they represent a very early attempt to explain the life of Jesus on a rational basis: the miracle of the resurrection, notably, is given a plausible interpretation. Second, they established in the lives of Jesus a fictional tradition, as distinct from the purely scholarly tradition, that can be traced in numerous details right down to Robert Graves's *King Jesus*.

Scarcely less inventiveness was displayed by the more academic school of thoroughgoing rationalism, which applied its imagination not to filling in the gaps of the Gospel narrative, but rather to finding a rational explanation for what is already there. The principal representative of this tendency was Heinrich Eberhard Gottlob Paulus (1761-1851), who came to rationalism in reaction against the mysticism of a father who compelled his son to pretend to be in communication with his deceased mother's spirit. As a professor of Oriental languages at Jena, Paulus became a friend of Goethe, Schiller, and the other intellectual and literary luminaries around Weimar. When he wrote his two-volume *Life of Jesus* (*Das Leben Jesu als Grundlage einer reinen Geschichte des Urchristentums*, 1828), he had become professor of theology at Heidelberg. Paulus succeeded in the remarkable accomplishment of doing away with every miracle in the Gospels except the Virgin Birth. The voice of God was nothing but thunder, while the appearance of angels was an individual or collective delusion suggested by meteors. Similarly, the transfiguration is explained as an optical illusion produced by the play of light upon mountain mists. For his healings Jesus used secret medicines and sedatives as well as rigorous diets. The raising of the dead was actually the deliverance from premature burial. And the feeding of the multitudes is interpreted as an example of his powers of persuasion: when Jesus and the disciples shared their small supply of food, their generosity encouraged the rich to distribute their own provisions to the poor.

During the first third of the nineteenth century, then, two radically different theologies existed side by side. The old-fashioned supernatural school insisted that the miracles of the Bible happened just as they are recorded and must be accepted as an act of faith. The rationalists, both the imaginative and the thoroughgoing varieties, maintained that there must be a reasonable and natural explanation for all the seemingly supernatural happenings. The work that attempted to overcome this dilemma was one of the most brilliant intellectual achievements of the nineteenth century: David Friedrich Strauss's *Life of Jesus* (*Das Leben Jesu*, 1835).

Strauss (1808-73) followed the classic educational route of Swabians destined for a theological career: after secondary studies at Blaubeuren, he moved on to the seminary at Tübingen, where he came under the influence of the rationalist, Ferdinand Christian Baur. Since from the outset Strauss had hoped to combine theology with philosophy, in 1831 he went to Berlin to continue his studies with the foremost philosopher of the age. Hegel, a fellow Swabian, had himself started out as a theologian at Tübingen, and his early theological writings included a rationalistic essay on "The Life of Jesus" (1795), in which Jesus is portrayed as the preacher of a Kantian system of ethics.[2] Hegel died only a month after Strauss's arrival, but Strauss remained in Berlin for a year to listen to the eminent old romantic theologian, Schleiermacher, who in 1819 had introduced the first university (that is, general education and non-seminary) course on "The Life of Jesus." Back in Tübingen as a junior lecturer, Strauss invoked the right of theologians to lecture on philosophy: he introduced a course on Hegel's logic that became hugely successful with the students. When disgruntled conservatives on the faculty objected to this innovation, Strauss attempted to resolve the problem by shifting to the philosophical division of the university, but he was prevailed upon to remain in the theological seminary. His *Life of Jesus*, however, was published just a short time later and turned out to be so controversial that it wrecked the young lecturer's chances for a professorship in Tübingen. For the remainder of his life he was unable to obtain a professorial appointment in any university or seminary.

Strauss, true to his Hegelian temperament and training, attempted to reconcile the thesis of the supernaturalists with the antithesis of the rationalists by synthesizing them into what he called a *mythic* interpretation. He had noted that many of the deeds and miracles attributed to Jesus were fulfillments of expectations pronounced in the Old Testament. Rather than accepting them on faith or explaining them away by rational means, he concluded that these elements were actually literary conventions added to the accounts of the life of Jesus by the authors of the Gospels, who wanted to make of the historical Jesus a figure that corresponded in every respect to the predictions of the prophets. It is difficult to exaggerate the epochmaking brilliance of Strauss's two volumes, in which he elaborated this

[2] G.W.F. Hegel, *Early Theological Writings*, trans. T. M. Knox. With an introduction and fragments trans. Richard Kroner (Chicago: Univ. of Chicago Press, 1948), pp. 205-81.

basic idea. Strauss was the first to distinguish systematically between the Christ of faith and the Jesus of history, who can be reached only by stripping away the "mythic" additives from the recorded life. Rationalism had attempted to salvage every incident of the Gospels by explaining everything logically. Strauss, in contrast, argues that much of the New Testament is in the last analysis fiction and that, as such, it belongs to Christian faith but not to historical fact.

In addition, his *Life* mapped out virtually every important area that New Testament scholarship was to explore in the following century. In his attention to "mythic" elements he provided the basis for the mythological studies of the History of Religions school. His consideration of the propagandistic role of the Gospelists paved the way for modern Form Criticism. His evaluation of what he called the "enthusiasm" and "fanaticism" in the character of Jesus anticipated the psychiatric interpretations of the early twentieth century. More immediately, however, his question concerning the reliability of the Gospels as historical documents—a question, by the way, that marks Strauss as a contemporary of Ranke and the great historians of the early nineteenth century—determined the direction of New Testament research for the next thirty years. Generally speaking, the scholars of the mid-nineteenth century were concerned with the so-called Marcan Hypothesis: they wanted to prove (what is widely accepted today) that the Fourth Gospel differs in aim and historical reliability from the three Synoptic Gospels, and that of these first three the Gospel of Mark deserves priority in time and authenticity.

Yet it was not the exciting work of Strauss and his followers that attracted broad public attention to the central theological problem of the century, but Ernest Renan's *Life of Jesus* (*Vie de Jésus*, 1863), a volume whose critical insufficiency is matched only by its aesthetic charm. Léon Bloy might rail against "l'abominable Ernest" and oppose his own violent, intolerant, militant reformer-hero Marchenoir to the saccharine-sweet Jesus of Renan.[3] Nietzsche, in the "Curse on Christianity" that he entitled *The Antichrist* (1888), might prove beyond any reasonable doubt that "Herr Renan" was nothing but a "Hanswurst *in psychologicis*."[4] Nevertheless, for all his alleged psychological ignorance, it was this abominable Ernest who provided the cultured public of Europe with its first literary biography of a humanized Jesus, written in a graceful language that the educated layman could read with appreciation. His book went through thirteen editions in the first two years, with fifteen more editions of a popularized revision in 1864; and it was almost immediately translated into more than a dozen languages.

Renan's book is in one sense a trivialization or skillful popularization of three decades of serious New Testament scholarship in Germany. Renan (1823-92) was destined for the priesthood, but he left the seminary of St. Sulpice in Paris in 1845 with his faith undermined by the German critical theology to which he had been exposed there. After a few years as a private tutor, he spent a decade preparing himself for the professorship of Semitic languages at the Collège de France, which he assumed in 1862. But Renan suffered almost the same fate as Strauss: the controversy aroused by his *Life of Jesus* compelled the government to remove him from office in 1863, and it was not until the Republic of 1871 that he was reinstated in his professorship.

Renan portrays an amiable young carpenter wandering through the lovely Galilean countryside in the company of gentle fisherfolk and urging upon his listeners a "délicieuse théologie d'amour." Renan is fully aware of earlier scholarship, which he exploits for his own purposes, but his attitude toward the sources is unproblematic, as though Strauss and his followers had not devoted a generation of

[3] In his novel *Le Désespéré* (1887); I have referred to the text in Bloy's *Œuvres* (Paris, 1932), II, 245.

[4] Friedrich Nietzsche, *Werke in drei Bänden*, ed. Karl Schlechta (München: Hanser, 1955), II, 1190 (= § 29).

painstaking analysis to the composition and relative reliability of the Synoptic Gospels and the Gospel of John. Blithely ignoring the Marcan Hypothesis, Renan proclaims his affection for the Jesus portrayed in the Fourth Gospel. In his introduction he attempts to reduce the thorniest theological dilemmas to grand simplifications. Taking the middle road between rationalism and supernaturalism, he considers the Gospels neither as reliable biographies nor as fictitious legends, but as "biographies légendaires." He proposes to examine the texts—as though it had not been done repeatedly—and to proceed carefully by induction, resorting to rationalization only in the case of clearly supernatural events.

Unlike the German scholars who preceded him and spent most of their time in seminary libraries, Renan wrote much of his book in Syria. As he traversed the country of the New Testament, he recalls, "I had before my eyes a fifth Gospel, torn, but still legible, and henceforth, through the recitals of Matthew and Mark, in place of an abstract being whose existence might have been doubted, I saw living and moving an admirable human figure" (p. 39).[5] Renan's conciliatory fifth Gospel did nothing to further the theological quest for the historical Jesus. In fact, Maurice Goguel, the leading modern French historian of Jesus, has complained that Renan's *Life* "compromised, or at least delayed, the critical education of the French public." But for all its theological inadequacies, it determined more than any other work of the nineteenth century the public image of Jesus as a living human being rather than an ethereal deity—Jesus rather than Christ, the man of history rather than the god of faith. "All centuries shall proclaim," the book ends, "that among the sons of men, there was none greater than Jesus."

If Strauss set New Testament scholars on a new and fruitful course, Renan awakened the general public to an awareness

[5] Renan, *The Life of Jesus*, translator not named (1864; rpt. Garden City, N. Y.: Doubleday-Dolphin, n.d.).

of Jesus as a historical figure. Strauss did not go wholly un-
noticed, of course: George Eliot at the instigation of her
free-thinking friends translated his *Life of Jesus* into English in 1846. But outside of groups with a specific interest
in liberal theology, it was years before Jesus could be presented to the public in his new humanized form. In 1840, in
his lecture on "The Hero as Divinity," Thomas Carlyle, who
was not known for his humility, noted with a modest aposi-
opesis: "The greatest of all heroes is one—whom we do not
name here!"[6] Similarly, Emerson recalled after reading
Renan's *Life*: "When I wrote *Representative Men*, I felt
that Jesus was the 'Representative Man' whom I ought to
sketch; but the task required great gifts,—steadiest insight
and perfect temper; else, the consciousness of want of sympathy in the audience would make one petulant or sore, in
spite of himself."[7]

After the publication of Renan's book there was no longer
any such restraint or the fear that the public might not sympathize with the new image of Jesus. Popular works began
to appear literally by the dozen. In 1864 Schleiermacher's
lectures on Jesus, originally delivered in 1819, were published for the first time. That same year Strauss brought out
a radically revised popular edition of his own *Life of Jesus*,
hoping to enjoy the public success denied his original work.
The political awakening of the German people, he noted in
his preface, had opened a freer arena for the discussion of
religious questions. Problems formerly reserved for the
halls of German seminaries had now become public issues.
The historical Jesus, ignored for eighteen centuries and
then for fifty years nothing but a controversial topic for theological argument, was suddenly liberated for popular consumption. The intense intellectual excitement of those years
is reflected fictionally in *Robert Elsmere* (1888). Mrs.

[6] Thomas Carlyle, *Heroes, Hero-Worship and the Heroic in History*
(New York: Alden, 1885), p. 15.
[7] *The Journals of Ralph Waldo Emerson*, ed. E. W. Emerson and
W. E. Forbes (Boston and New York: Houghton, Mifflin, 1909-14),
IX, 579.

Ward had met Renan in 1874, and the characters of her novel refer not only to his *Vie de Jésus*, but also to Strauss and the leaders of contemporary German scholarship, which had been made known in England through the Oxford Movement and the efforts of such Balliol liberals as Benjamin Jowett and T. H. Green. Mrs. Ward's uncle, Matthew Arnold, introduced the notion of the "sweet reasonableness" of a very human Jesus in a series of works beginning with *St. Paul and Protestantism* (1870). And J. R. Seeley, in his best-selling *Ecce Homo* (1865), emphasized Jesus' "Enthusiasm of Humanity."

Just as Strauss's *Life of Jesus* was followed by three decades of careful study of the composition and reliability of the Gospels, Renan's *Life* produced thirty more years of so-called "liberal" lives of Jesus. The representative German example is undoubtedly David Schenkel's popular *Sketch of the Character of Jesus* (*Das Charakterbild Jesu*, 1864). Schenkel, the director of the seminary at Heidelberg, had outgrown conservative beginnings to become a leading liberal. Especially during the sixties he was acclaimed as a champion of the rights of the laity, and in the General Synod of 1861 he was instrumental in establishing the new constitution of the German Protestant Church. In 1863 he summoned the Protestant Assembly at Frankfurt to consider Church reforms. This liberal impulse clearly colors his image of Jesus, who is presented as a bourgeois Messiah having no "enthusiastic" elements. Instead, he is a sober social critic whose cleansing of the Temple is construed not as an act of violence, but as a gesture of reform.

For all their variety, these "liberal" lives in German, French, and English have three things in common. First, they all "modernize" Jesus in an attempt to make him relevant to the present; this tendency is related in large measure to the reform movements in the various Churches, which opposed the teaching of a living Jesus to the rigid dogmatism of ecclesiastical authority. Second, they shift their attention away from problems of eschatology to the message of Jesus for life in this world; this change of focus is related to the growing social consciousness in Church reform. And, finally, they try to compensate for the sketchiness of the Gospel accounts by a psychological reconstruction of events: they see Jesus as a man moved by human concerns and not as an inscrutable deity whose reasons and motivations cannot be comprehended.

It was this conception of a humanized Jesus—initiated by Strauss, popularized by Renan, and elaborated in the "liberal" lives—that became useful to the Christian socialism emerging during these same years as a powerful force within the Churches. In his introduction to *The Quest of the Historical Jesus*, Albert Schweitzer argues that the greatest lives of Jesus were written with hate—hate of the false nimbus with which conventional Christianity has surrounded and obscured the true figure and teaching of Jesus. Schweitzer's *bon mot*, coined with specific reference to Reimarus and Strauss, also applies to Christian socialism, which gratefully appropriated from the liberal lives an image of Jesus as social reformer with which they lambasted the orthodox Church of the late nineteenth century. But his notion of hate, which we can interpret as anticlericalism coupled with a more human understanding of Jesus, can also help us to approach three works in which the full-fledged transfigurations of modern literature are tentatively anticipated.

Goethe's *The Sorrows of Young Werther* (*Die Leiden des jungen Werther*, 1774), Stendhal's *The Red and the Black* (*Le Rouge et le noir*, 1831), and Melville's *Billy Budd* (1888-91) are not full-fledged transfigurations: in none of them is the life of the hero prefigured consistently by the events of the Gospels. But in all three works conspicuous parallels to the Passion are introduced for particular effect in the concluding pages.

The hero of Goethe's novel, for all his charismatic appeal

41

to children and his sympathy for sinners, is no more of a Christ-figure than Thomas Mann's Peeperkorn. Yet in his own tormented mind, toward the end of the book, he begins to think of himself in terms of Jesus—a delusion that is perfectly plausible in the light of the essentially religious theme of the novel. The motif is first introduced about a month before Werther's suicide (in the letter of November 15) when, playing on the word "father," he slyly substitutes himself for Jesus: "Doesn't the Son of God Himself say that those will be with Him whom His Father gives unto Him? But what if my Father wants to keep me for Himself, which is what my heart tells me?" Werther goes on to paraphrase Jesus' words about the cup that must be drunk—words repeated again two pages from the end. And the letter concludes with the cry from the cross: "My God, my God, why hast Thou forsaken me?" Goethe does not employ the motifs in such a systematically exact order as Thomas Mann; but enough references are introduced to make it clear that the author is playing with this added dimension of meaning. Three times Werther stresses the fact that his suicide is intended as an act of sacrifice for Lotte and Albert. He speaks of his death as going to join his Father: "I am going on ahead! to my Father, to your Father." On the evening of his death he orders a meal of bread and wine and, after this "Last Supper," goes out into the garden for his lonely meditations—despite the pounding rain. In his final letter to Lotte, after stressing that he wants to be buried in the clothes he is wearing, he envisages a scene that is virtually a parody of the resurrection and ascension: "My soul floats over the coffin." The fact that Goethe transposes the date of Werther's suicide from October (the date given in the source that he otherwise follows quite scrupulously) to the midnight of December 22 seems also to hint at a Jesus analogy.

The narrator's laconic last paragraph, finally, consists of two tableaux that are easily recognizable as conventional scenes: a Lamentation and an Entombment.

The old judge came bursting in as soon as he heard the news. With the hot tears streaming down his cheeks, he kissed the dying man. His oldest sons soon followed him on foot. They fell on their knees beside the bed in attitudes of the wildest grief, kissing the dying man's hand, his mouth. The oldest one, whom Werther had always loved best, clung to his lips as he expired and had to be forcefully removed. At twelve noon, Werther died. The presence of the judge and the arrangements he made silenced the crowd. That night, at about eleven, he had the body buried in the spot Werther had chosen. The old man and his sons walked behind the bier; Albert found himself incapable of doing so. They feared for Lotte's life. Workmen carried the body. There was no priest in attendance.

It would be difficult to find two characters more dissimilar than Werther and Julien Sorel, yet a very plausible case can be argued that the cold-blooded hero of *The Red and the Black* also achieves an unexpected dimension at the end of the novel as the result of parallels to the Passion of Jesus. Stendhal's novel moves very rapidly to its conclusion—so rapidly that some critics have objected to an alleged lack of motivation in the closing pages. After Julien shoots Mme de Rènal, he is taken to Besançon and brought almost immediately to trial. Since Mme de Rènal was only wounded and since Julien is such a handsome and appealing defendant, it is generally assumed that he will be acquitted. Then, just when his acquittal seems assured, Julien leaps to his feet to make a speech in which he insults the jury by telling them that they are about to condemn him—not because he is guilty of any crime, but because he threatens them socially by aspiring to move upward in society, from the peasantry to the bourgeoisie. The incensed jury returns a verdict of guilty; after another brief period in prison Julien is executed.

Within the simple framework of this concluding action (especially chapters 41-45), however, there are several seemingly inexplicable details. Julien refuses to defend himself at his trial. After his condemnation he calls himself, not without a touch of pathos, the son of a "carpenter" (*charpentier*), although up to this point his father has been designated more precisely as a sawyer or wood merchant. Julien makes a special point of having been condemned on a Friday, though otherwise the days of the week have been of little or no importance. In prison, with no apparent motivation, he invites two hardened criminals to share a bottle of wine with him. In one of his last monologues he reflects upon the nature of truth ("Où est la vérité? Dans la religion. . . ."). And after his execution his body is taken to a grotto for burial, followed by the mourning Mathilde de la Mole. It seems likely that Stendhal is here exploiting the emotions attached to certain episodes from the Passion: the absence of a defense, the Friday trial, Pilate's speculations on truth, the two thieves on the cross, and the entombment.[8] But like Goethe, Stendhal has introduced this dimension, virtually without preparation, only at the end of the novel; the sequence of events is not precise; and there is more than a suspicion that both writers are utilizing the Passion for purposes less than serious.

Half a century later Herman Melville built equally unmistakable allusions to the Passion into the culminating passages of *Billy Budd*, where the "Handsome Sailor" is hanged for the accidental killing of an officer: "At the same moment it chanced that the vapoury fleece hanging low in the East, was shot through with a soft glory as of the fleece of the Lamb of God seen in mystical vision, and simultaneously therewith, watched by the wedged mass of upturned faces, Billy ascended; and ascending, took the full rose of the dawn." This crucifixion and ascension is followed, in the final pages, by other legendary details. The ship's crew cuts

---

[8] Richard B. Grant, "The Death of Julien Sorel," *L'Esprit Créateur*, 2 (1962), 26-30. Grant mentions all of these parallels except the Pilate allusion. He also includes the fact that Mathilde de la Mole buries Julien's head with her own hands; but that detail would seem to suggest John the Baptist rather than Jesus.

relics from the yard-end on which Billy was hanged: "To them a chip of it was as a piece of the Cross." And when Captain Vere later dies from wounds suffered in battle with the French man-of-war *Athéiste*, he murmurs "Billy Budd, Billy Budd" in a prayer-like incantation. In Melville's complex allegory of innocence and depravity we seek in vain for any consistent structure based on the Gospels, even if we take into account such incidental hints as Billy Budd's foundling birth or the Judas-like kiss of the chaplain shortly before his execution. Like Goethe and Stendhal before him, Melville has used the Jesus motifs to give structure to a single section of his story, and not to lend shape to the entire work.

Is Goethe seriously suggesting, as one critic claims, that Werther's suicide is to be taken as a straightforward secularization of Christ's agony? That the title (*Die Leiden*) should properly be translated as "The Passion" rather than "The Sorrows" of Young Werther?[9] Do Stendhal and Melville really regard their heroes as Christlike figures? In the context of the works it hardly seems likely. Werther is an emotionally deranged young man suffering from a number of delusions; the fact that he feels impelled to act out the events of the Passion is designed to characterize his own endangered state rather than to suggest that Goethe seriously identifies him with Jesus. Julien Sorel, for all his impressive talents, is a scheming *arriviste*. Billy Budd may be as innocent as a lamb, but he is also just as dull-witted. In fact, once we note the structural pattern of these three scenes, we rapidly go on to conclude that the additional dimension achieved in each case might well be parody instead of pathos. At this point analysis must yield to interpretation as we cast a quick glance at the religious views of the authors.

[9] Herbert Schöffler, *Die Leiden des jungen Werther: Ihr geistesgeschichtlicher Hintergrund* (Frankfurt am Main: Vittorio Klostermann, 1938). Though I disagree with Schöffler's interpretation of *Werther* as an inspirational work, my analysis of the Jesus parallels coincides in most essentials with his.

Goethe wrote *Werther* at a critical time in his religious development: while his attitude was shifting from the pietistic faith of his youth to a more mature understanding of Jesus as a sublime and yet wholly human ideal of perfection.[10] This process, which was coupled with a strong anti-ecclesiastical feeling, was complete by 1782 when he called himself "a pronounced non-Christian."[11] But his attitude is sufficiently clear as early as December, 1773—shortly before the composition of *Werther*—when he wrote to Betty Jacobi regarding the education of her sons: "It doesn't make any difference whether they believe in Christ, or Götz, or Hamlet; just make sure that they believe in *something.*" This attitude, which reduces Jesus to a level with other heroic figures of history and literature, is echoed in a more scurrilous tone when Goethe rigorously distinguishes between the man Jesus and the dogma of Christianity: "If only the whole Christian teaching were not such a shitty thing that, with its impoverished limitations, infuriates me as a human being, then I would be fond of its object of veneration."[12] The implication is clear: Christ has been de-mythified and secularized into a very human Jesus while institutionalized Christianity is regarded with a suspicious hostility. In the poem "Celebrität," written a number of years later, "Herr Werther" and "Herr Christ" are associated once again: both are reduced to the rather ignominious common denominator of woodcuts or copper engravings produced for mass consumption by a mindless public.

It is necessary to go no further than his novel to find evidence of Stendhal's rabid anticlericalism, which comes out in the characterization of priests, who are "impertinent scoundrels" and guilty of "base hypocrisy." Even during Julien's final days in prison, his confessor falls victim to a "Jesuit intrigue." This anticlericalism, however, is merely

---

[10] See Gerhard Möbus, *Die Christus-Frage in Goethes Leben und Werk* (Osnabrück: A. Fromm, 1964), esp. pp. 89-112 (the discussion of *Werther*) and pp. 113-49 ("Entscheidung gegen Christus").

[11] "ein dezidierter Nichtkrist": letter to Lavater of July 29, 1782.

[12] "ein Scheisding": letter to Herder of May 12, 1775.

46

the manifestation of a more deep-seated hostility to Christianity. It can probably be assumed that Stendhal, like several of his heroes, was well acquainted with the Scriptures: it is said that Julien knows the Holy Bible by heart from beginning to end (chap. 40), and he recites appropriate passages to himself from time to time. After his condemnation Julien reflects on the possibility of an afterlife: "But if I meet the God of the Christians I'm lost: he's a despot and, as such, he's filled with ideas of vengeance; his Bible speaks of nothing but horrible punishments. I've never loved him, and I've never been able to believe that anyone else could love him sincerely" (chap. 42). Later he characterizes the God of the Bible as "a cruel, petty despot with a thirst for vengeance" (chap. 44). He longs for a true Christianity whose priests would be paid no more than were the Apostles. How is it possible, he concludes, to believe in the great name of God "after the terrible abuse our priests make of it?" It seems likely, then, that Stendhal introduced the parallels for the double purpose of contrast and parody. Julien seizes every possible opportunity to re-enact the role of Jesus in order to unmask the fundamental lack of Christian sentiment in his own society. At the same time, the fact that Julien is so un-Christlike turns his role into a parody.

With Melville we encounter a similar situation. Lawrance Thompson has persuasively traced Melville's shifting views from a youthful Christian idealism to his later anti-Christian agnosticism, from the "divine and gentle Jesus" of *Typee* through the skepticism of *Mardi* to the covertly sneering allusions to Jesus in *The Confidence-Man* and the blatant satire in *Billy Budd*.[13] It is possible for "the superficial skimmer of pages," in Melville's phrase, to regard Billy as a serious parallel to Christ. Indeed, some critics read the story as a confession of Melville's orthodoxy.[14] But Thomp-

---

[13] Lawrance Thompson, *Melville's Quarrel with God* (Princeton, N.J.: Princeton Univ. Press, 1952), pp. 50, 65-67, 303-304, 405-408, and *passim*.

[14] This is the thrust of Dillistone's interpretation in *The Novelist and the Passion Story*.

son makes a strong case for the view that Billy Budd represents a Jesus who has been "double-crossed" by God through his needless crucifixion.

It is unnecessary to go into greater detail, for the religious beliefs of Goethe, Stendhal, and Melville are not at issue here. What matters is simply this: the authors of three fictions that exploit the technique of fictional transfiguration in rudimentary form—for special effects in the concluding pages of their works—were writing either before the critical New Testament scholarship of the nineteenth century (Goethe, Stendhal) or without any particular study and awareness of it (Melville). But in each case we are able to ascertain a conspicuous attitude of skepticism, even hostility, toward conventional Christianity and its view of Jesus. It was this hostility that afforded these three authors the necessary detachment—what Schweitzer called "hate"—to contemplate the figure of Jesus with undogmatic eyes and to presume to utilize the events of his Passion for their emotional value in literary creations.

By the end of the nineteenth century, however, the liberal view of Jesus had become so widespread that it was no longer necessary for a writer to generate his own "hate": it was available in any bookshop. But it was not simply by providing a new secularized image of Jesus as a social reformer that liberal theology made his figure programmatically interesting and useful for Christian socialism. Before writers could undertake conscious and consistent fictional transfigurations, in contrast to the concluding parallels adduced almost on second thought by Goethe, Stendhal, and Melville, it was necessary for them to become accustomed to a wholly new way of looking at the life of Jesus. In this connection Strauss's mythic interpretation turned out to be productive and suggestive for many writers. But Strauss's method amounted in fact to the rediscovery of an ancient Christian way of thinking, which he inverted for the purposes of higher criticism.

The mode of thought known as "figural" is specifically Christian in origin. As Erich Auerbach has demonstrated in a classic article, "Figural interpretation establishes a connection between two events or persons, the first of which signifies not only itself but also the second, while the second encompasses or fulfills the first."[15] The Old Testament is regarded as a series of incidents anticipating or "prefiguring" the life of Jesus in the New Testament. For instance, Abraham's readiness to sacrifice his son Isaac prefigures God's willingness to let his son Jesus die on the cross. Conversely, though no causal relationship is intended in the modern sense of the word, the events surrounding Jesus' life are arranged in such a way as to verify the predictions in the Old Testament. This accounts for those frequent passages in which it is reported that Jesus or others acted in a certain way so that an older prophecy might be fulfilled. For instance, Joseph departs for Egypt with Mary and Jesus "that it might be fulfilled which was spoken of the Lord by the prophet, saying, Out of Egypt have I called my son" (Matt: 2:15). And on the occasion before the triumphal entry into Jerusalem when Jesus sends two of his disciples to fetch an ass and a colt tethered nearby, it is said: "All this was done, that it might be fulfilled which was spoken by the prophet, saying, Tell ye the daughter of Sion, Behold, thy King cometh unto thee, meek, and sitting upon an ass, and a colt the foal of an ass" (Matt: 21: 4-5). Passages such as these sometimes make us feel that we are dealing with a determinism more rigid than any conceived by nineteenth-century science.

Now this kind of thinking clearly differed from other modes of thought—e.g., allegorical or symbolical—available to early Christian authors in pagan antiquity. For it is the

[15] Auerbach's essay, "Figura," appeared originally in 1938. I refer here to the English translation in Auerbach's *Scenes from the Drama of European Literature: Six Essays*, trans. Ralph Manheim (New York: Meridian, 1959), p. 53.

essence of figural interpretation that the two poles of the figure, though separate in time, be concrete, and not concepts or abstractions. In symbol and allegory, in contrast, only one pole is concrete while the other is abstract. To take a simple example: according to Christian symbolism the cross (a concrete object) stands for redemption through self-sacrifice (an abstract notion). Similarly, in the famous allegory of the Christian's armor (Eph: 6: 13-17) the Christian virtues are enumerated through a systematic explication of the concrete object: "Wherefore take unto you the whole armour of God, that ye may be able to withstand in the evil day, and having done all, to stand. Stand therefore, having your loins girt about with truth, and having on the breastplate of righteousness. . . ." We do not need to discuss in further detail the differences between symbolism and allegory. It is sufficient for our purposes to establish the difference in quality between those two common pagan modes of thought, on the one hand, and Christian figural thought on the other.

Figural thinking emerged in early Christian times as a response to a specific historical situation and need. As long as it was felt that the millennium was imminent, there was little need to seek any external authority for Jesus' teaching: its authority resided in its truth and in his presence. But when it became apparent to his followers, shortly after his death, that the Second Coming had been delayed and that the upstart religion might have to compete for years to come with well established and popular pagan cults, it became desirable to assure the legitimacy of the new teaching through some pedigree.[16] This could be accomplished most effectively by linking Jesus to the Hebrew past from which he had emerged and which was already conveniently available in the Old Testament. This simple move had two immediate effects. As far as Gentile Christians were concerned, it provided the new cult with a history as venerable

[16] J. H. Plumb, *The Death of the Past* (London: Macmillan, 1969), p. 76.

as any other and made the Old Testament relevant to non-Jews by transmuting it from a book of laws for a specific people into a series of *figurae* anticipating Jesus. And as far as the Jews were concerned, it legitimized Jesus by relating him to the prophecies of the Old Testament. On the basis of the available evidence many New Testament scholars assume that Jesus himself was not yet accustomed to thinking in figural terms, for this kind of thinking is not attributed to him consistently in all of the Gospels. (It is most pronounced in the Gospel of Matthew, for Matthew was writing for a Jewish community in Syria, which needed to be persuaded by evidence linking the new savior to the old prophecies.) Figural thinking developed only after his death, and notably in the later Gospels (Matthew and John), for propagandistic purposes.

Owing to the authority of such early Christian scholars as Tertullian and Augustine the technique of figural interpretation became firmly established in the Christian West. Virtually every passage in the Old Testament was eventually interpreted in such a way as to "prefigure" the events of the New Testament. In addition, this mode of thought deeply affected the literature and art of the Middle Ages. Auerbach has shown, for instance, how extensively the structure and incidents of the *Divine Comedy* are determined by figural forms. With the gradual secularization of the West during the Renaissance, typological or figural thinking became less dominant as men turned increasingly to such classical modes as symbol and allegory. But it by no means vanished. Among such religiously conservative groups as the Puritans, for instance, figural thinking was imported to the United States, where it became an element, by derivation, in the writing and critical thought of such writers as Emerson, Hawthorne, Melville, and Poe.[17]

[17] Ursula Brumm, *Die religiöse Typologie im amerikanischen Denken* (Leiden: Brill, 1963), pp. 17-29. Miss Brumm also demonstrates, pp. 6-16, that the American Puritans distinguished rigorously between allegorical and typological (= figural) interpretation.

Strauss helped to reawaken the awareness of figural thought because his mythic interpretation of the life of Jesus is in effect nothing but figural interpretation applied in reverse. Whenever Jesus "fulfills" a prophecy of the Old Testament, thereby establishing a precise figural parallel, Strauss, assuming that the literary imagination of the Gospelists has been at work, strips away their additions in order to get at the verifiable historical Jesus. To be most precise, we should probably speak of a "postfigurative" rather than a "prefigurative" interpretation in Strauss's *Life*. For prefiguration implies a mystical belief that the Old Testament miraculously anticipates events that took place hundreds of years later. Postfiguration, in contrast, suggests the conscious construction of a fiction to conform to existing predictions in earlier texts. One might almost say that Strauss interprets the Gospels as though they were fictional transfigurations of the historical Jesus.

Now most of the Christian socialist authors, as we shall have occasion to observe, were well acquainted with Strauss's work, both at first hand and indirectly through liberal theology. It was this newly rediscovered and popularized figural mode of thinking, I suggest, that prompted writers to undertake the first conscious and consistent fictional transfigurations of Jesus. The fictional transfiguration stands in precisely the same relationship to the New Testament as does, in traditional figural thinking, the New Testament to the Old. For Strauss, Jesus was a plausible figure whose skeletal historic life was fleshed out with incidents suggested by the Old Testament. For Christian socialists, the modern hero was a historically plausible character, the course of whose life was suggested by the events of the New Testament. We might even go a step further in the argument. Figural thinking was originally developed at a time of crisis in order to link the then new religion of Christianity to the older traditions of Judaism. By analogy, the first Christian socialist transfigurations were initially undertaken in a clear mood of crisis: they represented an attempt to remind a forgetful Christian society, once again, of its true source in the person of Jesus.

If this turns out to be the case, then what are we to make of T. S. Eliot's claim in his essay on *"Ulysses,* Order, and Myth" (1923) that Joyce's "parallel use of the Odyssey" has the importance of a scientific discovery? "In using the myth, in manipulating a continuous parallel between contemporaneity and antiquity, Mr. Joyce is pursuing a method which others must pursue after him. . . . It is simply a way of controlling, of ordering, of giving a shape and a significance to the immense panorama of futility and anarchy which is contemporary history."[18] Eliot's description of the technique of postfiguration is exemplary. What gives us pause is his assertion that "no one else has built a novel upon such a foundation before"—an assumption that has been echoed by many critics and scholars. But in fact several novels employing precisely this "continuous parallel between contemporaneity and antiquity" were written in the forty years preceding the publication of *Ulysses*: the earliest fictional transfigurations of Jesus established a continuous parallel between the contemporaneity of the late nineteenth century and the antiquity of the Gospels.

Given the existence of such a well-defined "literary" technique as figural interpretation and its recent sensational popularization through Strauss's *Life of Jesus*, what is more reasonable than that this technique of explicitly Christian origin should first have been reintroduced into literature by means of a Christian subject—the transfiguration of Jesus— rather than a non-Christian subject? It is one of the arguments of this book that the technique of typological postfiguration, which Joyce used so brilliantly in his novel, was possible there only because it had already been employed and rather fully explored in a variety of fictional transfigurations of Jesus extending back half a century before the

[18] Eliot's essay first appeared in *Dial*; rpt. in *Forms of Modern Fiction*, ed. William Van O'Connor (1948; rpt. Bloomington, Ind.: Univ. of Indiana-Midland, 1959), pp. 120-24.

publication of *Ulysses*. To point this out is not to denigrate Joyce's accomplishment, which is superlative, nor his originality, which goes unchallenged. As a matter of fact, the postfigurative method is often employed very clumsily in the early transfigurations and stands in the same relationship to Joyce's virtuosity as does the style of Edouard Dujardin's *Les Lauriers sont coupés* to Joyce's more sophisticated use of stream of consciousness. It is not simply a question of the priority of lesser writers: priority is hardly a factor in critical evaluation. But an interesting point of literary history is involved. The very self-consciousness with which the early authors of fictional transfigurations use the technique suggests that they were fully aware of their innovativeness in appropriating the ancient device of figural parallels for new novels. But this brings us to a more detailed consideration of those first tentative transfigurations of Christian socialism.

3. The Christian Socialist Jesus

ONE OF THE STOCK TYPES of late nineteenth-century literature is the renegade clergyman who forsakes theology in order to work for grand humanitarian goals. Ibsen's Johannes Rosmer (*Rosmersholm*, 1886), the scion of two centuries of Norwegian ministers, shocks his brother-in-law by proclaiming proudly that he has "given up his faith." Turning instead to the "great world of truth and freedom" that has suddenly been revealed to him, he resolves to devote his life to "the creation of a true democracy." Similarly, Hauptmann's Johannes Vockerat (*Lonely Lives*, 1891), disappoints his pious parents by renouncing his promising career as a theologian in order to dedicate himself to his "philosophical" work. The hero of Mrs. Humphry Ward's *Robert Elsmere* (1888) resigns his orders and goes out among the workingmen of London to establish a New Brotherhood. During the last decades of the century cassocks and collars fall to the right and the left as clergymen, both in literature and in life, come to feel that intellectual responsibility and social reform—"truth," "freedom," "democracy," and all the other grand ideals—are unattainable within conventional ecclesiastical structures.

The radical break with organized religion was simply a dramatic gesture for a mood increasingly shared by thoughtful men and women, who sensed an incompatibility between a living Christianity and the fossilized institutions and dogmas that Kierkegaard lampooned under the label of "Christendom." The variety of movements in many countries through which Christians increasingly sought to apply the spirit and principles of the New Testament to social reform is known, loosely and collectively, as Christian socialism.

Though some of its proponents flatly rejected the Church and sought to work outside its framework, Christian socialism generally implies not only social reform but also reform of the Church itself. It should be clearly understood, as well, that in the nineteenth century the term had almost none of the political significance that it later assumed. Christian socialists of the age took great pains to distinguish their thought from the more politically oriented forms of socialism. In *The Heart of the World: A Story of Christian Socialism* (1905) Charles M. Sheldon expressly excludes "any other economic theories than those which have been so plainly stated in the Bible, and especially in the New Testament."[1] The hero of the novel, the Reverend Frederick Stanton, explains that "Christian Socialism is nothing but a term which means that if the plain teachings of the Son of God were obeyed in human society, the world would begin to enjoy a peace, a strength, a prosperity, a brotherhood, such as it does not now know." Similarly, Alfred Barry in his *Lectures on Christianity and Socialism* (1890) carefully differentiated Christian socialism from the "many theories of thorough-going Socialism": "Other forms of Socialism will tell us that all our evils come from forgetting or neglecting this or that law or condition of life. But Christian Socialism will ask, with Carlyle, 'Is it not the root of all our confusions and bewilderments, that we have too much forgotten God?' "[2]

Christian socialism was inspired by the new image of a humanized Jesus that had emerged from the nineteenth-century lives of Jesus. At the same time, we should not overlook the fact that the later "liberal" lives were often colored very much by what the social reformers wanted to see in them. When Albert Schweitzer wrote *The Quest of the Historical Jesus*, he came to the conclusion that it was the characteristic feature of lives of Jesus around the turn of the century to subordinate historical accuracy to a particular interpretation: "Men who have no qualifications for the

[1] (New York and London: Fleming H. Revell, 1905), p. 113; see also pp. 113-43: "To Be Skipped by the Thoughtless Reader" and "The Programme of Socialism."

[2] *Lectures on Christianity and Socialism* (London: Cassel, 1890), p. 32.

task, whose ignorance is nothing less than criminal, who loftily anathematise scientific theology instead of making themselves in some measure acquainted with the researches which it has carried out, feel impelled to write a Life of Jesus in order to set forth their general religious view in a portrait of Jesus which has not the faintest claim to be historical" (p. 325).

We have already noted that such early utopian socialists as Constant, in *The Last Incarnation*, seized eagerly upon the image of Jesus as a social reformer, and the tendency toward social betterment is implicit in Renan's *Life*. Toward the end of the century "The Social Teaching of Jesus" began to be stressed more and more, as was the case in an influential book of that title by Shailer Mathews (1897). Mathews had been a historian and political economist at Colby College before he became professor of New Testament history and interpretation at the Chicago Divinity School. His work, which bears the subtitle "An Essay in Christian Sociology," is representative of the new trend. To the objection that Jesus left no systematized social teachings, Mathews replies that "he certainly was no more a systematic theologian than he was a sociologist." Two factors have delayed the understanding of his social teaching. First, theology since the Reformation has been concerned with the salvation of the individual believer: "A new man and not a new society has been the objective point of most preaching." Second, dogmatic theology has all too frequently "mistaken what they think Christ ought to have taught for what he really did teach." As an heir of the nineteenth-century critical tradition, Mathews concludes: "There is but one way to the apprehension of the teaching of Jesus, whether religious or social, and that is the patient study of the gospels with the aid of all modern critical and exegetical methods."[3]

It is to this kind of Christian socialism that the Reverend

[3] *The Social Teaching of Jesus* (New York: Macmillan, 1897). All quotations are taken from the Introduction.

David Burkley is converted in Archibald McCowan's novel *Christ, the Socialist* (1894). Burkley, pastor of the "First Presbyterian Church of Springford, Connecticut," at first resists the teachings of his friend, the village schoolmaster Robert Stewart. "I made a mistake in confounding socialism with anarchy and lawlessness," he later reflects. "Christian socialism, the socialism of Robert Stewart, has no more connection with these, than the archangel Michael has with Satan" (p. 255). The novel concludes with a manuscript of Stewart's entitled "Socialism and Christianity," in which it is flatly stated: ". . . the greatest, purest, truest socialist the world has ever seen, was our Lord and Saviour Jesus Christ" (p. 335).

A few writers of the generation, to be sure, claimed the authority of Jesus for more specifically partisan purposes. In a novel called *Jesus and Judas* (*Jesus und Judas*, 1891) the German writer Felix Hollaender argued that "the first epoch-making Social Democrat, the Social Democrat par excellence, was none other than Jesus Christ." And the leading theoretican of German naturalism, Arno Holz, put very much the same thought into verse in the dedicatory epistle to his *Book of the Times* (*Buch der Zeit*, 1885):

> Für mich ist jener Rabbi Jesus Christ
> nichts weiter als der erste Sozialist.
>
> (As far as I am concerned, that rabbi Jesus Christ
> is nothing more than the first socialist.)

In general, however, the impulse to write the first fictional transfigurations of Jesus came from Christian socialism in the broader sense of the term. The writers, moved to what Schweitzer called "hate" by the sterility of the conventional Church—particularly its unwillingness to accept liberal ideas and its resistance to social reform—set out to depict this clash between "Christendom" and "Christianity" by portraying the life of a Jesus-like hero in conflict with the Church of his day. In view of the renegade theologians, the "imitations," the "revived" Jesuses that were currently popular, it is perhaps inevitable that a writer, sooner or later, would stumble onto this new form.

Possibly the first full-length transfiguration was *The True History of Joshua Davidson*, which appeared in England anonymously in 1872. It is an appallingly bad novel—a Christian socialist tract suspended on the barest framework of plot. But its very clumsiness reminds us of two considerations. First, these early transfigurations were conceived in a tendentiously religious sense. The Christian socialist theme of *Joshua Davidson* is stated quite clearly: *"The obstacles to practical Christianity come from professing Christians"* (p. 7).[4] Second, the authors of the first transfigurations were faced with a double problem: their own lack of experience with the technique, and the fear that the audience might miss the parallel. As a result, the fiction is carried out with the same heavy-handed explicitness that marks, say, Constant's *The Last Incarnation*. (After all, they could not count on a generation of readers trained on *Ulysses* and *Doctor Faustus*.)

The "theory" of *Joshua Davidson*, this so-called "theoretical novel," is expounded explicitly in the preface to its third edition: "Let us ask ourselves candidly what would be the manner of man, the course of action, and what the reception JESUS CHRIST would meet with, if He came among us now, in circumstances parallel to those of His own times." The author is in no doubt whatsoever as to the answer: "He would be a working man, and He would speak with a provincial accent; He would attack the capitalist, the political economist, the Sabbatarian, and the bench of bishops; He would live at the East End among the roughs and gaol-birds of Tiger Bay, who are our lepers, and He would denounce the luxury and respectability of the West End as He formerly denounced Dives and the Pharisees . . ." (p. 8). The theoretical characterization goes on

[4] I quote from the Tauchnitz reprint of the 3rd London edition (Leipzig: Tauchnitz, 1873).

for another page. Since the author is persuaded that "the world has not changed in essential feeling since the days of Pontius Pilate and Barabbas," the "Christ-man" is doomed from the start: "If Christ has not died, neither has the Cross been taken down; and characters are crucified, if men are not" (p. 11). And the whole story is written to bear out the narrator's cynical observation that "to live according to Christ in modern Christendom was, as we found out, to be next thing to criminal" (p. 155).

The novel itself achieves no more fictional spontaneity than the preface suggests. Ostensibly a first-person account by Joshua Davidson's closest associate (who, like most of the characters in the book, remains nameless), it is essentially a series of conversations strung together on the flimsiest of plots. Whether he is talking to a member of Parliament, a wealthy philanthropist, or a friendly aristocrat, Joshua repeats basically the same message over and over: "Let us then strip our Christianity of all the mythology, the fetichism that has grown about it. Let us abandon the idolatry with which we have obscured the meaning of the Life; let us go back to the MAN, and carry on His work in its essential spirit in the direction suited to our times and social conditions" (p. 84). Going slightly beyond pure Christian socialism, Joshua asks his friends to understand that "Christianity is not a creed as dogmatised by churches, but an organization having politics for its means and the equalization of classes as its end. It is Communism" (p. 85).

Now this doctrine of "practical Christianity" or "Christian Communism" is advanced within a basic pattern that is clearly dependent upon the Gospels. "Joshua Davidson was the only son of a village carpenter, born in the small hamlet of Trevalga on the North Cornwall coast, in the year 1835" (p. 15). (In the absence of any other reason and in view of specific references to demythologizing, it would seem that the author chose that date as a gesture toward the publication of Strauss's *Life of Jesus*, which represented, so to speak, the birth of the historical Jesus.) The only incident narrated from his childhood is a dispute with the local clerical authority—the vicar, Mr. Grand—on the nature of Christianity. Otherwise, Joshua "wrought at his father's bench" and held prayer meetings and Bible readings with his friends beside the sea—"Their aim was to be thorough and like Christ" (p. 29). Eventually Joshua moves from this British Galilee to London, where he senses a wider sphere for his activities: "He interested himself in politics, in current social questions, especially those relating to labour and capital, and in the condition of the poor" (p. 80). During this period one of his friends is Félix Pyat, a future French Communard, who is in England "as an exile, chiefly reading at the British Museum, . . . when he gained the love and admiration of all who knew him by the dignity, the devotion, the earnestness of his life" (p. 145). For a time Joshua attempts to accomplish his goals by working "on the Christ plan" with no one but his friends and disciples: he rescues a prostitute named Mary Prinsep as well as a burglar called Joe Traill—acts of Christian charity that do not endear him to the authorities. But eventually, recognizing the need for class organization, he joins the International Working Men's Association (an organization established in the years following 1848 by Charles Kingsley, J. M. Ludlow, and other early Christian socialists). And he continues to work for his "religion of politics" (p. 206): "No man was more convinced than he that sin and misery are the removable results of social circumstances, and that poverty, ignorance, and class-distinctions consequent, are at the root of all the crimes and wretchedness afloat" (p. 207).

In the spring of 1871, attracted by socialism in action, Joshua goes to Paris to work for the Commune. For a few weeks it seems that the Christian socialist utopia has arrived. But during the repression that soon follows, Mary Prinsep is shot to death; Joshua's friend and biographer is beaten within an inch of his life. On his return to England, Joshua finds that he is now besmirched even among the workingmen as a Communist and, worse yet, a French atheist. Joshua makes a last futile attempt to explain to the English workers the truth about the French struggle for equal rights. He announces a lecture on Communism in which he intends to show "how Christ and his apostles were Communists, and how they preached the same doctrines which the Commune of Paris strove to embody; allowing for the differences of method inherent to the differences of social arrangements that have grown up during a lapse of nearly two thousand years" (p. 243). But the inevitable happens. Incited by Mr. Grand, the conservative clergyman and Joshua's old enemy, the crowd attacks and tramples Joshua to death: "The man who had lived the life after Christ more exactly than any human being ever known to me . . . was killed by the Christian Party of order" (p. 250). The book ends with the rhetorical question of Christian socialism: "Which is true—modern society in its class strife and consequent elimination of its weaker elements, or the brotherhood of communism taught by the Jewish carpenter of Nazareth? Who will answer me?—who will make the dark thing clear?"

Though the Christian socialism, or communism, of the book is apparent, the transfiguration is so sketchy and clumsy that we might not notice it without the author's repeated reminders that Joshua Davidson is acting out a modern imitation of Christ. His name and parentage remind us of Jesus, as does the disputation of the child in the temple. He saves a prostitute named Mary and takes pity on sinners. And he is finally killed by a mob incited by conservative religious forces in a scene calculated to suggest the violence of the crucifixion. In addition, the entire work is written in an intentionally artless form that, like a Gospel, plays down biographical narrative for the sake of inspiration. "As I am neither a gentleman nor a scholar I have not pretended to any graces of style; and I have not tried to make an amusing story," the narrator avers in his Preface. "My little book is more a record of what JOSHUA said and thought than of what happened to him through others"

(p. 13). The narrator also refuses to give his name: he was Joshua's nearest friend, and "those who know JOSHUA will know who I am well enough" (p. 14).

For all its aesthetic ineptness, *The History of Joshua Davidson* was an instant sensation, and its originality—that is, the use of the postfigurative technique—was noted by the critics. It went through three editions in as many months, and many subsequent editions were published with slight alterations of the title: *The True History of Joshua Davidson, Communist* (Philadelphia, 1873); *The Life of Joshua Davidson; or, The Modern Imitation of Christ. A Theoretical Novel* (New York, 1882). It was translated into German by none other than the socialist leader Wilhelm Liebknecht,[5] and it was included in such popular series as the Tauchnitz Collection of British Authors and Mr. Stead's Penny Series.

It was soon revealed that the author was that great-grandmother of today's liberated women, Elizabeth Lynn Linton (1822-98). A strong-willed young woman, Eliza Lynn left home at an early age to become a journalist in London. From 1851 to 1854 she was the Paris correspondent for several London papers. She wrote dozens of essays with nasty titles, and topics, that did little to endear her to the public. As a result, she had a notable lack of success with the many novels that she turned out in the fifties and sixties. It was only after her marriage in 1858 to William James Linton, the radical editor-translator-engraver, that her literary fortunes began to change. And with *The History of Joshua Davidson* she found the subject that was ideally suited to her abilities: the loose structure provided by the transfiguration compensated for a weak sense of plot and characterization, while the subject provided a suitable occasion for her strong social and political commitment and her sharply crit-

[5] I have been unable to verify this fact bibliographically; my sole source for the information is Heinrich Weinel and Alban G. Widgery, *Jesus in the Nineteenth Century and After* (Edinburgh: T. & T. Clark, 1914), pp. 241-42, which quotes briefly from a " 'revised' translation by Liebknecht."

ical eye for weaknesses in individuals and institutions. These are hardly the qualities that make for creative genius, but wrapped up in the package of the then fashionable Christian socialism they afforded Mrs. Linton her greatest success.

A Singular Life (1894) is somewhat better as fiction, and no one could have been more unlike the sharp-tongued and emancipated Mrs. Linton than its author, Elizabeth Stuart Phelps Ward (1844-1911). Elizabeth Phelps was the natural heir of her religious impulse as well as her fictional bent. Her mother, Elizabeth Stuart Phelps (1815-52), had written a number of successful sentimental novels whose nature is characterized adequately by their titles: *Sunny Side, or, The Country Minister's Wife* (1851) and *A Peep at Number Five, or, A Chapter in the Life of a City Pastor* (1851). Her father was a Congregational minister who later became a professor at the Theological Seminary at Andover, Massachusetts. With a background like this, a talented young girl could hardly avoid becoming the author of best-selling novels with a sentimental religious tone, four of them suggesting an obsession with "gates" that would delight a Freudian critic: *The Gates Ajar* (1868), *Beyond the Gates* (1883), *The Gates Between* (1887), and *Within the Gates* (1901).

A *Singular Life* draws, first of all, upon the author's own life in the seminary town of Andover and the discussions regarding the German "higher criticism" that she heard in her father's house. It is, second, an American version of *Robert Elsmere*: instead of the Oxford, London, and Surrey of Mrs. Humphry Ward's England, we find here the Andover, Boston, and East Gloucester of late nineteenth-century Massachusetts. These two elements are synthesized, finally, by a conspicuous use of the fictional transfiguration, which is employed with no greater sophistication but with far more dogged consistency than in *The History of Joshua Davidson*. The story begins when the hero, Emanuel Bayard, is a thirty-year-old student about to graduate from the Theological Seminary in a New England town with the unlikely name of Cesarea, where he resides in Galilee Hall. Emanuel not only has theological problems; he also is emotionally involved with his professor's daughter Helen Carruth, who bears a striking resemblance to Elizabeth Stuart Phelps herself.

In a flashback close to the beginning of the novel we learn that Emanuel is an orphan. His mother, Mary Worcester, came from a prominent Boston family. One summer, in the vacation village of Bethlehem, she met and married Joseph Bayard, a minister and part-time carpenter. Both Mary and Joseph died soon after Emanuel's birth, and Emanuel was raised by wealthy relatives in Boston.

After this flashback, which establishes the transfigurational technique for even the densest reader—though, it must be conceded, without all the pointing and theorizing of Eliza Lynn Linton—the story gets under way. Emanuel, though one of the most brilliant students of his class, has received no call because his "theology" is not sufficiently orthodox. When his ordination is rejected by the prosperous church in the seaside resort of Windover, Emanuel is invited by the poor fishing people of the town to be their pastor. Here, in "Angel Alley," Emanuel soon comes to be known as "the gospel cap'n" or, like Joshua Davidson, the "Christman." As he gives himself more and more selflessly to his work, Emanuel begins to realize that his theological education has not equipped him to deal with the simplest and most pressing problems that arise every day in his new position: "We were not taught such things in the Seminary. . . . Predestination, foreordination, sanctification, election, and botheration,—and never a lesson on the Christian socialism of our day, not a lecture to tell us how to save a poor, lost woman, how to reform a drunkard . . ." (p. 153).[6]

Emanuel begins to win his first "disciples" when he performs what is generally regarded as a "miracle" by the peo-

6 *A Singular Life* (Boston and New York: Houghton, Mifflin, 1898).

65

ple in the fishing village: he swims out during a storm to save a shipwrecked sailor—obviously the contemporary equivalent of Jesus' walking on the waters. As he turns increasingly away from "Christendom" and begins to put his Christian socialism into practice, the rumor begins to spread of his miraculous powers of persuasion: " 'I hear when you talk to folks they stop drinking.' " And a public scandal arises when Emanuel tries to help a local prostitute with the predictable name [Magda]Lena. (Given the Christian socialist obsession with prostitution and alcoholism, whores and drunkards play a prominent role in these novels.) In order to attract a following and—another Christian socialist ideal—to lure the workingmen back to the church, Emanuel dispenses with conventional services and holds a series of outdoor revival meetings.

To make sure that the reader will not miss the parallels, the author and her characters point them out to us from time to time without the slightest smile of irony. For instance, when the family attends one of the celebrated revival meetings, Mrs. Carruth finds herself reminded of a scene from literature. After toying in her mind with George Eliot, Foxe's *Book of Martyrs*, and the Memoirs of Whitefield, it finally occurs to her that the occasion reminds her of a scene from the New Testament: the Sermon on the Mount. Similarly Emanuel's initial decision not to marry Helen Carruth is compared to the Temptation: "So Emanuel Bayard entered into his Wilderness. Therein he was tempted like other men of God who renounced the greatest joy of life for its grandest duty" (p. 242). (Shortly before his death he marries Helen Carruth when he comes into a small inheritance.)

But by the time Emanuel is thirty-three, all this Gospel felicity has inevitably aroused the hostility of the stalwart Christians of Windover. The wealthy members of the congregation up on the hill are offended by the unconventionality of his teaching and methods. (One is reminded of

Mrs. Linton's assertion that "the obstacles to practical Christianity come from professing Christians.") When he befriends Lena, public resentment reaches such a pitch that his chapel is burned down. In addition, Emanuel has alienated the powerful "liquor interests" of Windover by causing many licenses to be revoked. On the day that his newly built chapel is dedicated, Emanuel is struck by a stone thrown by "Judas"—the nickname of the owner of a seamen's grog shop. He dies a week later.

In this early transfiguration many of the parallels are no more than onomastic: *Emanuel* Bayard, *Mary* and *Joseph*, *Cesarea, Galilee* Hall, *Lena,* and so forth. Yet the Christian socialism has here been provided with a much livelier narrative framework than was the case in *The History of Joshua Davidson.* For this reason it is worth stressing the fact that the author was quite familiar with the exciting theological questions of the day: she uses the postfigurative technique with such a degree of consciousness and consistency that we conclude it could only be the result of the literary application of the figural interpretation known from New Testament scholarship. This seems to be borne out by the frequent references, within the novel, to the controversy on the authenticity of the Fourth Gospel. In fact, while Emanuel is struggling to assert his Christian socialism in Windover, Professor Carruth makes a trip to Germany in order to pursue his theological investigations.

As Shailer Mathews stressed, Christian socialism resulted directly from the critical exegesis of liberal theology, which had separated the social teaching of Jesus from the dogma of the Church. It is somewhat ironic, therefore, that in *A Singular Life* and other Christian socialist novels, this very scholarship is often attacked as a distraction from the true and proper mission of a Christian minister. We have already noted that Emanuel Bayard felt that the seminary had prepared him for everything except the very problems with which he had to deal every day. And at the end of the novel even Professor Carruth is made to feel that he "had been so occupied with the misery of the next world that he had never investigated the hell of this one" (p. 385).

Although Benito Pérez Galdós does not advance any such unambivalent and naively optimistic program for reform, the impulse that we have called Christian socialist is conspicuous in his thought and works. Galdós (1843-1920) was born in the Canary Islands and attended the English school at Las Palmas, where he developed the Anglophilia—and the taste for Dickens—that remained with him throughout his life. It was only after he departed for the University of Madrid in 1862, however, that the previously sickly and submissive young man was able to give vent to a secret lust for liberalism, in part as a gesture of rebellion against a domineering mother. Coming under the influence of the currently fashionable *krausismo*—the philosophical effort, deriving from the minor German thinker K.C.F. Krause, to reconcile faith and reason in a "harmonious rationalism"— Galdós rapidly accommodated Darwinism to his basic religious faith. His voluminous library in several languages included the works of Renan as well as Strauss's *Life of Jesus* alongside Thomas à Kempis and tomes of a more inspirational nature. Caught up in the fervor for liberal reform that marked Madrid in the years before the Revolution of 1868, Galdós was made keenly aware through his journalistic activities of the specific needs for social reform. He gradually arrived at the conclusion that the national accidie, which had prevented Spain from sharing in the general European progress of the nineteenth century, must be attributed in large measure to the debilitating struggle between the Liberals and Clericals, which had wasted the creative energies of the people. At the same time, his deeply religious nature, which expressed itself in the conviction that social reform could ultimately be achieved only as the result of a religious renewal, saved his anticlericalism from developing into the agnosticism or atheism of many of his contemporaries.

It is the history of this essentially religious struggle that Galdós began to trace in the fictional series that is still the mainstay of his popularity in his own country as the greatest Spanish novelist since Cervantes—the forty-six volumes of his monumental *Episodias nacionales* (1873-1912). At the same time, in a parallel series of twenty-four social novels entitled *Novelas españolas contemporáneas* (1881-1915) he analyzed the impact of that malaise on his own society. In *Doña Perfecta* (1876), one of his novels best known outside of Spain, he attacked the stultifying clericalism of the provinces, which destroys a young engineer of liberal tendencies. It is to this group of works devoted to the analysis of present social problems that *Nazarín* belongs (1895).[7]

Both of the previous transfigurations used the device of a first-person narrator who claims to have known the hero and who thereby authenticates the doctrine of Christian socialism, which is presented as being more than a mere fiction. *The History of Joshua Davidson* was allegedly written down by the hero's closest disciple. Similarly, *A Singular Life* is recorded by a narrator who repeatedly intrudes with first-person comments: "I see no reason why one should hesitate to give a man full credit for personal beauty because one chances to be his biographer, and do not hesitate to say that the attractiveness of this young man was extraordinary" (p. 11). In *Nazarín* we find a similar technique, which is obviously suggested by the very nature of a mod-

---

[7] In the secondary literature on Galdós, *Nazarín* has been conspicuously neglected until quite recently; many of the biographies barely mention it in passing. The studies that I have found most helpful are Sherman H. Eoff, *The Novels of Pérez Galdós: The Concept of Life and Dynamic Process* (St. Louis: Washington Univ. Studies, 1954); Gustavo Correa, *El Simbolismo Religioso en las novelas de Pérez Galdós* (Madrid: Gredos, 1962); and *Anales Galdosianos*, 2 (1967), an entire issue devoted to *Nazarín* (esp. pp. 83-101: Alexander A. Parker, "*Nazarín*, or the Passion of Our Lord Jesus Christ according to Galdós").

ern gospel. But here it is used, paradoxically, not to certify the facts but to cast doubt upon the narrative and, ultimately, upon the hero's rather quixotic mission.

According to the fiction, the narrator first meets the priest Don Nazario Zaharín, popularly known as Nazarín, when he accompanies a friend, a newspaper reporter, into the slums of Madrid. The reporter, his curiosity piqued by Nazarín's refusal to prosecute someone who has robbed him, interviews the priest. Somewhere between thirty and forty years old and the son of Moorish shepherds—he is frequently called "the Arab" or "the Semite"—Nazarín has neither a parish nor, for that matter, much contact with the Church and other clergymen. Living from alms and the occasional mass that he says, Nazarín is attempting to withdraw from the world. His notion of what he calls "the faith of Christ in all its purity" (p. 1731)[8] includes not only total altruism toward others, but also total passivity in life and silent acceptance of adversity and suffering. Although he is frequently exploited and robbed by his slum neighbors, he refuses to lodge complaints with the police because he believes neither in private property nor in such institutions as courts of law, which serve only to oppress the poor, or book learning, which merely distracts our attention from the work of God.

The reporter comes away from this astonishing interview, which fills the first of the five parts of the novel, convinced that Nazarín is a complete scoundrel, the most talented cynic he has ever met, a man who cultivates social parasitism with supreme skill. Others, like Aunt Chanfaina, the owner of the rooming house where Nazarín lives, are certain that the priest is a saint. The narrator is unable to make up his mind, and his uncertainty catalyzes the novel. Long after the reporter has dismissed the peculiar priest from his memory, the narrator is still obsessed with him and finds

---

[8] To my knowledge there is no translation; I quote in my own translation from *Obras Completas de Don Benito Pérez Galdós*, ed. F.C.S. de Robles (Madrid: Aguilar, 1942), v, 1723-1814.

himself unable to decide whether the Nazarín he recalls is "a true and real personality" or simply a figure "constructed from materials extracted from my own ideas" (p. 1737). On the one hand, the narrator maintains throughout the novel the fiction of historical objectivity and pretends to rely on a corpus of specific sources. At one point, for instance, he is unable to report the name of a village "since the Nazarín-ist references are somewhat obscure in the designation of this locality" (p. 1783). On the other hand, he is not sure whether the story he intends to recount is true or merely "an illusion of reality" (p. 1737). In the last analysis, he can-not even state with assurance who wrote the story he is tell-ing. "The narrator conceals himself," the first section ends. But he is persuaded that the story is in essence "clear, pre-cise, and sincere."

The novel turns out to be not, like *Joshua Davidson* or *A Singular Life*, the ostensibly firsthand account of events ex-perienced or witnessed, but rather an experimental or the-oretical novel in the most precise sense of the word. Stimu-lated by his encounter with the real Nazarín in Part One, the narrator writes the remainder of the novel as a sort of experiment to see what would happen to Nazarín if he should be forced to put his theory into practice. Will the priest, transported out of his retreat into the world of real-ity, turn out to be a saint, a scoundrel, or simply a fool? This ambivalence, needless to say, casts a new light on the fic-tional transfiguration.

Part One, then, constitutes a theoretical introduction to Nazarín, his personality, and his theory of Christianity. The remainder of the novel falls roughly into two parts: the picaresque adventures of Parts II-III and the Passion of Parts IV-V. Nazarín willy-nilly becomes involved with real-ity when the prostitute Andara—once again, this stock figure of Christian socialist novels—takes refuge in his room after stabbing another girl in a knife fight. Nazarín is glad of a chance to put his theory of altruism into practice by aiding the wounded girl, who is being pursued by the police. Within a short time, however, his good intentions are frustrated: he is reproved by the ecclesiastical authorities for living in sin with a whore; and when Andara tries to conceal traces of her presence by setting a fire in Nazarín's room, he is accused of arson as well as harboring a criminal. Instead of making any attempt to exonerate himself of accusations of which he is totally innocent, Nazarín decides to take to the roads and to live in reality the life of possessionless altruism that he has preached in theory.

Very soon, however, Nazarín discovers that he cannot simply run away from responsibilities. Andara implores him to let her accompany him on his wanderings, and she also brings along her friend Beatriz, who hopes that Nazarín's saintly influence will cure her of a disastrous passion that she feels for the horse-trader El Pinto. From the outset, therefore, his pilgrimage is marked by two symbolic Christian disciples, the militant Andara and the sweet, pacifist Beatriz. For all his demurrals, Nazarín cannot escape his reputation as a saint. In one village the simple peasants fall down and worship him because they believe that his presence has miraculously healed a sick child. And when the three pilgrims enter a region that has been stricken by a smallpox epidemic, they devote themselves selflessly to the care of the villagers. On another occasion Nazarín softens the heart of a fierce and tyrannical landowner named Don Pedro de Belmonte, to whom he outlines his theory of Christian humility and poverty.

After the quixotic adventures of Parts II–III, which reveal a rather Cervantean view of the teaching and healing Jesus, the plot is channeled into the tighter structure of the Passion in the last two sections. On their way from one plague-stricken village to another, the three exhausted pilgrims take refuge for a few days in the ruins of an old castle. Beatriz is recognized by her former lover, El Pinto, who threatens to come up to the castle and take her by force from her companions. This attempt is frustrated when a heavy fog sets in, but it is intimated that El Pinto betrays their presence to his cousin, the village *alcalde*. In any case, the next evening they are warned by Andara's admirer, a dwarf, that the local authorities have learned of their presence and intend to arrest them on charges issuing from Madrid. They share what turns out to be their Last Supper, after which, in the dilapidated garden, Nazarín speaks words of consolation to the two disciples who have accompanied him so faithfully. Still protesting that they are innocent and have nothing to fear, Nazarín refuses to flee and waits in the Gethsemane-like setting for the mob of citizens approaching to arrest him. (During the arrest Andara attacks one of the guards with her kitchen knife and thus acts out the role of Peter.)

The subsequent interview with the local *alcalde*—the secular power acting on instruction from the ecclesiastical authority in Madrid—gives Nazarín another chance to expound his views. After declaring his innocence of all charges, Nazarín asserts that his sole purpose is to "teach the Christian doctrine, the most elementary and simple one, to anyone who wants to learn it" (p. 1796). And he teaches it, he adds, by word of mouth and by example. If, for this reason, he has been mistaken for a criminal, God knows better: "My conscience accuses me of no wrong." Recapitulating once more his principle of altruism and love, Nazarín concludes with a sentiment familiar from many Christian socialist works: "I allow myself to believe—indeed, it is my conviction—that if Our Lord Jesus Christ were alive, he would think just as I do" (p. 1797). The more realistic mayor, playing Sancho Panza to Nazarín's Quixote, replies that he is neither a learned man nor a theologian. But it is his surmise that "el Jesucristo nuevo," should he return to earth, would be put straight into jail. He would not be crucified, for "that kind of scaffold is out of style nowadays" (p. 1797). And he would enter the capital city not seated on a donkey, but in a chain-gang of the Civil Guard.

The *alcalde*, for all his sympathy, considers Nazarín to be no more than a fool, who will be acquitted of all charges in

Madrid; his allusion to the New Testament parallels is purely ironic, by way of contrast rather than comparison. But just as the *alcalde*, in his Sancho Panzan realism, wholly secularizes the Passion by reducing the triumphal entry into Jerusalem to the shuffling of a chain-gang, Nazarín expands his adventures into a kind of quixotic grandeur. As he sets out to Madrid, escorted by the Civil Guard, the road takes on, in his imagination at least, more and more characteristics of the *via crucis* (his own term). He is taunted by several of the other criminals, who mock him for aspiring to sanctity and piety while traveling with whores. That night, in the cell, he is tormented with blasphemies and finally beaten up by the criminals until one of them, a church-thief nicknamed "Sacrilege," takes pity and comes to his defense (in obvious analogy to the repentant thief on the cross at Golgotha).

Suffering from his beating, his feet bloodied from the road, and racked by fever, Nazarín is less and less able to distinguish between reality and the figments of his imagination. In one great vision he witnesses a cosmic battle between his adherents, led by a transfigured Andara and "Sacrilege," and the *antinazaristas* of the world. Then his agony increases: "his head ached as though an axe were buried in it, and on his right shoulder he felt an irresistible weight" (p. 1814). Burdened by this imaginary cross, he has to be supported by his disciples and consoled by the sympathetic guards, who assure him that he will be acquitted on grounds of insanity. But Nazarín, totally unable at this point to distinguish between vision and reality, endures his Passion to the end: "At the end of the street he saw that a huge cross rose up, and if for a moment the joy of being nailed to it inundated his soul, he immediately came to his senses, saying: 'I do not deserve, O Lord, the exalted honor of being sacrificed upon your cross'" (p. 1814). This vision, finally, gives way to another that amounts virtually to an ascension: separated from the teeming masses of humanity, Nazarín sees himself celebrating mass with sublime devotion upon a pure and untouched altar. He awakens from these hallucinations to find himself in a hospital in Madrid. The novel ends with a vision in which Jesus appears to tell him that what he has experienced was only "an insane figuration of your mind," but suggests that Nazarín will yet accomplish much more for his sake.

The ambivalence that marks the beginning of *Nazarín* is intensified in the sequel entitled *Halma* (1895). Here it turns out that Nazarín has indeed been found insane by the courts and remanded to the estate of the Countess Halma-Lautenberg to be cured of his *melancolía religiosa* (p. 1863)[9]—which, according to good nineteenth-century medical theory, is assumed to have been brought on by that Dostoevskyan affliction, "epileptic neurosis." The established Church, in other words, has rid itself of the nuisance of Nazarín in the traditional fashion by calling him mad. At the same time, we learn that his vision has been in part fulfilled: his teaching, institutionalized into *el nazarismo*, is hotly debated in certain religious circles; the account of his adventures—that is to say, the novel *Nazarín* that had appeared earlier that same year—is circulated as reverently as a Gospel;[10] and journalists flock to interview this new Spanish mystic. Here again Galdós casts doubt on the meaning of his novel. One journalist inquires, for instance: "'Do you know whether he has read a slender volume that bears his name and is circulating hereabouts?' 'He has read it,' replied one of those who came with Flórez, 'and he says that the author, moved by the desire to fictionalize facts, exalts him unduly and gives excessive praise to ordinary actions that do not belong to the category of heroism, nor

[9] To my knowledge there is no translation; I quote in my own translation from *Obras Completas*, v, 1815-1921.

[10] A similar Shandean playfulness shows up seventy years later in John Barth's fictional transfiguration, *Giles Goat-Boy*; at one point the hero meets a girl who is reading the novel in which they are both characters. This intermingling of fiction and reality was quite common in German romantic fiction.

even of extraordinary virtue' " (p. 1859). Similarly, Andara is furious because the novel accuses her of arson: "If I was you, I'd put it in the papers that the writer of this book is a liar" (p. 1860). And a cousin of Don Pedro de Belmonte claims that the novel is "a fabric of lies" because the conversation between Belmonte and Nazarín is wholly out of character and improbable. All of these words tend to corroborate the idea that *Nazarín* is an experiment, a projection of the narrator's imagination, rather than a (fictional) account of events.

But what are we to make, after all this irony, of the meaning of *Nazarín?* The hero's "pure Christianity" is undeniably qualified by the objections of such realists as the reporter and the *alcalde*, just as the reliability of the narrative is impugned by other witnesses. To this extent Galdós' Christian socialism is far more problematic than that of some earlier writers, and it should not be identified directly with the teaching of his hero. Galdós would accept the anticlericalism of Nazarín, but his hero's anti-intellectualism would be absurd for such a modernist as Galdós. Similarly, there is much to admire in Nazarín's lived Christianity; his example converts Andara and the thief, cures Beatriz, and persuades, at least temporarily, Don Pedro. At the same time, events make it repeatedly clear that Nazarín's passive acceptance of everything is not only ineffectual, but even dangerous in the complexities of modern society. In fact, in Nazarín's withdrawal from reality Galdós seems to be attacking the lethargy and accidie that he and his fellow liberals diagnosed as the affliction of Spain itself. If society is to be helped, then Christian altruism and love need to be expedited by the techniques of liberalism and social reform. All of these ambiguities are present in the conclusion. For Nazarín's vision of the pure altar suggests that despite all his bitter experience of reality and despite the Passion that he undergoes in his imagination, he has still not escaped his sterile longing for withdrawal. The fact that he docilely accepts the Church's reproval and, in *Halma*, sets out to tame his "madness," suggests that any true reform must ultimately come about through the Church, not through quixotic efforts outside.

Another question that is discussed in *Halma* and that has obsessed some Galdós scholars is the extent to which *nazarismo* is indebted to *rusismo*. In view of Galdós' interest in Tolstoy—and he admired the Russian as greatly as he admired Balzac or Dickens—it is only reasonable to expect certain parallels in their thought. But although those passages in *Halma* are designed in part to make fun of influence-seeking critics, there is no reason to doubt Galdós when his spokesman says: "It could occur only to the devil to seek the source of this man's ideas in Russia of all places. You have asserted that he is a mystic. Very well. But why bring from so great a distance something native to our household, something we have in our soil, our air, our speech" (p. 1858). Our exercise in the history of ideas and comparative literature bears out this claim. The Christian socialist impulse was so pervasive in late nineteenth-century Europe that it is not particularly helpful to single out specific influences or to speak, as critics did until recently, of Galdós' "Tolstoyan phase."

Nazarín is no more able than *Joshua Davidson* and *A Singular Life* to deny its origin as a fictionalized Christian socialist tract. The novel is tied down at three important points by long dialogues that contribute absolutely nothing to the action and are justified solely as a platform for the expression of Nazarín's ideas: all of Part One, the long conversation with Don Pedro de Belmonte, and the scene with the *alcalde*. At the same time, Galdós has moved considerably beyond his predecessors in the sophisticated manipulation of the fictional transfiguration: indeed, here we are dealing with a first-rate novelist who happened to write a Christian socialist tract, whereas Mrs. Linton and Mrs. Ward were tract-writers who happened to express themselves in the form of the novel. There are, to be sure, certain external parallels between Nazarín and Jesus: his name, his

77

age, his clothing, his "Semitic" appearance, and his attitudes; he gives solace to a whore and performs what are taken to be miracles of healing; he disputes with the Scribes and Pharisees on the nature of Christianity; and he selflessly aids the destitute and the sick. He is accused of crimes of which he is innocent; he is betrayed and tried before a Pilate-like *alcalde* who turns him back over to the ecclesiastical authorities for punishment.

But within this external framework, which is so realistically plausible that we accept it, the author has made a major change: he has shifted the most problematic moment of the transfiguration, Nazarín's Passion, into the hero's own consciousness. Galdós is a much better psychologist than his precursors; as a matter of fact, he is one of the better psychologists of nineteenth-century fiction altogether. Although the ecclesiastical court attributes Nazarín's disturbances to religious hysteria produced by "epileptic neurosis," Galdós does not suggest at any point that Nazarín is clinically ill: his so-called madness is exposed as no more than an attempt of the Church to discredit what is anticlerical in his teaching; for the rest, Nazarín is healthy and reasonably normal up to the time of his beating and illness on the march to Madrid. The feverish hallucination is merely a passing state of mind, but it enables Galdós to motivate the hero's experience of the Passion with great plausibility. In his temporarily deranged mind the weight of the cross, the crown of thorns, the whole *via dolorosa* attain a degree of eidetic reality that is fully the equivalent of any external reality.

Nazarín is the first novel by a major European writer conceived and executed consistently from start to finish as a fictional transfiguration of Jesus. But around the turn of the century the Christian socialist impulse found in this literary form an increasingly popular vehicle that could be adapted easily to local circumstances. The American Emanuel Bayard, the British Joshua Davidson, the Spanish Nazarín would instantly recognize their German cousin in *The Stranger* (*Der Fremde*, 1901) by Hans von Kahlenberg.[11] "Von Kahlenberg" was actually the pseudonym of Helene Kessler (née Monbart, b. 1870), the daughter of a Prussian officer, who acquired a veneer of European sophistication through studies in France and England and then began turning out a series of piquantly salacious and highly popular novels of social criticism, usually focusing on the corruption of Wilhelmine Germany as seen from the standpoint of a dynamic and liberated young woman. In *The Stranger* she stumbled upon the increasingly fashionable form of the fictional transfiguration, which she applied with tedious rigor. Here, much as in Max Kretzer's *Vision of Christ*, a mysterious stranger appears in the Berlin of the late nineties and then moves across Germany doing all the things expected of a Christian socialist hero. He cures headaches and allays anguish by laying his hand on foreheads; he befriends prostitutes and succors the unemployed; he wins the affection of children and gradually assembles a group of devoted followers who are attracted by his gospel of love, humility, and common property. The modern Sermon on the Mount sounds like this:

> "The rich man is poor and the poor man is rich. He is strong who stands firm within himself. He who has become wise in God can not be affected by storms, the hatred of men, or need. The world is given to mankind. Above the world stands the man who bears the world within him. God is within you, and you belong to God. Awaken to your glory! A royal people without kings, masters all, and free men who have become masters over themselves."

Von Kahlenberg's "parable"—the subtitle of the novel—consists largely of unrelated episodes or encounters that

[11] To my knowledge there is no translation; I refer to *Der Fremde: Ein Gleichniss* (Dresden und Leipzig: Carl Reissner, 1901).

permit the author to introduce many parallels to the Gospels and to invent little allegories that illustrate various New Testament sayings. The episodes, however, are framed loosely by a plot consisting of the Ministry and Passion of Jesus. The story opens on a Christmas Eve, when the unnamed "stranger" meets a fiery unemployed workman who becomes John the Baptist to his Jesus. (This "great preacher of the Socialists" is subsequently imprisoned when he criticizes the prince for using troops to put down a riot of the unemployed. The prince orders his execution after he has a dream-like vision of Power, who dances before him like Salome.) After a time the newspapers become interested in the carryings-on of the strange new prophet. Looking into his background, they find out that his name is Joseph Schäppli and that he is the son of a carpenter in the small town of Bing an der Enz in Württemberg. His mother seems to have been subject to visions, and Joseph himself had been a quiet religious introvert until he disappeared from home at the age of thirty and set out on his wanderings. For a time the "stranger's" popularity and influence spread among the people: his activities are reported in the press, and he manages to outwit all the clever ruses designed to entrap him in the salons of the intellectual scoffers. (These scenes enable the author to introduce conversations on such currently chic topics as comparative religion and religious hysteria.) Eventually his activities begin to alarm the official clergy, who accuse him of stirring discontent among the people. Above all, they fear the disruption of their authority and tranquillity through the appearance of this man whom many regard as Jesus. "What would you do with the new Christ?" one preacher is asked. "You can just pack up your shop, pastor!"

Brought to trial on the charge of being a communist, the "stranger" soon convinces the secular authorities that he is in no sense guilty of any political offense. With reference to the currently popular theories of Charcot and Lombroso on criminality and insanity, he is then examined for sanity by a judge who translates Pilate's "What is truth?" into the modern legal equivalent: "What is reason?" Though the secular authorities are convinced that the man is no criminal, they condemn him to the madhouse, like Nazarín, in order to satisfy the clerics. When his alleged mother is brought from Württemberg for purposes of identification, the stranger denies her. Here, at the end of the novel, the Passion-parallel is brought to its completion. In the chapel of the madhouse the stranger is literally crucified by a crazed inmate, who ties him to the crucifix, drives a spike through his skull, and pierces his side with a sharpened stake. This "crucifixion" is wholly unmotivated; but the maddened murderer mumbles imprecations that seem to be borrowed from Nietzsche—an elaborate allegorical commentary, perhaps, on Nietzsche's attitude toward Christianity. At the end of the novel: "The Son of Man, from the cross, dead, pitying, sublime, gazed down." Nothing is left to the imagination.

The Stranger is a largely mechanical exercise in the invention of parallels between contemporary life and the Gospel narrative. The stylized tone, which is modeled more closely on Nietzsche's *Thus Spake Zarathustra* than on the Gospels, is calculated to lend an air of mystery to the events. It is clearly the author herself who creates and insists on the parallels: they are not attributed to the consciousness of the hero (as in *Nazarín*), nor is it left to the reader to draw his own conclusions. Instead, we come to resent the heavy-handed pointing and gesturing. The novel is fashionably anticlerical and advances all the proper Christian socialist ideas. In fact, its episodic structure permits the author to touch upon every conceivable social problem—including, of course, those old hobbyhorses of Christian socialism, alcoholism and prostitution. But as a novel it is no more than clever and timely, with none of the playfulness and psychological insight that distinguished *Nazarín* and raised it above the level of the other largely dated novels of the period.

For all the interest and controversy that these works aroused nationally among interested readers, none of the Christian socialist transfigurations had an international success until 1905, when Fogazzaro's *The Saint* (*Il Santo*) was published. The novels by the three ladies are trivial and minor, and only *Joshua Davidson* had a notable *succès de scandale.* Galdós was of course a major European writer, but *Nazarín,* long regarded as one of his lesser works, was scarcely known in Spain or abroad until 1959, when Luis Buñuel produced a film version that followed the original very closely and presented the story in such a way as to bring out its relevance for the present. (The only significant change that Buñuel made was to transpose the scene from Spain to Mexico.)

The huge and instant success of *The Saint* can be attributed to at least two factors. First, Fogazzaro was the first writer who succeeded in transmuting the Christian socialist transfiguration of Jesus from a tract into a novel. *The Saint* constitutes the third volume of a trilogy long considered to be the finest Italian fiction since Manzoni's *The Betrothed* —and admired, incidentally, by James Joyce. Second, the novel was vouchsafed the attention that automatically accrues to any work of a world-famous living writer that is placed on the Catholic *Index. The Saint* appeared in November, 1905; in April, 1906, it was listed on the *Index*; by the end of that same year it had been published in French and German periodicals and had appeared in London and New York, in English translation.

Why was the Church especially aroused by *The Saint*? The other fictional transfigurations that we have considered were directed outward toward the impact of practical Christianity on society. Moreover, the Church could hardly have cared less about their anticlericalism since it was aimed at Protestant Churches. (*Nazarín,* the only one of the four that appeared in a Catholic country, ended with the submission of its hero to ecclesiastical authority.) In *The Saint* the case is quite different: Fogazzaro, for all his concern with social problems, is obsessed above all with corruption within the Church; and his novel attacks the Church in its most sensitive area, the Vatican. This means, in turn, that Fogazzaro might more accurately be called a Modernist than a Christian socialist.

Modernism, like Christian socialism, constitutes one aspect of the general trend toward religious reform in the second half of the nineteenth century. But whereas Christian socialism comprises those movements that sought to apply the principles of Christianity to social reform, Modernism is a loose collective designation for the movement toward ecclesiastical reform and reform of Church doctrine. The Modernist attempt to reform the Church from within and to make it accessible to the liberal ideas of the times showed up, like Christian socialism and often hand in hand with it, in most Christian lands. In England the term "Modernism" came to be used by the Anglican opponents of theological liberalism to categorize any writers or thinkers who sought to effect a reconciliation between the dogma of the Church and such liberal notions as Darwinism and the German "higher criticism." George Eliot for her translation of Strauss, the so-called "Seven against Christ" of *Essays and Reviews* (1860), Matthew Arnold, Mrs. Humphry Ward, and anyone else who attempted to liberalize the accepted dogma fell into this category. And Modernism moved by way of the Andover Theological Seminary into the novels of Elizabeth Stuart Phelps Ward.

Catholic Modernism is associated with such names as Alfred Loisy and Maurice Blondel in France, George Tyrrell in England, and Ernesto Buonaiuti in Italy.[12] (Spanish *krausismo* can be regarded as a form of Modernism, and Galdós certainly shared many of its liberal ideas.) Modernism flourished during the twenty-five-year papacy of Leo

---

[12] Among the many works on Modernism I shall cite only Michele Ranchetti, *The Catholic Modernists: A Study of the Religious Reform Movement, 1864-1907*, trans. Isabel Quigly (London: Oxford Univ. Press, 1969), because it includes chapters on the role of Fogazzaro and *Il Santo*.

XIII; but when he was succeeded in 1903 by the "peasant pope" Pius X, the situation changed. Within two months the new pope issued a notorious encyclical (*E supremi apostolatus cathedra*), in which he attacked the "lying science that lays open the way to the errors of rationalism and semi-rationalism." Between 1903 and the encyclical of 1907 (*Pascendi dominici gregis*), which in effect put an end to Catholic Modernism, Church history was a succession of attacks, reprimands, and excommunications. *The Saint*, a fictional appeal for Modernist reforms within the Church, appeared at the height of the papal counterattack and hence received immediate Vatican attention: within half a year it was on the Index.

If Catholic Modernism in Italy spread beyond the Church to interest and involve a broader lay public, this growth was in large measure due to the impact of Fogazzaro's novels, all of which deal generally with the problems of religion and religious reform. Antonio Fogazzaro (1842-1911), though a layman, was a man of considerable theological learning. As a boy in Vicenza, he was infected with the ideas of Modernism by his teacher, the religious poet and liberal priest Giacomo Zanella. He subsequently studied the ideas of religious renewal that had emerged in Italian Catholicism, most particularly those of Antonio Rosmini (1797-1855), whose Order of the Brethren of Charity influenced the conception of a "League of Catholic Laymen" in *The Saint*. And he was widely read in the Modernist writings of liberal theologians outside Italy. Italian Modernism, in contrast to the more philosophical Modernism of French Catholicism, had a strong social commitment. Fogazzaro allegedly introduced the political concept of Christian Democracy into Italy in his novel *Daniele Cortis* (1887), and as a lawyer and Senator he had much experience in the practical matters of social reform. In addition, Fogazzaro was firmly grounded both in the Bible and the liberal "higher criticism." In 1902 he wrote to his friend, Monsignor Geremia Bonomelli, that "a thorough knowledge of Bible criticism is indispensable." In fact, he continues, "a knowledge of the firmly established results of the study of the Scriptures, although it may kill a faith that is weak, is not only invigorating to a faith that is strong, but also broadens and deepens the conception of the divine, and is therefore most efficacious in preparing that evolution in the interpretation of dogma which the times demand."[13] Both Christian socialist and Modernist impulses are conspicuous in *The Saint*.

The Saint was the third and most sensational volume of a trilogy rendering a panoramic view of Italian society in the second half of the nineteenth century. The hero, Piero Maironi, is born at the end of the first volume (*The Patriot*, 1895), which tells the story of his parents and their role in the struggle for independence from Austria in 1850-60 in Lombardy and Venetia. In the second volume (*The Man of the World*, 1901) Maironi has grown to become a deeply religious yet vacillating man, torn in a tragic triangle of love between his wife, who has gone mad, and a beautiful agnostic named Jeanne Dessalle; the novel ends when Maironi, after suffering a fit of remorse, decides to purify himself through a life of prayer and simple Christian service. In *The Saint*, which takes place three years later, we find Maironi living as a lay brother in a Benedictine monastery, where he has assumed the name Benedetto.[14]

The novel has all the Gothic complications of plot that characterize the fiction of European *décadence*—clandestine meetings in churches, exchanges of secret letters between malevolent princes of the Church, and papal audiences in remote chambers of the Vatican. The opening chapters are burdened by a rather tedious recapitulation of the background from the preceding two volumes. In ad-

[13] Quoted in Tomaso Gallarati-Scotti, *The Life of Antonio Fogazzaro*, trans. Mary Prichard Agnetti (London: Hodder and Stoughton, n.d.), pp. 205-206.

[14] I quote from *The Saint*, trans. M. Agnetti Pritchard (New York and London: G. P. Putnam, 1906).

dition, the basic theme is complicated by the continuing relationship between Benedetto (Maironi) and Jeanne Dessalle, who attempts first to win her beloved back from the Church and then to protect the idealistic dreamer from the subtle machinations of the Vatican. Benedetto represents in his whole being the forces of Catholic renewal that were advocated around 1900 by Modernists within the Church and the Christian socialists outside its hierarchy: a turn away from the ossified organism of the ecclesiastical structure and a return to an evangelical Christianity as exemplified by the Jesus of the Gospels. Benedetto's anomalous position is typified by the fact that he stands *in villeggiatura* —a lay brother who is neither in the Church nor in the world.

The novel begins in Bruges, where Jeanne Dessalle is residing with her brother Carlino and her friend Noemi d'Arxel, who has just returned from a visit in Italy. Noemi tells Jeanne of Don Clemente, a young Benedictine she met at her sister's home. The description suggests to Jeanne that it must be her former lover Maironi, whom she has been seeking ever since his mysterious disappearance three years before. The two young women decide to leave immediately for Italy. After this largely expository beginning the scene switches to Subiaco in the Sabine hills, where Noemi's brother-in-law, Giovanni Selva, is entertaining a group of friends, including Don Clemente. The elderly Selva, "the truest representative of progressive Catholicism in Italy" (p. 5), is writing a book on the conspicuously Modernist theme of "Reason in Christian Morality." He has assembled his friends on this May evening for preliminary discussions of certain Church reforms and the constitution of a league of Catholic intellectuals.

After the discussion, which advances many of the ideas of Modernism and Christian socialism, a skeptical abbé anticipates the plot by proposing ironically: "Science and religion progress only through the individual, through the Messiah. Have you a saint among you? Do you know where to look for one? Then find him and let him march forward. Fiery language, broad charity, two or three little miracles, and your Messiah alone will achieve more than all of you together" (p. 63). But later a warning, reminiscent of the *alcalde* in *Nazarín*, is added: "If you had a saint, he would immediately be cautioned by the police, or sent to China by the Church" (p. 74). As the meeting breaks up, Noemi and Jeanne arrive from Bruges. Jeanne sees that Don Clemente is not Maironi; but she does not catch sight of his gardener, Benedetto.

Don Clemente, who has been Benedetto's spiritual adviser during his three years at the monastery, sends him immediately to the nearby village of Jenne, so that he will not meet Jeanne Dessalle and be tempted once again to leave his life of Christian purity. However, the young women, arriving shortly after his departure, learn that Benedetto has stopped at the nearby monastery of Sacro Speco. Following him there, Jeanne sees Maironi face to face for the first time in three years. He exacts from her a promise not to seek him out again until he summons her. Meanwhile, she must devote her life to the poor and the afflicted if she truly loves him. (The parallels to the earlier Christian socialist works are, of course, conspicuous: we have noted repeatedly the motif of the sinful or hot-blooded woman who sublimates her passion into charity.)

A month passes, Giovanni Selva's League of Catholic Laymen is destroyed by Church intrigues and pressures even before it gets under way, and Selva's own works are condemned in a leading clerical journal. Selva, his confidence undermined by these events, is incapacitated by his own doubts and intellectuality. Meanwhile, in the mountain village Benedetto has already become known as the Saint of Jenne for the "miraculous" cures he is said to have effected. Unable as a lay brother to say mass, he addresses the throngs outside the church from time to time. The Selvas and Noemi decide to go to Jenne to see the new saint, whose identity they do not know. There they meet Don

Clemente, who has been sent to reclaim Benedetto's habit:
he has been accused of preaching unorthodox doctrine and
of pretending to work miracles. They find a great crowd
assembled with many sick persons; one woman appears to
be healed simply by touching Benedetto's dwelling. Benedetto scrupulously obeys the ecclesiastical commands: he
surrenders his monk's habit and decides to leave Jenne
since rumors have already begun to circulate about his relationship with a village schoolmistress. Before he departs,
however, he meets Selva for the first time and tells him how
deeply the older man's thoughts and writings have influenced his own ideas on Church and social reform.

After a fit of illness, perhaps typhoid, Benedetto sets out
in July for Rome, where he is engaged as a gardener by
Selva's friend, Professor Mayda. In Rome Benedetto begins
to expand his field of activities: he works among the poor
of Testaccio; two or three times a week he speaks to a group
of followers in a secret meeting place known as the "Catacombs." And in October he addresses a group of Catholic
laymen, to whom he lays out his dreams: "I see, in the future, Catholic laymen striving zealously for Christ and for
truth, and finding a means of instituting unions different
from those of the present" (p. 294). For all these activities
and for his conspicuously Modernist reform tendencies,
Benedetto gradually wins the reputation of being "an enthusiastic religious agitator and miracle worker," and he is
kept under close surveillance by the priests.

Finally, in a mysterious scene in which he finds his way
through the Vatican at night in accordance with a vision,
Benedetto is granted a secret audience with the Pope. He
is first accused of miracle-working, of preaching "Protestant" (that is, Modernist and Christian socialist) thought,
and of over-intimacy with the schoolmistress at Jenne. (The
charges are almost precisely those that were leveled at
Nazarín.) Benedetto answers the accusations and then
claims, in turn, that four evil spirits have entered the body
of the Church: falsehood, domination of the clergy, avarice,

and immobility. (In this indictment we recognize the attitudes of anticlericalism, the socialist attack on property, and the Modernist attack on a rigidified dogma that refuses to accept the new scientific truth.) He implores the Pope, who is not at all unsympathetic to his aims, to come forth from the Vatican and help poor, suffering humanity. The Pope, explaining that he has a responsibility to the entire College of Cardinals and not simply to the liberals, ends the audience by inviting Benedetto to return in the future.

During the following days and weeks the conservative elements in the Vatican have many grounds for disgruntlement because the Pope carries out some of Benedetto's proposed reforms: we learn, for instance, that he has removed Giovanni Selva's writings from the *Index*. As a result, the Vatican conspiracy attempts to dispose of Benedetto by denouncing him to the Public Prosecutor for a trivial offense (an alleged failure to perform jury duty several years earlier). Benedetto is summoned at night for an interview with the Director General of the Police, who warns him of the political pressures in the Vatican and urges him to leave Italy. Benedetto, refusing this obvious ploy, demands a hearing and is conducted to an interview with the Minister of Interior. The Minister, who says that he is anti-Catholic "because he is Christian," is eager to hear Benedetto's thoughts on reform and even suggests that "we might perhaps become apostles of your ideas" (p. 371). But Benedetto, charging the statesmen with "practical atheism," refuses to cooperate with them for their political aims. He concludes the interview by claiming that they are even worse than the professors and intellectuals, who at least have little or no power. Ill and exhausted from the hearing, Benedetto is brought back to the Villa Mayda.

The novel now moves rapidly to its close. Benedetto, who has rejected every compromise, has been given three days to leave Rome. But since he is desperately ill, Jeanne Dessalle has arranged for him to be hidden in a different house until he recovers. On Sunday afternoon Jeanne goes with the Selvas to the Villa Mayda. The black sky is streaked with white—"a mystic symbol of death"—and the people are muttering angrily in the streets: "Dio!—He had been taken away by the police, and returned in this state. A mournful, continuous rumbling of thunder, and the loud steady splash of the rain, drowned both the sorrowful and the angry whisperings." That same day Benedetto dies after a final meeting with his closer followers, and the workers from Testaccio file sadly past his bed.

This outline of the plot, apart from suggesting that the novel revolves around Modernist and Christian socialist reform, gives little indication of the extent to which the action is determined by the prefiguring influence of the Gospels. But if we look more closely, a number of points emerge. We note, first, that Benedetto's mission is initially proclaimed by an older man, the Catholic intellectual Giovanni Selva, whose very name suggests an association with John the Baptist, crying in the wilderness (*selva* = "woods" or "wilderness"). Benedetto's "public ministry" is preceded by several years of quiet reflection and by a scene, the flight from Jeanne Dessalle, that is explicitly compared to the Temptation. In Jenne it is widely believed that Benedetto performs miracles of healing; he preaches his doctrine of simple Christianity to the people in parables; and his principal speech is delivered before a crowd assembled on a steep hillside or mount. When he takes his mission from the provinces to the capital, he soon incurs the hostility of the ecclesiastical authorities, who betray him to the secular tribunal on trumped-up charges. When he refuses to accept the compromises proposed by a Pilate-like Minister of the Interior, he is threatened not with crucifixion but with exile. Yet the pattern of the Passion is completed when Benedetto dies of his illness under circumstances explicitly similar to those of Golgotha (e.g., the mysterious "darkness at noon").

But these details and other similar ones are less telling than the often ironic consciousness among the participants themselves that they are re-enacting the Passion; and it is hardly an accident that Thomas à Kempis is mentioned three times in the course of the novel. Early in his ministry Benedetto has a vision in which he sees himself proclaimed "the reformer of the Church, the true Vicar of Christ, set upon the threshold of the temple." But "at that moment there flashed across his mind the thought of Satan offering the kingdom of the world to Christ. He fell upon the ground, stretching himself face downward on the rock, groaning in spirit: 'Jesus, Jesus, I am not worthy, not worthy to be tempted as Thou wast!'" (p. 116). (This is almost precisely the thought that occurs to Nazarín at the end of his hallucinations.) Repeatedly in the course of the novel Benedetto's "transfiguration" is mentioned (p. 141, p. 242, p. 451)—when he is sent away from the monastery, when he appears to the people in Jenne, when he dies, and elsewhere. On another occasion, after Benedetto has addressed the progressive Catholics in Rome, an old gentleman tells him: "You will suffer insults and blows; you will be derided by the Pharisees and the heathen; you will not see the future you long for, but the future is yours; the disciples of your disciples will see it" (p. 295). Even the cynical and anti-Catholic Minister of Interior is aware of the role that he is playing in this drama. He knows full well that the Church is accusing Benedetto on false charges merely in order to rid itself of a troublesome miracle-worker. "My friend is not Herod," he assures Benedetto, "nor am I Pilate" (p. 371). But Benedetto refuses to compromise. "You say you are not Pilate. But the truth is that I am the least of Christ's servants, because I have been unfaithful to Him, and you repeat to me Pilate's very words:—Quid est veritas? Now you are not disposed to receive truth, as Pilate was not disposed to receive it." When Benedetto dies during the strange darkness at noon, "his one prayer had been to be able to speak with his favorite disciples." It should be mentioned, finally, that in the sequel *Leila* (1910), which was also condemned by the Vatican, the hero is one of Benedetto's disciples, who carries out his mission; and in a scene specifically reminiscent of the entombment of Jesus, Benedetto's remains are transported from Rome to Valsolda for interment.[15]

With *The Saint* we have come far from the earliest Christian socialist transfiguration, which was quite frankly a tract just barely supported by the outlines of plot. Here, in contrast, the transfigurational structure is almost lost in the lush vegetation of the Gothic plot. For all *The Saint*'s similarity in quality and theme to *Nazarín*, it is necessary to point out one essential difference between the two works— apart from the playfulness and humor, which are totally missing in Fogazzaro's somber fiction. In *Nazarín* the hero becomes explicitly aware of his role only at the end, and then his delusion is justified as an attack of temporary insanity. In Fogazzaro's novel we are dealing with characters of a much greater sophistication. There are some simple people, to be sure, who believe that Benedetto is a saint or even Jesus reincarnate, notably the peasants of Jenne and the workers of Testaccio (precisely the same classes with whom Nazarín comes in contact). But for the most part Benedetto is dealing with men of far greater subtlety and education, men who know that Benedetto is simply a reformer and not Jesus, but who are clever enough to see that history has forced him into a role vis-à-vis his own society that bears a remarkable resemblance to the role of Jesus in his time. As a result, they take cognizance of the parallels consistently throughout the novel, but usually with the note of ironic awareness that characterizes the Minister of Interior. Benedetto himself is conscious of the analogy from the moment of his temptation at the beginning of the novel. Yet he resists the transfiguration and tries not to pursue the *imitatio*, believing himself to be unworthy of any parallel with the Jesus in whom he so devoutly believes. Although

---

[15] Robert A. Hall, Jr., "Fogazzaro's Maironi Tetralogy," *Italica*, 42 (1965), 248-59, argues that the three preceding novels should be taken, along with *Leila*, as a tetralogy linked by the spiritual presence of Piero Maironi.

there are many outward similarities between *Nazarín* and *The Saint,* then, the attitude of the characters toward the transfiguration differs as radically as madness and irony.

The Saint represents the high point and, in effect, the end of the Christian socialist transfigurations. All of these novels, adapted as they are to the local conditions of the countries from which they emerged, share the common basic impulse toward social reform according to principles of practical Christianity as it had been exposed by the liberal theology of the late nineteenth century. Since there is no presumption of influence among the five works, their similarity is produced by the common pattern of the Gospels as seen and highlighted by the limiting viewpoint of Christian socialism. In all five novels a good but incredibly naive man, seeking merely to live according to the dictates of the Gospels, comes into conflict with ecclesiastical authority, which feels threatened by his activities. (In every case these activities involve alleged therapeutic miracles and aiding a fallen woman, or a woman consumed by her own passion, with subsequent accusations of impropriety.) In all the novels but one, the Christian socialist hero dies as a result of his conflict with the Church—three times violently; and Nazarín must recant and submit to ecclesiastical discipline. But despite these and other conspicuous similarities, certain differences have also emerged that point toward future developments of the genre.

It is too easy to say that *Nazarín* and *The Saint* achieve a literary quality that the other three works lack because Galdós and Fogazzaro happen to be better writers. We must go on to note that the two men, precisely because of their literary abilities, managed to find unique and imaginative ways of justifying the parallels between their modern fictions and the Gospels. If *Joshua Davidson, A Singular Life,* and *The Stranger* strike us today as poor novels, it is not only because our temporal perspective makes their tract-like nature stand out more sharply. (After all, the novels of Fogazzaro and Galdós cannot conceal their under-lying Christian socialist impulse.) Rather, it is because in those works the transfiguration is imposed mechanically and heavy-handedly by the author or narrator. No attempt is made to justify the action psychologically; we are simply expected to take the narrator's word for every parallel, however farfetched it may be. It is noteworthy that these authors of the earliest fictional transfigurations use the still unfamiliar technique with a great deal of self-consciousness. Von Kahlenberg calls *The Stranger* "a parable"; Emanuel Bayard's life is "singular" because it so closely parallels the Gospels; and the same sense of singularity is expressed in Mrs. Linton's theoretical introduction to her "Modern Imitation of Christ." The narrator's reflections in *Nazarín* suggest a similar self-consciousness about the technique, but Galdós avoids the usual heavy-handedness by shifting the Passion largely into the hero's deranged mind. Fogazzaro achieves the same effect of plausibility by moving many of the parallels into the ironic consciousness of sophisticated characters. This is worth noting because these two novels anticipate two types of fictional transfiguration that appear when the Christian socialist impulse dies out: the psychiatric orientation that regards the modern Jesus as a paranoid suffering from hallucinations, and the cynical but historically sophisticated Marxist view that discerns structural parallels between the undercover provocateur in the thirties and Jesus in Jerusalem. In this sense Galdós anticipates Hauptmann and Kazantzakis just as clearly as Fogazzaro prepares the way for Silone and Koestler. The three ladies, in contrast, do not look beyond their own generation, and their novels are deservedly forgotten.

Shortly after the turn of the century the Christian socialist transfiguration expired. And, setting aside *Nazarín* and *The Saint*, which are memorable precisely because they rose above the group in several respects, we note this demise with no particular regret. This category was a response to a very specific set of circumstances. But as theology shifted its attention from Jesus the social reformer to other problems, as Modernism was stamped out in the Catholic Church, and as social conditions gradually improved, Christian socialism became less of a central issue. As a result, when a very late example of this type shows up, it would suggest a parody if the author were not so deadly serious throughout.

Harold Kampf's *When He Shall Appear* (1953) employs the framework of a three-day trial in a London magistrate's court. The thirty-three-year-old Janek Lazar is charged with "committing blasphemy in that you have falsely set yourself up to be the Son of God and have mocked the established religion of this land, which is Christianity, and have preached its abolition" (p. 6).[16] If the circumstances were not specifically contemporary, we would think from these charges that we were back at the turn of the century with Emanuel Bayard or Benedetto. In this case the accused is the son of Russian immigrants, a blacksmith and his wife who never bothered to change their nationality. Janek, the younger son, was far ahead of the other children in school and took an "extraordinary interest" in the Bible. He left home six years before, shortly after the death of his father, as the result of a prophetic dream: "My son, for four years you will go among men, learning their ways. Then you will start your ministry in many lands, preaching the message which lies in your heart. And for this I will send you a sign" (p. 51).

Janek's "miracles" began, it turns out, when he encountered a beggar who pretended to be blind. Wrathful at such deceit, Janek made him truly blind and then well again. The beggar became the first of his disciples and organized his public appearances, which featured acts of faith-healing. After Janek is run out of town for creating a public nuisance, he is interviewed by a reporter, whose article portrays him as a crusader for mankind. After these events the plot becomes predictable. Janek wins additional disciples;

16 *When He Shall Appear* (Boston: Little, Brown, 1953).

he receives donations, which he distributes to the poor; the clergy of all denominations consolidate themselves against Janek, denouncing him from the pulpit and ridiculing him in the journals. At the same time, others believe in his religion of simplicity—like the American newspaperwoman who wants to arrange an American tour for the marvelous faith-healer.

This Jesus-like life, which emerges from the testimony of various witnesses, is reinforced by other more conspicuous parallels. At the very beginning, for instance, the judge is reminded of his own symbolic role in the proceedings: "'Surely whatever happens, I cannot be held to blame,' whispered Mr. Roulton to himself. And there flashed before him the startling thought that Pontius Pilate may also have said something of the kind" (p. 4). Similarly, Janek's brother reminds the prosecuting attorney of John the Baptist: "That big frame; the shock of black hair; the great deep evangelical voice when it's roused" (p. 74). Janek is arrested on a *Thursday* in the *gardens* of Leicester Square, where he is preaching that Christianity has degenerated to dogma and ought instead to be a way of life. On the third day of the trial the judge dismisses the charges, a highly popular verdict. But the Church dignitaries meet secretly with the prosecutor in a scheme to have Janek deported: "If his Christ-hood became a certain fact, the church would completely sink. No, gentlemen! To my mind the Christianity we have established is too important to allow *anything* to interfere with it—even a new Messiah of this nature" (p. 170). (This sentiment echoes almost literally the words of the clergymen in *The Stranger*; and it precisely reflects Christian socialist conviction in *The True History of Joshua Davidson*: "The obstacles to practical Christianity come from professing Christians.") The Home Secretary accedes to this powerful ecclesiastical pressure, but Janek has disappeared. The prosecutor manages to obtain his address from one of the witnesses. When Janek is appre-

96

hended and deported to Russia, the betrayer, conscious of his Judas-role, dies of a seizure.

In theme, Kampf's novel has not moved a single degree beyond the simple Christian socialism of Eliza Lynn Linton. In technique, there is not a touch of psychological insight or ironic consciousness to lighten the author's pedantic insistence upon the parallels. The only novelty in the volume is the courtroom device that permits the story to narrate itself through the testimony of various witnesses. But even this device is not sufficient to resuscitate the Christian socialist novel that had died a natural death some fifty years earlier and deserved to be left in peace. To be sure, when we read those early novels we are moved by a certain empathy. After all, Nazarín was a ghetto priest of the nineties; Emanuel Bayard operated out of a storefront church; and Benedetto's League of Catholic Laymen anticipated some of the religious action groups of our own day. In fact, though alcoholism and prostitution are no longer the most obsessive social problems, the perennial conflict between progress and conservatism, between action and dogma, between compassion and indifference, is certainly still with us. To this extent we can sympathize with the Christian socialist heroes and their problems. But nothing ages faster than yesterday's social protest, which more often strikes us as quaint rather than compelling. For this reason these novels have not stood up well to the test of time. Only a contemporary religious reform movement, desperately seeking a pedigree for its radicalism, could be seriously interested in the novels of Eliza Lynn Linton or Elizabeth Stuart Phelps Ward. And if we can still read Nazarín and The Saint, it is not so much the Modernism and Christian socialism that we appreciate, but the irony and psychological insight: they have survived despite their theme. For after The Saint wholly new impulses motivated both the popular view of Jesus and the fictional transfigurations.

97

4. The Christomaniacs

AT FIRST GLANCE Hauptmann's *The Fool in Christ Emanuel Quint* (*Der Narr in Christo Emanuel Quint,* 1910) bears a close resemblance to the Christian socialist transfigurations of the turn of the century. The novel was regarded primarily as a work of social criticism by most of his contemporaries: the author of one early appreciation cited the work as an example to prove that socialism is a "logical consequence" of Jesus' thought.[1]

Hauptmann's story concerns a life that is just as "singular" as the ones we have just considered. The action is set around the year 1890, during the period of intense Christian socialist activism. And the mission and Passion of Hauptmann's twenty-eight-year-old hero, the illegitimate son of an impoverished carpenter in the Silesian mountains, seems calculated to expose at every juncture the bigotry, dogmatism, and pharisaic behavior of the "Christians" with whom Quint comes in contact. Eliza Lynn Linton would surely have felt that the book was a perfect illustration of her claim that "the obstacles to practical Christianity come from professing Christians." The most respected members of the Christian establishment turn out to be the least Christian in their behavior; and with few exceptions the clergymen are worst of all. (It becomes clear, toward the end of the novel, that Quint was fathered by a Catholic priest.)

The critical thrust seems particularly emphatic because the novel ends with a jibe at good "Christians" who shy away from any possible confrontation with Christ, a motif familiar from the stories of *Jesus redivivus.* Rumors crop up from place to place in Germany about a man who knocks at doors and begs for bread and lodging, saying, when asked, that he is none other than Jesus Christ: "The alarm he produces wherever he turns up can readily be imagined,

---

[1] Georg Lomer, *Das Christusbild in Gerhart Hauptmanns 'Emanuel Quint'* (Leipzig: J. A. Barth, 1911).

although he seems to be quite a harmless lunatic. He cannot be doing a very brisk business, for the housewives usually slam the door in his face the moment he utters the ominous name, and quickly secure it with lock and key and bolt and whatever other means of safety they possess" (pp. 472-73).[2] In addition to blatant criticism of this sort there are repeated references to socialism and socialistic reform proposals. A political agitator presents Quint's disciples with a copy of the *Communist Manifesto*, but the heady political philosophy makes no impression on the simple-minded peasants. A socialist newspaper first draws public attention to Quint by recording his first sermon and reporting his activities in an ironic yet sympathetic tone.

Hauptmann had the proper credentials to suggest intentions of social criticism. Like many young intellectuals and writers of emergent naturalism in the eighties, he went through a socialist phase during which he studied Marx's *Das Kapital* as well as the writings of Lassalle, Kautsky, Bebel, and other theoreticians. As a student of sculpture in Breslau and during his few semesters at the University of Jena, he and his friends organized a "Pacific Society" with the goal of establishing a utopian commune in America after the pattern of Étienne Cabet's ill-fated "Icarian" settlements in Texas and Illinois. As a result of these activities, enthusiasms, and associations, Hauptmann was among those indicted in Breslau in 1887 on suspicion of supporting the Social Democratic Party, which had been declared illegal by Bismarck's government. On that occasion and later, Hauptmann denied being a socialist in any partisan sense. Indeed, his ideas were always utopian in the tradition of such older socialistic thinkers as Saint-Simon and Fourier. Like most of his own dramatic heroes, however, Hauptmann was long on talk and ideas, but short on political action.

This combination of utopian socialism and the pro-

---

[2] I quote from the translation by Thomas Seltzer (New York: Huebsch, 1911).

nounced anticlericalism that shows up in many of his works led Hauptmann to an intellectual position closely resembling that of Christian socialism. At the same time, for all its external similarity, it would be a mistake to confuse Hauptmann's novel with such transfigurations as those by Elizabeth Stuart Phelps Ward or Antonio Fogazzaro. For in *Emanuel Quint* the social commentary and ecclesiastical reform are almost peripheral. Hauptmann, as his title suggests, is interested far more in the psychological phenomenon of the "Fool in Christ." How is it possible for an individual to come to identify himself with Jesus Christ, and through what process of mass psychology does it happen that a large group of followers accepts him in that role?

This radically different point of view affects the novel in a variety of ways. First, the narrator can now afford to assume a much more detached attitude toward his subject. Unlike the disciple-gospelists of most of the Christian socialist works, Hauptmann's narrator does not need to establish the parallels between his hero and Jesus; this function is left to the psychically disoriented characters within the fiction. Second, the psychic affliction of the transfigured hero casts him into a far more ambivalent light than the largely positive heroes of the Christian socialist novels, who are without exception admirable—in fact, almost tediously good—men. Finally, the psychological focus determines in large measure the kind of character portrayed here. We are explicitly not dealing with the educated clergymen and sophisticated laymen of the earlier works, men who remain clear-headed and modest about their activities even when simple and over-grateful recipients of their charity regard them as "saints" or "Christmen." Rather, Hauptmann is concerned with a backward society of peasants and mountaineers who are fundamentalist in their faith, literalist in their belief in an impending millennium, and often hysterical in their worship. Against such a social background Quint's hallucinations and the mass delusion of his followers become plausible in a manner that would be unthinkable in

Fogazzaro's sophisticated Rome, in Mrs. Ward's sober Massachusetts, or in Galdós' cynically realistic Spain. To the extent that Hauptmann's interest has shifted from the Christian socialist critique of Church and society to the psychogenesis of Christomania, he reflects an intellectual development that characterized the first decade of the century.

In 1913 Albert Schweitzer published an "exposition and criticism" of *The Psychiatric Study of Jesus*[3] that was accepted as a doctoral dissertation by the medical faculty of the University of Strassburg. It was no doubt inevitable that psychiatry, which by the turn of the century had emerged as one of the most exciting intellectual disciplines, would turn its attention to the most spectacular religious problem of the day: the *Zeitschrift für Religionspsychologie* was founded in 1907 for the express purpose of combining psychiatry and theology. Immediately after 1900 the international world of psychiatry produced a variety of studies of Jesus. Georg Lomer, writing under the name of Georg de Loosten, published *Jesus Christ from the Standpoint of a Psychiatrist* (1905), in which he suggested that Jesus' hypertrophied self-consciousness and his delusions came from an excessive study of the Old Testament.[4] The French professor of psychology Charles Binet-Sanglé brought out a four-volume work on *La Folie de Jésus* (1908-15), which portrays a tubercular and anxiety-prone hypochondriac whose hereditary inclination toward religious mysticism first manifested itself in a hebephrenic crisis of the twelve-year-old in the temple. And the New York specialist in mental illnesses, William Hirsch, wrote his "Conclusions of a

[3] *Die psychiatrische Beurteilung Jesu: Darstellung und Kritik* (1913; rpt. Tübingen: J.C.B. Mohr, 1933); trans. Charles R. Joy (Boston: Beacon, 1948).

[4] *Jesus Christus vom Standpunkt des Psychiaters* (Bamberg, 1905); Lomer, the same man who later wrote the socialist interpretation of *Emanuel Quint* (see Note 1 above), was by profession a doctor and the director of a German mental institution.

Psychiatrist" on *Religion and Civilization* (1910). The common denominator of these and the other works that Schweitzer treats in his monograph is the fact that they all call Jesus "paranoid." Schweitzer, with his dual training as theologian and physician, found it easy to refute this thesis on four fundamental grounds: much of the material on which it is based is not historically valid; the interpretation is often vitiated by a misunderstanding of biblical times and conventions; the hypothetical case of madness derived from these false premises is not clinically verifiable; finally, the only two indisputable facts in the entire arsenal of proof— Jesus' self-consciousness of his mission and his hallucination at the time of his baptism—do not in themselves suffice to prove insanity.

The paranoiac interpretation was never accepted by New Testament scholars. The reasons for this rejection were reviewed fully by the American theologian Walter E. Bundy in a book that defended *The Psychic Health of Jesus* (1922). Schweitzer's refutation was so resounding that psychiatry turned from the methodological uncertainties of the historical Jesus to the investigation of such modern phenomena as religious hysteria, the psychology of occultism, the relations between sin and disease, or the psychology of guilt. Meanwhile, the Jungian school of analytical psychology began to concern itself increasingly with the history and interpretation of various religious symbols (e.g., the fish, the cross). G. Stanley Hall—the noted psychologist, friend of Freud and Jung, and president of Clark University—stated that "modern psychology, which has of late grown by leaps and bounds, is already competent to grapple with many of the questions hitherto hopelessly insoluble by older methods." Given the triumphant achievements of nineteenth-century New Testament research, "the inevitable next step with all this wealth of material must be psychological."[5] Hall, to be sure, had in mind goals far more

[5] *Jesus, the Christ, in the Light of Psychology* (Garden City, N. Y.: Doubleday-Page, 1917), i, vii.

reasonable than those of the psychiatric analysts, whose studies of Jesus he criticizes; he was fascinated not with the historicity of Jesus, but rather with "how men came to believe the things of Christianity."

The vogue of psychiatric interpretations in the first decade of the century, then, is more important as a symptom of the times—the era of Freud—than in its accomplishment. It was the inevitable outcome of the liberal lives, which regarded Jesus as a human being whose mind could be comprehended psychologically. For all the insufficiencies of the psychiatric interpretations, the paranoiac hypothesis in conjunction with the new interest in religious hysteria opened fascinating avenues for writers. It suggested that Jesus, or his transfigured counterpart, need not be presented only as a good man, a social reformer, a redeemer. The far more interesting question of the savior's mentality was also a legitimate area for investigation.

The notion that Jesus was psychically disoriented did not, of course, spring into existence overnight. It is implicit in Strauss's *Life*, where Jesus is called an "enthusiast" (*Schwärmer*) with "adventurous notions." Another impulse came from Nietzsche's *The Antichrist*. After arguing that Jesus was a "political criminal" crucified for inciting the lower classes to anarchy, Nietzsche turns to the problem of "the psychology of the savior" (§29-31). Dismissing Strauss's New Testament philology as irrelevant and Renan as a "Hanswurst *in psychologicis*," Nietzsche insists that he cares only about "the psychological type of the savior." What matters is not what he did, what he said, how he died, but rather: Is his type conceivable and plausible? (By putting the question to the type rather than to the specific case, Nietzsche saves himself from the mistakes of the psychiatric critics, who rely too much on unverifiable details of the Gospel text.) Nietzsche finds that Renan's categories of "génie" and "héros" are totally inapplicable to Jesus' primary characteristics: his inability to resist, and his life of love. "To speak with the rigor of the physiologist, an entirely different word would be in order here: the word *idiot*." Maintaining that the personality of Jesus can be understood only as a charming mixture of "the sublime, the sick, and the childlike," Nietzsche expresses his regret that "no Dostoevsky lived in the vicinity of this most interesting *décadent*." It is quite clear from these paragraphs of *The Antichrist* that Nietzsche had a great deal of admiration for Jesus as a man: "basically there was only one Christian, and he died on the cross." It is institutionalized Christianity, especially as associated with St. Paul, for which Nietzsche reserves his most vitriolic contempt. The Gospels are irrefutable evidence, he claims, of the "already insuppressible corruption *within* the first community"; and he warns the reader to put on gloves when he reads the New Testament in order to protect himself against so much filth (§46).

It is no accident that Nietzsche longed for a Dostoevsky to chronicle the life of Jesus, for the Russian shared Nietzsche's awareness of the problematic psyche of the savior. The novel in which he attempted to portray "a positively good man" is entitled, characteristically, *The Idiot*. Prince Myshkin is a truly Christlike man—in his manuscript notes Dostoevsky once refers to him as "Prince Christ"—of great moral beauty. But to make him plausible as a human being Dostoevsky found it necessary to mar his moral beauty with certain flaws. In contrast to Cervantes, who balanced Don Quixote's goodness with his often ridiculous naiveté, Dostoevsky drew his Christlike man as a severe epileptic who eventually, at the end of the book, is reduced to babbling idiocy—the savior as idiot! In part both Dostoevsky and Nietzsche were exploiting the ancient *topos* that associates divine truth with madness: in the eyes of society the savior or redeemer appears as a fool. At the same time, Nietzsche's repeated references to "the sick" in the character of the savior and Dostoevsky's portrayal of his Christlike man as an epileptic indicate unmistakably that they thought of this madness in a more than merely symbolic light.

All of these factors had a pronounced impact on Hauptmann, who was led to the critical New Testament scholarship by a personal religious crisis, who along with the other young intellectuals of his generation admired Nietzsche and Dostoevsky, and who was one of the most eager students of the new field of psychiatry. Hauptmann (1862-1946) was not exposed to the same rigorously religious upbringing as most of the writers of Christian socialism. During his school years at Breslau his favorite teacher was a Dr. Schmidt, who rather daringly introduced his pupils to a mild form of New Testament criticism. In 1878 Hauptmann dropped out of school because of poor grades and motivation. His family, prosperous hotel-owners in a Silesian resort village, suddenly suffered dire financial straits as a result of the economic crises of the seventies. Hauptmann went to live on the farm estate of his aunt and uncle Schubert to learn agriculture. His sense of failure in school coupled with a feeling of guilt at being a burden to his family aggravated the emotional turmoil that is the normal condition of adolescence.

When Hauptmann arrived at Lohnig, he was fit prey for the hysterical atmosphere of pietism that he encountered in his aunt's home. Having lost her son a year before, the devout woman devoted herself to a cult of the dead and to an excessive Christian charity. Hauptmann found a household filled with a circle of religious parasites. In his autobiography Hauptmann recounts the stages of his religious crisis, which was intensified by the wild sermons of itinerant preachers, who threatened their listeners with the fires of hell. A sixteen-year-old with intellectual or religious reserves to fall back upon might not have succumbed so readily to these backwoods hysterics. But Hauptmann had been a poor student; his upbringing had not been religious.

And since there was no responsible adult to whom he could talk, for several months his only solace was a copy of the New Testament: "I carried it on my heart and do not deny that I was calmed somewhat by its constant presence" (p. 300).[6]

Within a year Hauptmann escaped from Lohnig and his youthful stability reasserted itself. But the religious crisis of 1878 is important for a variety of reasons. In the first place, Hauptmann's forced exposure to remorseless preachers turned him against the organized Church and contributed to his strong anticlericalism. Furthermore, his experience with religious hysteria prompted his subsequent and lasting interest in the psychiatric aspects of religion. In addition, his experiences at Lohnig provided the background for many of the scenes in *Emanuel Quint*. Finally, his attempts to escape the religious fundamentalism to which he had been exposed led him, in the following years, to devote himself to a rather systematic study of New Testament criticism. His friend Wilhelm Bölsche recalls seeing Hauptmann, around 1890, surrounded by works on the composition of the Gospels. Hauptmann himself mentions such obvious sources as Strauss and Renan. His library included a copy of the "comparative psychopathological study" *Jesus* (1905) by the Danish theologian-turned-novelist Emil Rasmussen (1873-1956), who presented the savior as an epileptic. And Hauptmann later claimed to have read "just about everything" in the field of New Testa-

---

[6] I cite Hauptmann's autobiographical writings—esp. *Das Abenteuer meiner Jugend* and *Das zweite Vierteljahrhundert*—in my own translation according to the text in *Die grossen Beichten* (Berlin: Propyläen, 1966). Among the numerous secondary studies the following works are most specifically relevant: Wilhelm Sulser, *Gerhart Hauptmanns Narr in Christo Emanuel Quint: Ein Beitrag zur Geschichte der deutschen religiösen Dichtung* (Bern: Paul Haupt, 1925); Frederick W. J. Heuser, "Frühe Einflüsse auf Hauptmanns geistige Entwicklung," in *Gerhart Hauptmann: Zu seinem Leben und Schaffen*, by F.W.J. Heuser (Tübingen: Niemeyer, 1961), pp. 7-26; Karl S. Guthke, *Gerhart Hauptmann: Weltbild im Werk* (Göttingen: Vandenhoeck, 1961); and Eberhard Hilscher, *Gerhart Hauptmann* (Berlin: Verlag der Nation, 1969).

ment scholarship, a claim to be taken *cum grano salis* in view of the immense assortment of titles that Schweitzer lists for those years. It is perfectly true, however, that Hauptmann remained a devoted reader and student of the New Testament to the end of his life: his well-thumbed copy, which he always kept at hand on his bedtable, was finally buried with him.

From the mid-eighties on, Hauptmann sought in various ways to give literary expression to these religious interests. We have already had occasion to observe that many of his works—e.g., *The Assumption of Hannele* and *Lonely Lives* —are concerned with such problems as religious hallucinations or faith versus reason. But during these years we hear repeatedly of certain "Jesus studies," which several friends saw and read around 1890. In the mid-eighties he outlined a historical drama about Jesus. He was preoccupied a few years later with the plan for a "fifth Gospel" in the form of a diary of Judas Iscariot. (The notion of an *Evangelium Judae* had obsessed him, in fact, ever since his teacher Schmidt had suggested that the Gospels give no evidence that Judas, whom Jesus trusted, was an evil man.) In 1897-98 Hauptmann returned to his old plan for a drama about Jesus, which was originally supposed to keep close to the events of the New Testament. Gradually his intentions shifted, however, and the fragment that has been preserved (six scenes in roughly one thousand lines of iambic pentameter) locates a modern Jesus among the Silesian weavers of Hauptmann's own native province.

The work that most clearly anticipated his novel of 1910 was the naturalistic "study" entitled "The Apostle" ("Der Apostel," 1890), the last prose narrative that Hauptmann published prior to *Emanuel Quint*. In Zürich in 1888 Hauptmann had met an itinerant preacher named Johannes Guttzeit, who embodied the same sort of fiery evangelism that had dismayed the young Hauptmann ten years earlier on his aunt's estate. Taking Guttzeit as the model for his "Apostle," Hauptmann depicted him with such remorseless

fidelity that Guttzeit easily recognized himself and registered an indignant objection. If Hauptmann was able to
avenge himself on the religious tyrants of his youth by a
satirical portrait, it was in part because he was now older
and more mature. But it was also due in large measure to
Hauptmann's acquaintance with August Forel (1848-1931),
the renowned psychiatrist who was director of Burghölzli,
the famed mental institution attached to the Zürich medical
school. "His disclosures had an overwhelming impact on
me," Hauptmann wrote in his autobiography. "He gave me
an indestructible fund of knowledge about the human
psyche" (p. 613). Under Forel's guidance Hauptmann investigated not only the principal forms of madness; he also
studied special problems that had a substantial influence on
the dramas of his naturalistic phase, notably syphilis with
all its symptoms, questions of heredity, and the degenerative effects of alcoholism. More specifically, Forel taught
Hauptmann to regard religious hysteria as a psychiatric
phenomenon. Observing the Salvation Army as well as the
fanatical apostles and anchorites who circulated around
Zürich, Hauptmann concluded that "these half-naked people . . . had closed the gates of their soul in every direction.
August Forel did not hesitate to call their behavior
pathological" (p. 615).

"The Apostle," which amounts to little more than a
sketch, sets out to describe half a day in the life of one of
these pathologically religious fanatics. We encounter the
unnamed apostle one evening around Pentecost when he
arrives in Zürich on his way from Italy to Germany. Setting
out from his inn early the next morning, he pauses to admire himself in the mirror and decides that in his sandals,
with his long blond hair and his monk's habit, he indeed
looks like a true biblical apostle. As he walks, meticulously
avoiding the least living things—flowers or beetles—and
congratulating himself on his humaneness, he gazes around
from time to time to see if anyone is there to appreciate the
fine sight of him. Gradually this unhealthy narcissism de-

teriorates into a more problematic state: he has the sensation of walking on water and, at the same time, thinks of Christ's triumphal entry into Jerusalem. As the citizens begin to emerge from their houses for the day and stare at him, his delusion grows: "He went deeper and deeper into himself until he penetrated space, far, high, infinite. And so wholly absorbed was he with all his senses in this second world that he moved along, without volition, like a sleepwalker." As he climbs up the mountain, his identification with Jesus becomes more complete. Peeling an orange, "he ate the fruit with reverence, as Christ consumed the host." In a vision he sees himself healing the dead Jesus, who rises in his wrappings and enters bodily into the apostle. "He experienced very precisely the entire mysterious process as the figure of Jesus dissolved within him. He now saw the disciples who sought their master. From among them Peter stepped up to him and said: Rabbi! It is I, he replied in answer." The sketch ends with the apostle sitting high on the mountain, listening to the noonday bells: "He listened, smiling, as though to the voice of an old friend, and yet it was God the Father who was speaking with his son."

With this psychological study of "The Apostle" Hauptmann was consciously attempting to emulate a literary work that he admired immensely: Georg Büchner's "Lenz" (1835), one of the first stories in which the state of madness is described from within, out of the consciousness of the paranoid himself. Hauptmann's contempt for these latter-day apostles, with their egocentric presumptuousness, clearly marks the language and characterization of his tale. But all satire aside, we find here something that is almost wholly missing from the Christian socialist transfigurations of the same period: an attempt to comprehend the savior-type in the sense of Nietzsche and Dostoevsky as a pathological case. (Only Galdós, it will be recalled, strove tentatively in the same direction; and Nazarín was depicted not as a pathological case, but merely as the victim of a temporary hallucination.) In "The Apostle" Hauptmann could do no more than render a quick naturalistic snapshot of the apostle's paranoia. He anticipates certain motifs that show up twenty years later in *Emanuel Quint*, notably the vision in which Jesus enters bodily into the apostle. But in the few pages of his study and in the few hours from dawn to noon he could neither account for the apostle's condition nor trace the development of his paranoia. To do that required a much longer novel that would allow time for the emotional growth of the hero and ample space to describe his mental state. Precisely this unique combination of interests in religion and psychiatry, coupled with Hauptmann's experience with religious fanaticism in the mountains of Silesia and his long-standing hostility toward organized Churches, ultimately produced *The Fool in Christ Emanuel Quint*.

Within the first few pages of Hauptmann's novel we become aware of a completely new narrative tone. We are dealing neither with an ardent disciple who wants to convert us (as in *Joshua Davidson* or *A Singular Life*) nor with an indifferent narrator who simply confronts us with the uncertainty of the events: Fogazzaro often retreats behind dialogue and interpolated letters; and Galdós invents a narrator who is less sure of his opinion than any other character in the novel. Hauptmann, in contrast, permits us to relax in the hands of a wise and experienced narrator who guides us carefully through the psychological mazes of his unusual tale. The narrator is quite modest about his abilities: "It is impossible to make the inevitable course of a man's destiny comprehensible in all its details. Every man from his birth to his death is a unique phenomenon with no exact counterpart in the past or in the future. The observer understands things only within the limits of his own peculiar nature" (p. 344). But despite this disavowal and his insistence on the limitations of narrative objectivity, it is clear that the narrator is far more than the simple "chronicler" as which he introduces himself.

110

Our narrator, in fact, is not only a historian of religion who is able to enlighten us, when events seem incredible, by referring to parallels from other periods; he is also a subtle connoisseur of the human psyche who knows how to make matters comprehensible through psychological analysis. In one of his attempts to explain how Quint's followers came to believe that he was Jesus, the narrator begins by reminding us that faith cannot be rationally comprehended: we must accept this inverted faith as an "absurd fact." Then he digresses briefly on the history of religion to remind us that men have always sought the security and consolation of divinity that is manifested in human form. Catholics, he points out, prefer to pray to saints because saints are deified men: "The Protestant, too, prays with greater fervor to Jesus the Savior, than to God, because God is far beyond his reach, while Jesus is humanly near" (p. 230). On another occasion he speaks of the "romantic impulse for the formation of secret societies" that is evidenced by the Gospels and the story of the apostles: "The individual lost in the crowd would fain single himself out by laying claim to the possession of a mystery, which invests him with knowledge and leaves the mass in ignorance" (p. 287). It should be noted that in such cases the narrator not only uses the history of religion to explain the modern psychological situation; conversely, he also interprets the historical event by means of modern psychology. Thus to explain the fanaticism of Quint's followers, the "Valley Brethren," he cites the parallel cases of medieval sects, of the great "Delirium of Münster," of the American Mormons, and of the Salvation Army: "A delusion, it is known, can seize whole nations, all the more so small communities such as the Valley Brethren" (p. 234).

This narrator, then, tells us a great deal more than the earlier narrators. He does not pretend to be recounting a "true history" that most people have already heard; nor is he dealing with current events. Instead, he is writing in 1910 about incidents that took place some twenty years earlier; as a result, he treats the story with a certain historical detachment. "From time to time there comes over the old world, in conjunction with a new or a revived belief, a feeling of rejuvenescence. And just at that time, about 1890, a new faith and a spring feeling hovered in the air of Germany" (p. 81). In another place he speaks in more detail about this apocalyptic euphoria, explicitly linking the religious phenomenon to the socialist reform impulse. "A mighty social upheaval which was to regenerate the world was in all seriousness counted upon at the very latest in the year 1900. As the poor peasant workmen who had followed the Fool awaited the millennium and the New Jerusalem, so the Socialists and the young intellectuals closely allied to the Socialists in their views awaited the Socialistic, social, and therefore ideal, state of the future" (p. 415).

Seen within the general framework of religious ecstasy and within the more specific context of the millennialistic fervor of the nineties, Quint's messiahship becomes psychologically quite plausible. Hauptmann's psychological understanding is based, here as well as in his dramas, on a sympathetic insight into the active spiritual life of the common man. "Sufficient recognition has not been given the significance of the imagination in the life of every man, especially the simple-minded man," he asserts (p. 233). In Emanuel's life, he reminds us repeatedly, profound, passionate imagination takes the place of education; he has absorbed Jesus into his own being through an act of the imagination. At the same time, the narrator makes it clear that Quint's imagination, uncontrolled by reason and education, goes to extremes that verge on the pathological. On two separate occasions he is examined by doctors who detect "degenerative signs" in his character. One even goes so far as to say that Quint is "cretin-like," while another concludes that for all his weakmindedness he can be held morally responsible for his actions. On another occasion the terms *"idée fixe"* and "paranoia" are used to characterize his state, terms that would have been wholly inapplicable in the novels of Christian socialism.

In his effort to view Quint's derangement with objective detachment, Hauptmann backs up his narrator with a variety of other "sane" points of view. In the case of Kurt Simon, the eighteen-year-old secretary of a farm estate, Hauptmann has sketched an autobiographically exact portrait of himself during his year at Lohnig. (The poems that Kurt Simon writes are actually poems subsequently printed in Hauptmann's own autobiography.) Simon reflects the ambivalent attitude of young Hauptmann toward itinerant ministers like Quint. His impressionable mind is tempted to succumb to the religious ecstasy that surrounds him, and he almost believes that he is himself one of the figures from the New Testament stories that he continually reads. At the same time, he is clear-headed enough to realize that the others are suffering from a delusion, from a case of hysteria. When he looks at Quint and his followers, "the word 'obscurantists' passed through his mind" (p. 40). Such passages as these, in conjunction with the narrator's own analytical coolness, keep us in a state of objective detachment and never permit us to believe, even for a moment, that we are actually dealing with a mystical case of *Jesus redivivus*. As a result, the tone of the book differs from the tone of the earlier transfigurations, which sought in general to arouse in the reader the sensations shared by the characters themselves.

Because Hauptmann is interested not only in the depiction of Quint's fixations, as in "The Apostle," but also in the psychogenetic process through which imagination gradually displaces reality in Quint's consciousness, time is an important factor in the novel, whose action lasts for roughly a year and a half. We first meet Quint on a day in May around 1890; and we lose sight of him sometime in the late autumn of the following year. From the standpoint of psychological development the novel can be divided into two roughly equal parts. During the first ten months (chaps. 1-15) Quint's "folly" amounts to little more than excessive zeal in the effort to emulate Christ; having little sense of identification with Jesus, he regards himself as no more than an apostle. During these same months, however, the notion that Quint is in fact Jesus grows stronger and stronger among his hysterical friends and followers. At the beginning of the second half (chaps. 16-30) Quint has recovered almost totally from his incipient delusions when his "disciples" send a delegation to fetch him. When he succumbs to their pleas to return, his reversion becomes more complete than before, and during the last eight or nine months of his life he seriously believes that he is Jesus reincarnate. As a result, the structure of the two parts is quite different: in the first part there are few conspicuous parallels to the New Testament, and the followers take them more seriously than Quint himself; in the second half the parallels become quite striking because Quint, now fully convinced that he is one with Jesus, sets out systematically to re-enact the events of the Gospels. To put it most simply: in the first part Quint is imitating Christ and in the second part Jesus; in the first part he thinks of himself as the apostle of Christ's ethical teaching, while in the second part he sees himself as a new redeemer; in the first part he still distinguishes between reality and imagination, and in the second the two coalesce into a paranoiac hallucination.

When Quint preaches his first sermon in the town square at Reichenbach, it is little more than an evangelistic announcement that the Kingdom of Heaven is near. Interrogated by the local preacher, he says that he is only a tool, "a worker in the vineyard of the Lord" (p. 4). On this first occasion Quint is released with a mild reprimand from the preacher and the police. But his words and appearance have made a deep impression on two local religious fanatics, Martin and Anton Scharf. They take Quint home with them, and when Quint's touch seems to heal their sick father, they begin to regard him as the reincarnation of

114

Christ. It is necessary to make a rigorous distinction here. Although Quint at this point never doubts that the savior is in him, there is no question of any absolute identity: Jesus has used him as the vehicle for "the power of miracle," and this miracle confirms what he regarded merely as his "apostolic calling." It should be pointed out that Hauptmann is not indulging here in any mysticism: Quint, of course, cannot heal; old father Scharf dies a few days later. But the two brothers are so anxious to regard the father's momentary improvement as a miracle of healing that even his subsequent death cannot shake their faith.

We see precisely the same syndrome at work with other characters. Brother Nathanael Schwarz, who preaches "like John the Baptist" and who proclaims himself as "the voice of a preacher in the wilderness," decides after his first conversation with Quint that the impressive young man may be the savior in person. But it is in Brother Nathanael's interest to regard Quint as Jesus, for only then can he be fulfilled in his own self-appointed role as John the Baptist. Hence, when Brother Nathanael leads Quint to a nearby stream and baptizes him, the narrator makes it clear that he was "carried away even more than Emanuel." And when he sees or, in his ecstasy, thinks he sees a pair of wild doves appear out of the birch trees and hover momentarily over Quint's head, "he seemed to himself like John the Baptist, and the heavens appeared to be opened unto him" (p. 41).

It cannot be stressed enough that Hauptmann's novel is in large measure a study of the subtle chemistry at work between Quint and those surrounding him. The various fanatics with whom he comes in contact have their own reasons for wanting him to be Jesus, and the influence of these often hysterical believers gradually has an effect upon the susceptible mind of the paranoically predisposed Quint, who from his tenth year on has virtually lived with and for the New Testament. In this connection we should note a motif that was not exploited in earlier transfigurations but that turns up frequently henceforward: the motif of illegitimate birth. Quint's religious mania and his identification with Jesus are ultimately attributable to his quest for a father. Mistreated by a foster-father who detests him and rejected by a natural father (the priest) who is unable to acknowledge him, Quint seeks his comfort in the New Testament image of God the Father. Although in the first months of his mission he still does not regard himself as Jesus, he nevertheless welcomes any interpretation that brings him closer to God. Quint had heard of Brother Nathanael when he was ten years old, and the itinerant preacher with the fiery eyes and thundering voice had long represented "authority" in his eyes. When he is baptized by Schwarz, Quint quite naturally takes the ceremony to be a "confirmation" of his apostleship. Uncertain afterwards whether the heavens had actually spoken to him or whether Schwarz had merely asserted this miracle, he hesitates to draw any conclusions. And yet the episode has made a profound impression on his eagerly receptive mind. For the first time he presumes to draw consolation from the parallels between his life and that of Jesus: "Jesus, therefore, like himself, Emanuel, was fatherless, and Emanuel ventured to compare all the secret sufferings he had had to endure on that account, all his tormenting shame and bitterness, with the Savior's sufferings for the same reason" (p. 45). It is obvious from such passages as these that Hauptmann has gone much farther than any writer before him in analyzing the causes for Quint's growing delusion. With his alternating moods of grandeur and despair coupled with frequent hallucinations, Quint is a textbook case of paranoia of the very sort that Hauptmann had observed in Forel's hospital.

It is unnecessary to recount in detail the events of the next few weeks: after his discovery by the Scharf brothers and his baptism by Brother Nathanael, Emanuel goes out into the wilderness in order to come to terms with himself; but in fact his religious ideas become only more confused. On his return, he wanders around the Silesian mountains for a short time, giving occasional evidence of his alleged ability to heal through faith and preaching two sermons—conveniently on outcrops that could be called mounts. Within a short time Quint is again picked up by the police and, after an examination by a qualified psychiatrist, sent back home to be kept under supervision. While he is in jail Quint has an eidetic vision much resembling that of "The Apostle": he dreams that Jesus visits him in his cell and then bodily enters into him so that Quint from that time forth contains the savior entirely.

Quint's incipient delusions of these first few weeks, from May to July, are diagnosed by the doctors as a curable state. Shortly after his return home Quint, like Nazarín (in *Halma*) before him, is sent to the estate of a noblewoman who has become interested in his case. Quint spends eight months at Gurau—from midsummer until the following March, just before Easter—gradually regaining his psychic "harmony" under the watchful eye of a doctor and sympathetic friends. Here, through the weeks and months of a beautiful fall and winter, Emanuel becomes acquainted with "the harmony of an intelligent, sunny Christianity" in contrast to the dire and hysterical preachings of the mountain fanatics. Quint's religious delusions turn out to be a sickness accessible of cure by thoughtful treatment. Hauptmann makes it absolutely clear, in other words, that Quint's christological "folly" is nothing sacred or mystical, but a purely psychological state, one to which he is susceptible by nature but which is precipitated primarily by the suggestion of others. It can be cured by removing these pernicious influences and settling Quint in a more "harmonious" way of life.

While Quint spends eight peaceful months of recovery at Gurau, his disciples reach ever greater extremes of fanaticism. The so-called "Valley Brethren" have established a religious commune, where they pray, have visions, interpret dreams, make public confessions, tell oracles from the Bible, heal by the laying-on of hands, indulge in sexual orgies, and practice all the excesses of the most exaggerated fanaticism. Now this whole sect revolves around the faith of its members in the divinity of Emanuel Quint. Several times during the course of the winter they send emissaries to their "Messiah Designate." Finally, at the beginning of March, a messenger informs Quint that a fierce doctrinal dispute has broken out among the Valley Brethren. Some assert that Quint is the new Messiah; others hold that he is the Redeemer, but that he has not yet revealed the Ultimate Secret; still others argue that his divinity has not yet been proved.

Up to this point Quint has been living in a newly won state of harmony, but now he begins suffering sleepless nights. The more he thinks, the greater his confusion becomes. Recalling his vision in the jail cell months before, he reasons that if he does indeed bear Jesus within himself, then he also bears the responsibility of Jesus toward his fellow man. In other words, he feels himself forced back into his role of Jesus by the acclaim of the Valley Brethren, whose hysterics outweigh the calm reason of his friends at Gurau. His Christian ethic of brotherly love paradoxically compels him to assume once again the cloak of the redeemer: "It may be said that Quint's consciousness of being the Savior coarsened in proportion as he was forced to adapt it to the gross, crude, sordid demands of his community" (p. 283). At the same time, he achieves precisely the opposite of the cure that he had hoped to effect by reasoning with fanatical followers. The more he tries to argue the Valley Brethren out of their faith in his divinity, the more he fortifies them in their belief. "Their error, which Quint desired to destroy, exalted him. They were devoted to him with all their foolish faith, with all their foolish desires, and with a wild, blind passion" (p. 286). Pushed even further by the demands of his followers, Quint's already susceptible mind is irremediably shaken: now for the first time accepting fully his identity with Jesus, he sets out purposefully to pursue his own Passion. As a result, the last part of the novel is marked by much closer parallels to the

Gospels because Quint arranges incidents in such a way that the correspondence will be obvious; he is determined to force reality to conform to the visions of his sick imagination: "In truth, Emanuel Quint scarcely saw the Savior in the Bible any more—he had already done violence to that book—but, horrible to say, only in himself and as himself. Since his dream in prison, in which Christ literally entered into him, his holy madness had been repressed and had found time to take firm root" (p. 306).

Whereas the first half of the novel consists of two separate narrative strands, the main story of Quint and the subsidiary one of the Valley Brethren, the second part is one unified action as Quint assembles his disciples around him and goes down from the mountains to Breslau, where he expects to suffer his Passion. Quint's language from the very start has been colored largely by the rhetoric of the New Testament, the only book he knows. But from this point on he speaks almost exclusively in parables and in direct quotation of Jesus, shaping the words to suit his own purposes. The real turning point comes on Easter Sunday, when in his confused imagination Quint confounds the risen Christ with himself: "Now I clearly feel that I am going to meet the enemy, Emanuel thought. . . . My enemy is as old as the world, and like a second Christ, I will go forth against him and conquer" (p. 332). When he is stoned by a mob of orthodox Christians for his presumptuous sermon, he regards his bruises as the stigmata of a heavenly sanction. Gathering his disciples around him—"the impatient citizens of the millennium-to-come, who had forced his fate upon him" (p. 368)—he implores them not to part from him until the day when all shall come to pass as he foresees. With these words, he leads them down toward Breslau, the city that he explicitly calls his Golgotha.

On the way to the city there occurs the curious scene— the cleansing of the temple—in which Emanuel stops to visit the Catholic priest who is clearly his father, but whose paternity Emanuel refuses to acknowledge. With no motivation but the precedent in the Bible he ravages the church with his shepherd's crook; but the desecration is at the same time, psychologically, a gesture of frustration because he does not wish to concede the paternity of a human father: "'I am Christ,' shouted Emanuel, all the arches and niches echoing to his voice. 'I say unto you'—and with a mighty blow he knocked down the cross on the high altar—'this is no house of prayer, it is a den of murderers'" (p. 378).

Through a paradoxical switch of motivation the last quarter of the novel amounts to an ironic inversion of the Gospel story. For almost in the instant when their importuning has finally won Quint over, his "disciples" begin to doubt him. Their arrival in Breslau is accompanied by no great revelations or apocalypses. Indeed, as they remain week after week, they notice that life in the city goes on as usual. In addition, Quint's curious messiahship, which encountered a certain invigorating hostility in the mountain villages, arouses nothing but mirth and scorn in the sophisticated metropolis. Their group is ridiculed by the intellectuals and kept under surveillance by the police. Finally, after an unruly evening that ends when Quint is struck in the face by an angry innkeeper, the disciples begin openly to criticize him. This situation sets off Quint's frantic search for a Passion scene that will legitimize his claims.

Several days later Quint organizes an outing for himself and his disciples, during the course of which it is reported that the police are looking for Quint on suspicion of murder. Seizing the opportunity, Quint assembles his group for a Last Supper and in an impassioned monologue manages to paraphrase many of the most famous passages of the Gospels. Despite Quint's careful staging, the occasion threatens to turn into another quarrelsome airing of grievances when a clap of thunder announces a summer rain storm. Suddenly sobered, the superstitious disciples now sit quietly as Quint says, "May God forgive you, for you know not what you do." He then proceeds to wash their feet in the ritual gesture, acting more out of instinct than reason.

120

Afterwards Quint steps out into the garden of the inn and even finds occasion to invert the words from Gethsemane: "The flesh is willing, but the spirit is weak." Then in the absence of a convenient Judas he sets out back into town, where he is promptly arrested at his lodging.

Quint is completely innocent of the murder of which he has been accused, but acting in accordance with his role as Jesus, he refuses to defend himself. As his delusion begins to collapse around him, as his disciples lose their faith, and as the millennium fails to come, Quint desperately requires an act that will somehow confirm the identity that he has now fully accepted. It is this need that compels him to assume the guilt, as an act of self-sacrifice, for a crime that he did not commit. (The irony is intensified by the reader's knowledge that he is sacrificing himself for a completely unworthy man.) But in this most ironic of fictional transfigurations even that last solace is denied him: Quint is a Jesus who cannot find his cross. Before the trial the real murderer is discovered: one of his disciples who, true to his role as Judas, has hanged himself. Quint, however, is released to the void of his own unfulfilled imagination.

Betrayed, with his Last Supper and his Gethsemane behind him, but denied his crucifixion and deserted by his disciples who have presumably gone back to the mountains to seek another prophet, Quint has no further option but to disappear. The fictional framework has ended, and Hauptmann has followed his hero to the emotional point of no return. For a few weeks, the narrator informs us, there are reports of his sporadic appearance in various parts of Germany, a beggar who announces himself to the Doubting Thomases as Jesus Christ. The trail leads from Berlin to Frankfurt am Main and on across South Germany and Switzerland to the Gotthard, where, the following summer, a body resembling Quint's is found frozen in the ice.

There are at least two reasons why few writers since Hauptmann have attempted the fictional transfiguration of a paranoid Jesus. In the first place, with a sure instinct Hauptmann created a classic model that was difficult to match. Given the basic premise—a febrile imagination uncontrolled by a "harmonious" personality breeds a paranoiac hallucination that ultimately succeeds in displacing reality—it would require more than ordinary psychological insight and ingenuity of plot to go beyond Hauptmann's ironic yet sympathetic portrayal of his Fool in Christ. In the second place, psychiatric investigation was soon able to demonstrate that fact is indeed stranger than fiction. In his fascinating study of *The Three Christs of Ypsilanti* (1964) Milton Rokeach discusses three actual cases of men—a farmer, a clerk, and an electrician—who believe that they are Jesus Christ. His case-record of social psychology describes what happens to these three modern Christs when they are confronted with one another in the state mental hospital at Ypsilanti, Michigan. The writer who hopes to compete with this kind of reality must go to great lengths indeed.

The Austrian dramatist and novelist Robert Michel (1876-1957) came up with the necessary artifice in his story of *Jesus in the Bohemian Forest* (*Jesus im Böhmerwald*, 1927).[7] Here it is the mother, rather than fanatic disciples, who forces her son into a re-enactment of the Gospels. The mother, Marie, is the mentally afflicted daughter of a charcoal burner in the remote depths of the Bohemian woods. Her illness manifests itself in the form of an abnormal coma into which she falls from time to time. On one such occasion she is raped in the woods by a young artist from Prague, whose name—ironically—is Christian. When she finds herself pregnant, seemingly by virgin conception, Marie begins to identify herself in her deluded mind with the Virgin Mary. She marries the local blacksmith's apprentice, but exacts from him the promise never to touch her in physical

[7] To my knowledge there is no translation; I refer to the original edition (Wien: Speidel, 1927).

love. From this point on, Marie arranges events whenever possible to conform to the Gospel narrative. Her child is born at Christmastime, and Marie makes sure that she is in the local stable for the birth. On Twelfth Night the revelers, dressed as Magi, arrive with gifts for the newborn child, whom Marie has named Jesus. Jesus turns out to be mentally retarded like his mother. Raising him in the seclusion of the forest and instructing him only from the New Testament, Marie teaches her son to arrange or interpret the events of his life in such a way as to correspond to the Gospel. When he miraculously heals his mother from her comas, she sends him forth on a cow to do good deeds among men. The remainder of the novel shows only tenuous parallels to the Bible as the plot becomes progressively more sensational. Jesus works a few wonders and assembles a group of children around him as disciples. An unlikely episode of mistaken identities results in his being thrown into jail with his father, Christian, who is suspected of murder. Released from jail, Jesus is seized by the true murderer, a brutal criminal who grants him the violent death he has longed for: he burns Jesus on a pyre in the presence of his mother. Marie, shocked out of her madness by this violence, responds to Jesus for the first time as a son rather than an idol and leaps after him into the fire.

Michel's novel, widely read when it appeared serially in the *Vossische Zeitung*, was favorably reviewed and won the prize of the Adalbert Stifter Society. But the plot is sensational rather than plausible; the psychology is outré rather than incisive. The author was forced to these extremes because Hauptmann's novel already occupied the sound middle ground as a brilliant fictional study of paranoia and because psychiatry itself had produced equally interesting case studies. Where minor writers fail, however, major authors may welcome the challenge. The psychiatric transfigurations, so few in comparison with the other categories, include in addition to *Emanuel Quint* a second major European novel. In fact, Nikos Kazantzakis' *The Greek Passion*[8] has become one of the best-known fictional transfigurations, both as a widely acclaimed novel and in the film version by Jules Dassin (*He Who Must Die*, 1957). (In 1962 it was also made into an opera by Bohuslav Martinu.)

Like Hauptmann, whose works he read and admired, Kazantzakis (1882-1957) was obsessed throughout his life with the figure of Jesus.[9] Always in search of spiritual heroes after whom he could model his own life, Kazantzakis first became fascinated with Jesus when, as a boy, he was placed in a school run by Franciscan friars on the island of Naxos. This early Christian zeal, which was accentuated by a conspicuous impulse toward asceticism, survived his law studies in Athens and even his philosophical training in Paris under Bergson. Like many of his heroes Kazantzakis was a man of violent extremes: determining to establish direct contact with the savior, he spent six months in a monk's cell on Mt. Athos in Macedonia. When spiritual and bodily exercises failed to produce the desired results Kazantzakis turned away from Christ and, during the following decades, experimented with a variety of intellectual positions. The allegiances that claimed him after his youthful mysti-

[8] Kazantzakis wrote the novel in 1948; but for various reasons—principally ecclesiastical opposition—he was unable to publish it in Greece for six years: *Ho Christos xanastauronetai* (Athens: Diphros, 1954). In the meantime, however, it became widely known in a variety of translations: Swedish (1950), German and Norwegian (1951), Dutch and Danish (1952), and English (1953).

[9] For the biographical background I have relied on Helen Kazantzakis, *Nikos Kazantzakis: A Biography Based on his Letters*, trans. Amy Mims (New York: Simon and Schuster, 1968), from which the quotations have been taken. See also Kimon Friar's informative introduction to his translation of Kazantzakis, *The Saviors of God: Spiritual Exercises* (New York: Simon and Schuster, 1960); and Colette Janiaud-Lust, *Nikos Kazantzaki: sa vie, son œuvre* (Paris: François Maspero, 1970). For additional information see F. W. Dillistone's discussion of *The Greek Passion* in *The Novelist and the Passion Story* (New York: Sheed and Ward, 1960); and the largely biographical chapter on Kazantzakis in Will and Ariel Durant, *Interpretations of Life: A Survey of Contemporary Literature* (New York: Simon and Schuster, 1970), pp. 269-98.

cism, he once remarked, were successively nationalism, communism, and nihilism. Some of the heroes besides Jesus to whom he devoted himself—the "Saviors of God"—-were Buddha, Odysseus, Don Quixote, Nietzsche, and Lenin.

When from 1948 to 1951 Kazantzakis finally wrote his two great Jesus novels—the fictional transfiguration *The Greek Passion* (whose technique is suggested more precisely by a literal translation of the Greek title: *Christ Re-Crucified*) and the fictionalizing biography *The Last Temptation of Christ*—his view of Jesus was tempered by the various intellectual positions he had held. After the mysticism of his youth Kazantzakis came to regard Jesus as a spiritual hero on a level with other heroic myths of mankind. In his retelling of the *Odyssey*, for instance, Odysseus says to Christ: "Tell me your myth that the whole world may turn to myth." This view of Jesus reflects an attitude that Kazantzakis shared with various scholars of religion and writers of the twenties. At the same time, during his Marxist phase Kazantzakis came to view communism as a religion, an attitude that affected the view of Jesus held by many writers in the thirties. Although the mythic and the Marxist views of Jesus, as we shall have occasion to observe in the next two chapters, produced clearly distinguishable categories of fictional transfiguration, neither dominated Kazantzakis' thought and work. At most, these positions justified the shift of his interest from the Christ of faith to the Jesus of human history. In his obsession with the psychology of the savior and his modern imitator, Kazantzakis is much closer to Hauptmann than to the next generation of writers.

In 1921 Kazantzakis wrote a verse tragedy on *The Christ* and in 1942 he contemplated composing the "Memoirs of Jesus," in preparation for which he made a careful study of the Scriptures as well as the Apocrypha. Four years later, his wife reports, he was still thinking about Jesus; but at that point he wanted to "cure Christ of His Messianic spirit through psychoanalysis" (p. 407). During that period a young Greek doctor regularly came to his apartment in

Paris to introduce Kazantzakis to the secrets of analysis. The direct product of this psychiatric view of Jesus was *The Last Temptation of Christ*, which Kazantzakis wrote "in a state of deep religious exaltation, with fervent love for Christ." As he wrote the novel, he recorded, "I felt what Christ felt. I became Christ" (p. 516). Kazantzakis' attitude is a curious mixture of the liberal hatred of the conventional distorted image of Jesus and the hallucinatory identification of Hauptmann's Quint: "It's a laborious, sacred, creative endeavor to reincarnate the essence of Christ, setting aside the dross, falsehood and pettiness which all the churches and all the cassocked representatives of Christianity have heaped upon this figure, thereby distorting it" (p. 505). It was his eminently human conception of Jesus that enraged the Greek Orthodox Church, causing it to threaten Kazantzakis with excommunication. "That part of Christ's nature which was profoundly human helps us to understand him and love him and to pursue his Passion as though it were our own," he wrote in the Prologue to *The Last Temptation*. "If he had not within him this warm human element, he would never be able to touch our hearts with such assurance and tenderness; he would not be able to become a model for our lives."

What Kazantzakis wrote about *The Last Temptation* suggests the spirit in which he composed *The Greek Passion* within two months of 1948. Since he was obsessed with the figure of Jesus as a literary subject from 1942 to 1951, we can assume that he was consciously aware at every instant of the parallels in his transfiguration. Secondly, his transfiguration would reflect precisely the same kind of Jesus that we find in *The Last Temptation*: a human savior whose image has been shorn of the inauthentic attributes bestowed upon it by conventional Christianity. Finally, the impulse motivating both books is an impulse toward psychiatric analysis: like Hauptmann, Kazantzakis wanted to understand what it is that causes a man to identify himself with Jesus. To a certain extent he was recording his own experience: as he noted during the composition of his later novel, "I became Christ." It is perfectly consistent, therefore, that Kazantzakis motivated the crucial psychological transformation of his hero with an incident that might strike us as implausible if we did not know of its autobiographical source.

In May, 1922, while in Vienna, Kazantzakis suffered an inexplicable outbreak of "eczema" of the face. Fascinated by a lovely woman beside whom he was sitting in the theater, Kazantzakis invited her to visit him in his room the following evening. But overnight a mysterious affliction set in: his face puffed up until his eyes were nothing but pinpoints in a blubber of flesh, and his lower lip dripped with a yellowish fluid. The affliction, which neither pathologists nor dermatologists were able to relieve, lasted until August and effectively put an end to Kazantzakis' amatory designs. Then one day, quite by chance, the author was approached by a doctor who expressed curiosity about the disfiguring disease; the doctor turned out to be the psychiatrist Wilhelm Stekel. After an examination Stekel diagnosed the affliction as "saint's disease," a neo-ascetic case of psychosomatic origin that stemmed from feelings of guilt associated with the temptation of the beautiful woman in the theater. On Stekel's advice Kazantzakis left Vienna, the site of his temptation, and almost immediately his face healed. Twenty-five years later Kazantzakis used an identical incident to motivate the hero of *The Greek Passion* to undertake his imitation of Jesus.

The Greek Passion[10] differs from *Emanuel Quint* in three important respects. The action, first of all, takes place within a historical framework that bears a startlingly close resemblance to the political circumstances in Jerusalem at the time of Jesus: in an Anatolian Greek village in the years immediately following World War I (presumably during

[10] I quote from the Ballantine Books edition of the translation by Jonathan Griffin (New York: Simon and Schuster, 1953).

the Greek offensive in Anatolia in 1921). This permits Kazantzakis to introduce very precise parallels that were impossible for Hauptmann: the Turkish agha who represents the political authority in the ethnically Greek village, for instance, is an absolutely appropriate equivalent to Pontius Pilate and the Roman authorities in Hebrew Jerusalem. Second, Kazantzakis has invented a brilliant fictional device to initiate the action: his hero has been chosen to play the role of Jesus in a re-enactment of the Passion that is performed every seven years in this Anatolian Oberammergau. Finally, since the historical circumstances and the plot make the parallels so obvious, Kazantzakis can dispense with the commenting narrator of Hauptmann: he leaves it up to the reader to work out most of the parallels for himself. To the extent that Kazantzakis is writing for a Greek audience about specifically Greek circumstances, this attitude can present occasional problems. Most Western readers need to consult a reference work to determine facts of time and place that are instantly clear to the Greek reader. In addition, the ceremonies, images, and holidays of the Eastern church vary slightly from those that are familiar in the Roman Catholic world.

The Greek Passion is wholly traditional in form: this was a conscious decision on the author's part when he wrote the novel as an act of liberation from several years of public service (most recently as Director of the UNESCO Bureau of Translations). As a result, there are few tricks and surprise disclosures; virtually the entire plot is implicit, for anyone who knows the New Testament, in the characters and the situation introduced in the first chapter. It is Easter Tuesday, and the village elders have assembled to appoint the citizens who are to play the roles of Jesus and the disciples in the following year's Passion Play. From the very start, therefore, everyone concerned—both the principals and the observers—is aware of the symbolic roles that are being acted out. The assignments are made initially because the villagers suit the various roles for which they are selected, according to the popular understanding of the Bible stories; and during the ensuing weeks and months they are expected to live more or less in accordance with the role that has been assigned to each.

Although the villagers take their Passion Play and their roles seriously, two unexpected factors are required to activate the potential plot: the paranoia of the hero, Manolios, and an unusual external event. On the very day that the roles are assigned, an entire village of refugees, driven from their homes by the Turks, arrives at Lycovrissi after three months of wandering and implores aid. This situation permits Kazantzakis to indulge in the satire and criticism of institutionalized Christianity familiar ever since Christian socialism. The prosperous "Christians" of Lycovrissi, who feel unthreatened by the Turks, are unwilling to render even the slightest assistance to their fellow Christians; instead, led by the priest Grigoris, they attempt to drive the starving refugees away. Indeed, the Turkish agha turns out to be more humane and charitable than the Christian elders. It is the villagers chosen for parts in the Passion Play who decide to live out their roles by coming to the assistance of the refugees, guiding them up to the sheltering caves of the nearby Mount Sarakina. The tension between these two parties generates the hostility that the other villagers come to feel toward their Jesus, the shepherd Manolios, and that eventually drives them to execute him. Whereas in *Emanuel Quint* a hallucination displaced reality in the mind of the hero, here an entire village of two thousand is driven to act out in reality the Passion Play that begins as simple illusion. Unlike Hauptmann, however, Kazantzakis is not interested in the phenomenon of mass hysteria. His villagers act out their role unconsciously and not because they believe in the divinity of Manolios.

The novel falls roughly into two halves: the first part deals with the hero's private religious development up to the point where he wholly assumes the identity that was initially thrust upon him by others (chaps. 1-10); and the second part expands the action to embrace the public and political involvements of the hero who now actively seeks out his own Passion (chaps. 11-21). Manolios is chosen for the role of Jesus mainly because of his pious behavior and his appearance. With his blue eyes and short yellow beard, Manolios is "a real Christ like an icon," the priest assures the village notables, adding as an afterthought: "and pious into the bargain" (p. 26). One of the elders remarks that "he's a wee bit crazy." But what none of them realizes is that, by chance, they have hit upon a man with a religious mania that already amounts to incipient paranoia. Left an orphan at an early age, Manolios was brought up first by an aunt and then, for years, by the monks at the monastery, where he early conceived a mystical desire to re-enact the Passion. When he is chosen for the role of Jesus, it is the fulfillment of a lifelong dream: "The thing to which he had aspired from his tenderest childhood, the thing he had desired during so many nights as he sat at the feet of his Superior, Father Manasse, listening to the golden legend— behold, now God was granting it to him. To follow in the footsteps of the martyrs and the saints, to pare away his flesh, to go to his death for his faith in Jesus Christ, and to enter Paradise bearing the instruments of martyrdom: the crown of thorns, the cross and the five nails . . ." (p. 39).

Manolios is suited for the strenuous role by virtue of his physical strength; but his emotional stability does not match this strength. In fact, he suffers from Emanuel Quint's paranoid inability to distinguish between hallucination and reality. On the very first day, for instance, he warns his fellow apostles against reading the lives of the saints in preparation for their roles: "When I was with the monks I used to read them, and I nearly went off my head. Deserts, lions, dreadful diseases, leprosy; their bodies were covered with boils, eaten by worms, or became like the shells of tortoises. . . . At other times temptations came like a beautiful woman. No, no! Only the Gospel" (p. 42). This capacity for eidetic re-experience of the Scriptures and Christian legends affords Manolios the same sense of identity with Jesus that Quint received through his vision in the jail cell: "Manolios dragged himself into the ray of light which fell from the skylight, pulled the little Gospel out of his waistcoat pocket, opened it at random and began to read, forgetting the others around about him. He entered into the boat with Christ, mingled with the apostles, they went sailing on the lake of Gennesareth, and toward evening a violent wind came up . . . " (p. 249).

Kazantzakis has given careful attention to the psychological plausibility of his hero in order to make the entire fiction acceptable. Manolios' background and his predisposition toward religious hysteria convince him that his selection for the role of Jesus represents more than a happenstance or a mere formality: like Quint's baptism by Brother Nathanael, it seems to confirm all his visions and dreams. "When I left Priest Grigoris's house," he confides to his friends, "my head was buzzing. It seemed to me that the village had become too small for me, that I wasn't any longer Manolios, the lowly shepherd of old Patriarcheas, the ignorant, the wretched, but as it were a man chosen of God and with a great mission: to follow the footsteps of Christ, to be like Him!" (p. 200). Whereas the other actors are able to distinguish clearly between their own identities and their assigned roles, Manolios gradually accepts the role as his new identity. This emerges clearly from his conversation with the peddler Yannakos, who has been chosen to be the Apostle Peter. When Manolios, who is engaged to be married, tries to persuade him that they must change their lives and live in purity for the coming year in order to be fit for their roles, Yannakos realistically points out the facts: " 'When you come before us to act Christ Crucified, you'll be newly married. They'll put you on the cross, but a lot that will mean to you! You'll know that it's all a game, that it's Another who was crucified, and at the moment when

131

you cry out on the cross: 'Eli, Eli, lama subachthani!' you'll say to yourself that soon you'll be home, after the crucifying . . ." (pp. 91-2). Manolios, shaken by the undeniable truth of Yannakos' statement, begins to tell himself that he's an impostor, while Yannakos reminds him that their enthusiasm on the day before was a different matter: "It was a holiday, don't you see? . . . Today, look, the donkey's loaded, our bellies are empty, Easter's over, trade's starting again. . . ."

The first half of the novel is given over largely to the psychological question: How does it happen that Manolios, alone among the actors, slips wholly into the role of Jesus? As we have just seen, his background and character make this delusion ultimately plausible. But at first he wavers, moved by the more cynical realism of his friends and afraid of his own presumptuousness. Then four days after his selection, stirred by a strong though subconscious longing, Manolios sets out to visit the beautiful widow Katerina, chosen to play the part of Mary Magdalene. Manolios rationalizes his sexual urge by telling himself that he really wants to visit her in his newly appointed role as Christ to save her from sin. But as he starts down the mountain in his Sunday outfit, with a vision of the sensuous widow in his imagination, his head suddenly begins to buzz, his temples throb, his face prickles. Passing his hand over his face, he perceives that his features are grotesquely swollen. When he looks in his pocket mirror, he sees that his face is completely bloated: "his eyes were no more than two tiny balls, his nose was lost between his ballooning cheeks, his mouth was a mere hole" (p. 133). This affliction, in which we recognize the "saint's disease" that Kazantzakis suffered in 1922, tips the emotional balance and causes Manolios to accept his delusion wholly. Horrified at his appearance, he hurries back up the mountain, where he remains in his hut for the following weeks. Breaking his engagement with his fiancée, he vows to live a life of total self-sacrifice in imita-

tion of Jesus. (On July 27, 1948, Kazantzakis recorded in his
notebook: "My lip began swelling just at the moment in my
novel where I describe the swelling on the face of the hero,
who enacts the role of Christ.")

Early in May Manolios and his three apostles attend a
Sunday service that the priest Fotis holds for the refugees.
Afterwards, as they sit and explicate the Beatitudes,
Manolios makes a great confession to his friends, telling
them of his childhood dreams, his presumptuous wish to
imitate Christ, his temptation by the widow Katerina, and
the frightful affliction by which God struck him down. But
Fotis interprets the events in a new light: rather than a punishment, the affliction is a protective mask that God has
clapped on Manolios in order to save him for salvation and
for a great deed. It is only a few days until Manolios seems
to have a chance to act out his role. The agha's young homosexual lover, Youssoufaki, has been murdered—as it later
turns out, by his giant bodyguard Hussein. At first the
furious agha suspects the Greeks and threatens to hang
them one by one until the murderer confesses. When
Manolios hears of these happenings down in the village, he
resolves to sacrifice himself for the sake of the town and sets
out down the mountain in an ecstatic hallucination, "as if he
were again following Christ's footsteps and they led down
to Lycovrissi" (p. 235). Almost miraculously, his face heals
from one moment to the next, now that his soul is purified
by the decision to sacrifice himself. Manolios, in turn, imagines himself to be nothing but the will-less tool of Jesus:
"You must realize that it's not me speaking, but Christ commanding me. I'm carrying out His orders, and no more"
(p. 236).

Entering the village, Manolios surrenders to the agha,
who releases the other hostages and promises to hang
Manolios at sunset. The widow Katerina, moved by
Manolios' example and words, makes a fruitless effort to
save him—it is remarkable how often this old Christian so-

cialist motif of the repentant woman of passion crops up!
—and earns nothing but her own death at the furious agha's
hands. But Manolios, like Quint, is deprived at the last
minute of his act of sacrifice. The agha's housekeeper, dismayed at the murder of Katerina, turns up evidence that
Hussein murdered Youssoufaki in a fit of jealousy. Releas-
ing Manolios, the agha hangs and mutilates his bodyguard.
But the total surrender of self implied by his resolved self-
sacrifice has welded Manolios completely with his role.
"Brothers," he tells the other disciples, "I have taken the decision to change my life completely, to reject the past, to
welcome Christ by the wayside. I shall walk before Him
with the trumpet, like His bodyguard, . . . When I open my
mouth, Christ will put the right words on my lips." And in
the darkness the disciples note that "his face was dazzling"
(p. 277).

In the first half of the novel, then, the emphasis is on the
psychogenesis of the hero, whose paranoia is traced
through a series of plausible stages, beginning with the
recollections of his childhood and moving through delusions of grandeur and the despair of doubt to the complete
displacement of reality by hallucination. The New Testament parallels remain rather general: the proclamation of
Manolios as Jesus, the gathering of the disciples, the
temptation, the sermon on the mount, and the transfiguration. In the second half, as his ministry becomes public,
the parallels become far more conspicuous, especially as
Manolios begins to pursue his own Passion.

The events of the first ten chapters last no more than
three weeks—from Easter (around April 22) until early in
May. After the high point of this section, Manolios' transfiguration, several months are passed over in silence. Up to
this point Manolios has been concerned only with his personal religious development; but now the action becomes
political as he comes into conflict with authority. During the
harvest season he appeals to the villagers to help the
refugees to prepare for the approaching winter. At the Fes-

tival of Elijah he addresses the congregation after asking the priest for permission to speak "about Christ."

" 'Christ?' said the priest, taken aback; 'but that's my business.' "

" 'Christ has ordered me to speak,' Manolios insisted" (p. 304). Although the villagers are persuaded by Manolios' words, his behavior arouses the hostility of the priest Grigoris, who sets about to destroy his work and to drive out the detested refugees along with their priest, who competes with his authority. Grigoris, clever enough to realize that he would lose by attacking Manolios' Christian charity on religious grounds, implies that he is a political threat. By accusing Manolios of bolshevism he achieves two goals: he anticipates and undermines the appeal that Manolios and Fotis make to the regional bishop regarding the behavior of the Lycovrissians; and he enlists the active aid of the agha, who was not even remotely interested in the affair as long as it was merely a religious squabble of the detested *romnoi*.

The priest's principal henchman in his schemes is the village saddler, Panayotaros, to whom Kazantzakis has devoted a care of characterization second only to that of Manolios. Panayotaros hates Manolios because the shepherd has displaced him in the affections of the widow Katerina; but he is doubly embittered because he was selected to play the role of Judas. "My wife calls me Judas, the kids in the street make long noses at me; the women bolt their doors when they see me pass. Plague take you, you'll make me into a Judas forever!" he tells the other apostles (p. 178). Throwing himself more passionately into his role than the others, but out of resentment rather than love, he helps the priest to gather information against Manolios and the refugees. One of the other disciples tries to dissuade him from his treachery by arguing—just as Yannakos had reminded Manolios—that "it's a play, a sacred play but only a play, not real," that he was chosen for the role of Judas only because he had a red beard (p. 381). But Panayotaros, albeit consciously and not in a hallucination, takes his role just as seriously as Manolios does his. And since every Jesus needs his Judas, he determines to act it out to the end.

Meanwhile, the situation of the refugees deteriorates as the season moves into winter. On December 22, the birthday of St. Elijah, they decide to march down into Lycovrissi to demand food from the villagers. A general brawl develops during which part of the village is burned and the schoolmaster is killed. The priest, furious, tries to persuade the agha to arrest Manolios, whom he calls a dangerous bolshevik: "He has one aim only: to overthrow the Ottoman Empire. Behind him stands the Muscovite, pushing him on. If we let him live, he'll have us all" (p. 490). Up to this point the agha has observed the happenings with an amused detachment, as "manias" of the foolish Greeks. "Let them shift for themselves; I smoke my chibouk, I sip my raki, and I don't care a fig! But now the Ottoman Empire's becoming mixed up in it, the Muscovite is there, things are getting out of hand. Yet, yes, if I let that abortion Manolios live the Ottoman Empire is in danger" (p. 491). Drinking himself into a stupor, the agha sends the saddler to arrest Manolios, and Panayotaros congratulates himself that his moment is at hand: "Bravo, Judas Panayotaros, my gallant, you've got him" (p. 493). When Panayotaros finally catches up with Manolios, he speaks like a true Judas: " 'When I've killed you, Manolios,' he bellowed, 'I shall kill myself afterward; I'm only living to kill you' " (p. 496). For Panayotaros, reality has been as radically displaced by his Judas-role as for Manolios by his Jesus-role.

From this point on the incidents fall neatly into the sequence of the Passion, a Passion that has been ironically inverted. When Panayotaros sets out, Manolios and his disciples are in a Gethsemane-like garden outside the village. But when word arrives that the search is on for Manolios, most of the men hide or take flight. Only one disciple remains as Manolios, with cocks crowing in the distance, sets out toward the village to give himself up; and that one,

Kostandis, goes off at a run as soon as he sees Panayotaros approaching. Since Manolios surrenders voluntarily, there is no proper arrest in Gethsemane. Yet Panayotaros, in order to play up his own role, embellishes his account of the apprehension so that it seems to conform more closely to the Gospel scene: "I've nabbed him, Agha. He was barricaded in the garden with his men, about twenty, armed to the teeth" (p. 497). So greatly does imagination take the place of reality!

The agha, in turn, is perfectly well aware that Manolios is innocent of the accusations: "Wolves don't eat one another; Greeks do. Here they are now, wanting, for all they're worth, to eat Manolios! Why? what's he done to them? He's innocent, poor fellow; a bit crazy, but he never did anyone any harm." But when Manolios refuses to defend himself, the agha resolves to let the Greeks have their way and falls unwittingly into the very words of Pontius Pilate. If Manolios insists on playing the saint, he must suffer the consequences. The agha, deciding that it would mean too much trouble if he tried to defend the shepherd, makes up his mind to hand him over: "There he is, take him, you blessed *romnoi*, and enjoy your meal! I wash my hands of it" (p. 497). But first, sorry for Manolios in his innocence, he tries to give him a chance to escape. Manolios, confessing to the crimes of arson and bolshevism, advises the agha to surrender him to the villagers, who are howling outside for his life. Finally agreeing, the agha orders Manolios to admit that he is a bolshevik so that he can surrender him to the mob in anger. Then he seizes Manolios by the neck and throws him down the stairs, where the mob is waiting. Led by the priest Grigoris and Panayotaros, the villagers drag him off to the church, where Manolios must again confess publicly to being a bolshevik. Three times he implores the mob to kill him, but they hesitate until they hear, outside, the voices of the refugees who have come to rescue Manolios. At this point Panayotaros strikes him down, and the villagers, hurling themselves upon his body

137

in a fury, tear at it with their teeth in an obscene travesty of the Eucharist.

The novel ends with an ironic inversion of the crèche scene, for it has meantime become Christmas Eve and the bells begin to ring, summoning the Christians to the church to witness the birth of Christ. Nearby Manolios is stretched out on a bed, "swathed like a newborn child": "About him his companions watched, pale and silent; Yannakos had rested his head on Manolios' feet and was weeping like a child . . . " (p. 507). Just as Manolios was proclaimed as Jesus at Easter, the time of Christ's death and resurrection, so he now dies on the day of Jesus' birth in a scene in which Nativity and Lamentation are curiously blended.

In Kazantzakis' novel the crucifixion is followed by no resurrection; the ending seems to be totally bleak: "Priest Fotis listened to the bell pealing gaily, announcing that Christ was coming down on earth to save the world. He shook his head and heaved a sigh: In vain, my Christ, in vain, he muttered; two thousand years have gone by and men crucify You still. When will You be born, my Christ, and not be crucified any more, but live among us for eternity?" (pp. 507-08). If there is any hint of redemption in this novel, it can be detected only in the sheer human perseverance that prompts the refugees—in the face of hostility on earth and, in heaven, the gloomy promise of an eternal cycle of crucifixions—to resume "their interminable march toward the east." The faith in Christ with which Kazantzakis began in his youth has given way to a more secularized faith in man's dignity and his ability to endure.

If we now pause to compare the novels of Hauptmann and Kazantzakis, we see that for all their distinctive differences they share many common features that, apart from the parallels already noted from time to time, set them off from the Christian socialist transfigurations. In both works the motivating impulse has shifted from social criticism to psychological understanding. This shift reflects, first of all, the basic interests of the authors: although Kazantzakis does not help the reader as much as Hauptmann's solicitous narrator, both novelists were long fascinated by psychology, psychiatry, and psychoanalysis and specifically applied the techniques of these disciplines to their novels. The shift also helps to account for the narrative humor that makes these two novels more enjoyable than the often deadpan tracts of Christian socialism. Although Hauptmann and Kazantzakis both had a keen eye for social injustice, they did not regard themselves primarily as ethical revivalists or crusaders for social reform. Both were writing some twenty years after the events depicted and the specific circumstances were often historically outmoded; and, in fact, their large human understanding permitted them to see the ridiculous side of such characters as the bigoted Silesian preachers and Priest Grigoris, the startled German housewives and the avaricious villagers of Lycovrissi. But above all, their narrative detachment and their psychological insight enabled them to view even their paranoid heroes with a certain warm humor that is completely missing from the fervid gospels or coldly objective narratives of Christian socialism.

Apart from these more general characteristics we can also recognize a few more specific similarities of setting and temporal organization. In both novels the milieu is kept simple. Instead of the mainly urban and cosmopolitan settings of the earlier novels—London, Rome, Berlin, Madrid—we are dealing here with isolated communities where primitive faith has not been eroded by sophistication and cynicism and where the individual is still not excessively hampered by the bureaucracy of modern civilization. Only in such a society, twenty years prior to the author's present, is it plausible that a paranoid hero would be permitted to nurture his hallucination to the point at which it transcends the private sphere and begins to affect public reality. (In a more controlled contemporary society Quint and Manolios would find themselves in Ypsilanti, Michigan, or its equivalent.)

139

Both novels, in addition, use a temporal sequence that begins around Easter and ends at Christmas—in *The Greek Passion* the nine months from April through December, and in *Emanuel Quint* the extended period of a year and a half. This temporal organization has the effect of inverting the Gospel sequence, an ironic inversion of structure that reflects the inversion of character in the paranoid hero. But it affords an additional narrative advantage. It is conspicuous that the finest novelists we have considered—Galdós, Fogazzaro, Hauptmann, and Kazantzakis—chose to focus on the concentrated weeks and months of mission and Passion whereas most of the others expanded their narrative into a less compelling and more loosely episodic sequence that permitted them to explore a variety of social situations and ills. In the novels of Hauptmann and Kazantzakis this concentration is dictated by psychological as well as by purely narrative considerations. Since the emphasis is on the development of the hero's paranoia, our attention must be focused on the period during which it develops and during which it exerts its impact on the surrounding reality. For this reason both novels fall into two nearly equal parts, the private obsession and the public action. Above all, in these novels we are willing to accept unusually close parallels to the Gospels as plausible. For they are not thrust upon us from the outside by insistent narrators who keep reminding us about the "parable" nature of their "true history" or "singular life." Rather, the parallels are motivated psychologically by the heroes who, as fantasy gradually displaces reality in their minds, actively seek out their own Passion in imitation of the Jesus with whom they have come to identify themselves.

Although the psychiatric interpretations of the historical Jesus were rejected by theology and psychiatry alike as insufficiently grounded in fact, the new interest in religious paranoia and hysteria around the turn of the century had far-reaching implications for the fictional transfiguration. In brief, it instantly expanded the potentialities of the form, shattering all the pious limitations that had been accepted by the Christian socialists. Notably after *Emanuel Quint* writers were no longer afraid to hint that the man who attempts to imitate Christ may not necessarily be saintly; he may simply be sick. And even though, for reasons suggested earlier, the fictional transfiguration of the paranoid Jesus could not be often repeated, its example enabled future authors to deal more shrewdly with the psychology of their transfigured heroes.

5. The Mythic Jesus

FOR ALL the differences between them, the Christian socialist and the psychiatric critics alike presumed the existence of a historical Jesus possessing sufficient human reality to be plausible as a social reformer or, as the case may be, a paranoid dreamer. But during the very heyday of this "romantic Cult of Jesus,"[1] of which the psychiatric interpretation is simply the most radical extreme, the inevitable reaction was setting in. First of all, the validity of much nineteenth-century research was undermined shortly after 1900 when such scholars as Wilhelm Wrede and Julius Wellhausen began to challenge the Marcan hypothesis, which had provided the basis for the historicity of Jesus. Now many scholars argued that the Gospel of Mark, far from being a historical document of greater reliability than the other Synoptics, was itself a "historicization" of Jesus, composed to conform to the faith of the community for which Mark was writing. However, a more telling threat to the historical Jesus emerged when theologians began to question not merely the validity of the image, but even its relevance.

As early as 1892 Martin Kähler had published an important book, *The So-Called Historical Jesus and the Historic Biblical Christ* (*Der sogenannte historische Jesus und der geschichtliche biblische Christus*), in which he pointed out, in opposition to the prevailing liberal view, that the sources of information regarding Jesus are neither adequate nor reliable enough to permit the reconstruction of any valid biography. But all questions of validity aside, it is not this alleged historical Jesus who has been of inspirational importance to millions of believers, but Christ as he is depicted in the New Testament: "the real Christ is the

---

[1] Arthur Drews, *The Christ Myth*, trans. from the 3rd (rev. and enl.) ed. by C. Delisle Burns (Chicago: The Open Court Publishing Company [1911]), p. 18.

142

preached Christ." Kähler argued, in fact, that it would be no loss to Christianity if the historical picture remained obscure, for faith is not and should not be dependent upon historical research. Essentially the same point of view was advanced by Albert Schweitzer after he had completed his survey of the lives of Jesus from Reimarus to Wrede: the Jesus popularly revered around the turn of the century, he concluded, was "a figure designed by rationalism, endowed with life by liberalism, and clothed by modern theology in an historical garb" (p. 398). But it was a figure wholly ir- relevant to Christianity: "The truth is, it is not Jesus as his- torically known, but Jesus as spiritually arisen within men, who is significant for our time and can help it" (p. 401).

The challenge to the existence of the historical Jesus was not really new, but it was effectively suppressed until the beginning of the twentieth century. As early as 1842 Bruno Bauer was obliged to cease lecturing at Bonn because his critical study of the Gospels had convinced him that there was not nearly enough material available to support any sort of life of Jesus. By the time Bauer wrote his two-volume *Criticism of the Gospels and History of their Origin* (*Kritik der Evangelien und Geschichte ihres Ursprungs*, 1850-51), his skepticism had given way to the totally negative con- clusion that the historical Jesus never existed. Bauer's bril- liant work, so incompatible with the theological attitudes of the mid-nineteenth century, had almost no immediate impact. But his work was rediscovered at the beginning of the twentieth century when certain critics, inspired by the work of the anti-Marcans, began systematically to question the existence of Jesus.

Bauer's views were enlarged particularly by the so-called Radical Dutch School, whose theories were popularized from 1906 on in a series of lectures, articles, and books by the influential professor of philosophy at Leyden, Gerardus Bolland (1854-1922). In Italy, Emilio Bossi, writing under the name Milesbo, advocated the non-historicity of Jesus in an often reprinted volume with the sensational title *Jesus*

Christ Never Existed (*Gesù Cristo non è mai esistito,* 1904). The German pastor Albert Kalthoff—in explosively controversial books on *The Problem of Christ* (*Das Christus-Problem,* 1902) and *How Christianity Arose* (*Die Entstehung des Christentums,* 1904)—concluded that Christ was nothing but the "personification" of the collective longing of the early Christian community.

To fill the vacuum produced by this growing suspicion that Jesus never lived and to account for the details of his portrayal in the Gospels, two responses emerged which dominated the first third of the twentieth century: the History of Religions school and Form Criticism (or History of Gospel Form). Strauss had prepared the way for the modern mythic interpretations by suggesting that many passages in the New Testament were written simply in order to fulfill prophecies or "myths" laid down in the Old Testament. And even before 1800 such rationalists as C. F. Dupuis and C. F. Volney had noted parallels between the life of Jesus and such classical myths as those of Hercules and Bacchus. But it was only after scholars became acquainted with the huge body of myths other than Hebrew and Greek that it became possible to point to a mythic source for virtually every motif or mythologem in the New Testament.

Particularly the scientific study of mythology and folklore inspired by Sir James Frazer's *The Golden Bough* (1890) opened entirely new avenues of interpretation. In a series of books beginning with *Christianity and Mythology* (1900) John M. Robertson argued that Christianity marked only the re-emergence of an older Semitic cult of Joshua. A similar theme was advanced by William Benjamin Smith, a professor of mathematics at Tulane University, who published a book in German to suggest that Jesus could be interpreted as a cult god in the faith of a pre-Christian Jewish gnostic sect (*Der vorchristliche Jesus,* 1906). The Marburg Assyriologist Peter Jensen attempted to prove that the story of Jesus was nothing but a variant of the ancient epic of

Gilgamesh (*Das Gilgamesch-Epos in der Weltliteratur*, 1904). During the first decade of the century a whole series of works was written that sought either to identify Jesus outright with major pagan deities or to interpret his figure as an amalgam of characteristics borrowed from other cultic heroes. Scholars exerted all their ingenuity in detecting astonishing parallels between the Passion—including even such details as the flagellation, the two thieves, the vinegar on a sponge, the lance wound, and so forth—and the sufferings of the Persian Mithras, the Phrygian Attis, the Syrian Adonis, the Egyptian Osiris, the Babylonian Tammuz, and a variety of other mythic deities. Since most of the mythic interpretations were advanced by philosophers, anthropologists, Orientalists, and classical philologists, they were for the most part rejected by professional theologians as irresponsible or, at best, uninformed.

If these mythic interpretations became popularly known, it was due in part to the inherently sensational nature of their appeal. But their success—or notoriety—in Germany, at least, can be attributed largely to the activities of Arthur Drews, a professor of philosophy at the Technical University at Karlsruhe, who wrote a widely discussed study entitled *The Christ-Myth* (*Die Christusmythe*, 1909). Drews' readable account of the various mythic interpretations—he was himself partial to Smith's theory of a pre-Christian cultic Jesus—produced slanderous attacks upon his person and professional competence, a series of acrimonious debates at the leading German universities, and a mass demonstration of protest in Berlin in 1910. Nevertheless—or, more probably, for this very reason—Drews was for a period around 1910 a highly fashionable lecturer in Germany and did much to popularize the view that the historical Jesus never existed. "It is in fact the fundamental error of the liberal theology to think that the development of the Christian Church took its rise from an historical individual, from the man Jesus," he concluded in the epilogue to the book. "It will be necessary to concede that the Christ-faith

145

arose quite independently of any historical personality known to us; that indeed Jesus was in this sense a product of the religious 'social soul.'" Drews and his fellow mythophiles were not trying to destroy Christianity or its belief in Christ as "the symbolic personification of the unity of nature in God and man, on the belief in which the possibility of the 'redemption' depends." The proponents of the mythic interpretation were, however, convinced of the utter irrelevance of the historical Jesus: "As a purely historical individual, as liberal theology views him, he sinks back to the level of other great historical personalities, and from the religious point of view is exactly as unessential as they." Paradoxically, Drews was contemptuous of the historical Jesus for precisely the reasons that endeared this conception to Christian socialism: his essentially human characteristics. The mythic interpretation served to do away with the liberal Jesus altogether. "This work seeks to prove," he noted in his preface, "that more or less all the features of the picture of the historical Jesus, at any rate all those of any important religious significance, bear a purely mythical character, and no opening exists for seeking an historical figure behind the Christ myth."

The myth theory, which reached its first peak of popularity around 1910 with Arthur Drews, managed to survive the war and to continue unabated into the twenties, when it received an unexpected new impetus from analytical psychology and the various studies of the Christ archetype and Christian symbols published by C. G. Jung and his followers. In France, P. L. Couchoud achieved the same kind of sensational success as Drews with a volume entitled *Le Mystère de Jésus* (1924), which was pre-published in the *Mercure de France*. Couchoud, synthesizing Kalthoff and the anti-Marcans, suggested that the legend of Jesus was the product of a collective mystical experience that was gradually humanized in the primitive imagination and finally transferred to the human plane in the Gospel of

Mark. Though its vogue is past, the mythic theory still survives in certain quarters. Recently the theory has been advanced—only half-seriously, to be sure—that "Jesus" was in fact nothing but a hallucinogenic mushroom and that the New Testament amounts to a mystical code for adherents of the cult.[2]

Three types of mythic interpretation turned out to be productive for fictional transfigurations. One view regards Jesus as a culture-hero parallel to the other great mythic figures of mankind. A second theory considers him as the syncretic product of elements appropriated from a variety of pre-Christian or pagan cults. A third view, finally, sees him as the spontaneous personification of the religious longing of the early Christian community.

History of Religions was interested primarily in accounting for the Gospel image of Jesus by establishing parallels between the myth of Jesus and other contemporary cultic myths; but in its basic premise it was related to the other leading critical impulse of the period: Form Criticism. Liberal theology—and, by derivation, both Christian socialism and psychiatry—had been obsessed with the presumed character of the historical Jesus. Now that the historicity of Jesus was disputed or at least declared irrelevant, attention shifted from the person of Jesus to the collective experience of the early Christian communities which shaped the image of Jesus. "In the Gospels we have nothing but the expression of the consciousness of a community," Arthur Drews wrote. "The life of Jesus, as portrayed by the Synoptics, merely brings to an expression in historical garb the metaphysical ideas, religious hopes, the outer and inner experiences of the community which had Jesus for its cult-god."

This thematic statement of myth theory would be largely acceptable to the form-critical school that is identified especially with the names of Rudolf Bultmann (born 1884) and

[2] John M. Allegro, *The Sacred Mushroom and the Cross* (New York: Doubleday, 1970).

Martin Dibelius (1883-1947). Form criticism does not necessarily deny the historicity of Jesus, and it tends to use terms more devout than "cult-god" to describe Jesus' role in the early Christian community. Nevertheless, the historicity of Jesus becomes just as irrelevant for form critics as for the myth critics since they are concerned primarily with the consciousness of the community that produced the Gospels.

Form criticism begins with the basic assumption that the Gospels do not represent documents of any great originality but, rather, the ultimate product and synthesis of isolated elements and traditions that had circulated orally within the Church for at least half a century before they were finally recorded in writing. Form criticism seeks to establish the original "form" of these elements—miracle stories, apothegms, proverbs, prophetic sayings, and so forth—in order to determine the modifications and editorial revisions that they underwent at the hands of the evangelists. If it is the primary problem to ascertain how the Gospel narratives were created from this original multiplicity of isolated elements, the second principal problem is suggested by the feeling that the Gospels, if they do not represent history, reveal the meaning of Jesus for the circles within which the various versions were composed. Matthew, writing the story for a community of Jews in Syria, had an entirely different point of view from that of Mark, who was responsible to a group of persecuted Christians in Rome, or from that of Luke, who sought to explain Jesus to a congregation of gentiles with no Jewish national consciousness. As a result, form criticism shifted its attention in large measure from the central figure of Jesus to the consciousness of the early Christian communities as it is reflected in the various Gospels. The hero in their studies is not the savior, but the gospelists themselves. This major shift of focus inevitably had an impact upon a generation of writers increasingly concerned with—indeed, self-conscious about—point of view and rhetorical effects in fiction.

It should be apparent that the syncretization of Jesus and Bacchus that we noted in *The Magic Mountain* reflects the mythic theory that was the prevailing popular view of Jesus at the time Thomas Mann wrote his novel. In fact, whether Mann was aware of it or not, there was even a mythic interpretation that explained Jesus in terms quite similar to those of his novel: as a ridiculous comic figure handed over annually to the Roman legionnaires as the "king" of their saturnalia.[3] But Thomas Mann needed no source; he was perfectly capable of constructing his own saturnalian Jesus in keeping with the character of Mynheer Peeperkorn. What he did need was a cultural climate in which it was possible, indeed fashionable, to regard Jesus as the transformation of a pagan myth or cult figure. As we have seen, dozens of books and articles since 1900 had created precisely that atmosphere.

Thomas Mann subsequently exploited the Passion in another novel. *Doctor Faustus* (1947) is an elaborately conceived postfigurative novel, based closely upon the sixteenth-century chapbook of Faust, but also introducing a variety of other sources. Here again, within the rather startling context of a hero who has signed a pact with the devil in order to become a great composer, we find toward the conclusion clear parallels to the story of Jesus. It has often been noted that Leverkühn's features, as he is progressively ravaged by syphilis and incipient insanity, take on a Jesus-like appearance.[4] The beard that he grows, coupled with his tendency to hold his head inclined toward his shoulder, "bestowed upon his countenance a spiritualized-agonizing, yet Christ-like character." And later, after

[3] Around the turn of the century the discussion of this point was so lively that Frazer devoted a special appendix to it in the 3rd edition of *The Golden Bough*. See Frazer, *The Scapegoat* (London: Macmillan, 1913), pp. 412-23: "The Crucifixion of Christ."

[4] See Leslie L. Miller, "Myth and Morality: Reflections on Thomas Mann's *Doktor Faustus*," in *Essays in German Literature in Honour of G. Joyce Hallamore*, ed. Michael S. Batts and M. G. Stankiewicz (Toronto: Univ. of Toronto Press, 1968), pp. 195-216.

his total collapse, we are told that his face has become a veritable "Ecce-homo countenance." Descriptions of this sort alert us to the fact that the last major scene of the novel —the occasion when Leverkühn assembles his friends to hear his confession (chap. 47)—evokes clear associations with the Last Supper and the crucifixion. The mood is prepared by the narrator's analysis of Leverkühn's last great composition, *Doctor Fausti Lament*, as an inversion of the Gethsemane scene. When Faust tells his companions to go to bed and sleep quietly, "it is difficult to avoid recognizing this admonition, in the framework of the cantata, as the conscious and desired reverse of the words in Gethsemane: 'Wake with me.'" Similarly, the narrator interprets Faust's last drink with his friends as having a "ritual" character. Prepared by this passage, we are willing to interpret the occasion as Leverkühn's "Last Supper" although the food consists of coffee, sandwiches, and apple juice, and although thirty people, not twelve, sit down to hear the composer's last words. Finally, there is an unmistakable allusion to the *via dolorosa* in the way in which Leverkühn, surrounded by three women, makes his way, weeping, to the piano, where he flings out his arms and emits a loud groan before he falls, unconscious, to the floor. This scene has none of the amusing irony of the chapter "Vingt et un," and the parallels are not worked out so closely. But in view of the conspicuously postfigurative technique of the novel as a whole, it seems undeniable that Thomas Mann is once again exploiting the pathos of the Passion, through mythic syncretization, to add a surprising new dimension to the story of his tormented Faustian hero.

Thomas Mann's comments on his biblical tetralogy *Joseph and His Brothers* (1933-43) as well as his correspondence during the thirties with the myth-scholar Karl Kerényi make it clear that Mann was not only a fascinated student of the history of religions in general but also, more specifically, consciously aware of the technique of figural interpretation that he appropriated for his fictional works. Yet for all the brilliance with which he used these devices to write his postfigurative novel of Faust and his mythic story of the biblical Joseph, Thomas Mann never exploited the Jesus myth as the consistent basis for an entire narrative, but simply as an additional dimension in the single scenes we have considered. To find a typical example of the consistent fictional transfiguration of the mythic Jesus we must turn to Thomas Mann's contemporary, Hermann Hesse (1877-1962).

Hesse once remarked that he considered the religious impulse as the decisive characteristic of his life and works, and his novels bear this out. *Siddhartha* (1922) traces a religious quest set in India at the time of Buddha; the heroes of *Narcissus and Goldmund* (1930) come to self-awareness in a medieval monastery; and for the background of certain sections of *The Glass Bead Game* (1943) Hesse did extensive research in eighteenth-century German pietism, and he patterned the spiritual realm of Castalia explicitly on the hierarchy of the Catholic Church. From his earliest childhood Hesse was exposed to history of religions in his daily life. His parents, as well as his maternal grandfather, had been missionaries to India; his grandfather, Hermann Gundert, was a noted authority on Indic languages and religions. Hesse grew up in an atmosphere saturated with the spirit of India, its culture and its myths. Hesse subsequently rebelled against the narrow pietism of his Swabian boyhood and ran away from school, where he was being prepared for theological study and a life in the ministry. But this was not a rebellion against religion; it liberated him to pursue his religious interests into more exotic channels.

Emerging from a Protestant background, he first became fascinated with Catholicism, which appealed to him as the paradigm of institutionalized religion. He wrote a popular biography of St. Francis (1904) and edited several volumes of saints' legends from the Middle Ages. It was obviously not faith, but his sheer delight in the mythic or legendary quality of these tales, that prompted him to retell a number of them in his own short fiction. And in 1924, in his report on "The Feast of the Madonna in the Ticino," he remarked jestingly that he should have been a Catholic so that he could properly indulge his aesthetic obsession with the madonna: "I permit myself my own cult and my own mythology of the madonna; in the temple of my piety she takes her place alongside Venus and Krishna."[5] Hesse's interests gradually expanded to include Church history, Chinese religious thought and myth, and the cults of antiquity. The list of titles that he reviewed during his many years as a book critic amounts to a catalogue of works on different aspects of religion and myth.

It is unlikely that a man of Hesse's predilections should have remained unaware of the controversy surrounding the mythic interpretation of Jesus that was aroused in 1910 by Arthur Drews. A few years later, in any case, he was well acquainted with the currently fashionable theories, which conformed so well to his own relativistic view of religion. In an essay entitled "Artists and Psychoanalysis" (1918) Hesse noted that a close and fruitful point of contact had arisen between art and psychology "ever since analytical psychology turned directly to popular myth, legend, and poetry."[6] Hesse confessed that he had not the slightest interest in what he called the "scientific psychology" of the day; but he was all the more attracted by the writings of Freud, Stekel, and Jung because of their literary and imaginative qualities.

In 1916 Hesse studied Jung's epoch-making work on *Wandlungen und Symbole der Libido* (1912), which signaled the beginning of Jung's break with Freud and the In-

---

[5] "Madonnenfest in Tessin," in *Gesammelte Schriften* (Berlin und Frankfurt: Suhrkamp, 1957), III, 896.

[6] "Künstler und Psychoanalyse," in *Gesammelte Schriften*, VII, 137-43.

ternational Psychoanalytical Society. In this volume—translated into English as *Psychology of the Unconscious* and, in a later revised edition, as *Symbols of Transformation*—Jung introduced a substantial amount of material gleaned from history of religions. He related Dionysos, for instance, to "the early Asiatic god who died and rose again from the dead and whose manifold manifestations have been brought together in the figure of Christ into a firm personality enduring for centuries." And in other passages he adduced elements of the Christ-myth from Agni, Wotan, Mithra, and a congeries of other mythic heroes. Between 1916 and 1922 Hesse met Jung on several occasions and even read from his works to Jung's circle in Zürich. For his acquaintance with Jungian theories and mythic interpretations in general Hesse was indebted to Jung's disciple, Dr. Joseph B. Lang, with whom he underwent some seventy-two analytic sessions during 1916 and 1917.

Lang was not only an analyst; he was also a student of myth and a scholar of Oriental languages. His notebooks record conversations in which he and Hesse discussed the mythic implications of various biblical stories.[7] It was wholly in the spirit of Lang that Hesse wrote, in a letter of 1930: "The myths of the Bible, like all myths of mankind, are worthless to us as long as we do not dare to interpret them personally, for ourselves and our own times." External evidence bears out what the internal evidence of the works makes sufficiently clear: Hesse was thoroughly familiar with the mythic theories of the day, which he found compatible with his own religious sense. If Hesse received much of this material through Lang's mediation, he acknowledged his debt by characterizing Lang symbolically in the figure of the mythologist Pistorius in the novel *Demian* (*Demian*, 1919), which he wrote in 1917 as the direct product of his psychoanalysis.

[7] Cited in Hugo Ball, *Hermann Hesse: Sein Leben und sein Werk* (1927; rpt. Berlin und Frankfurt: Suhrkamp, 1947), pp. 156-58.

On the surface Hesse's novel is wholly unlike those that we have considered up to this point.[8] *Demian* is allegedly the first-person account of a young man named Emil Sinclair, who soon after the end of World War I records certain crucial episodes from his life between the ages of ten and twenty. His boyhood revolves around his friendship with the mysterious Max Demian, an older boy who rescues him from a childhood bully and then challenges him to liberate himself from the sheltering confines of a narrow pietism by thinking independently. When Sinclair goes off to boarding school, he at first slumps into profligacy. But the ethereal love he conceives for a girl he glimpses in the park sets him back on the path to self-discovery, whose goals are brought into focus by the mystical teachings of the renegade theologian Pistorius. At the university Sinclair encounters Demian again and enters into an ambivalent relationship with his friend's mother, who is known to her circle as Frau Eva. This year of happiness and spiritual maturity is ended by the war, which soon claims Demian as a victim. Demian's death forces Sinclair to the final stage of spiritual independence, where he discovers that he no longer has need of external mentors to guide him on his way.

At first glance this plot reminds us neither of the earnest Jesuses of Christian socialism, whose lives are carefully laid out by their authors in accordance with the Gospels, nor of the paranoid Jesuses who monomaniacally seek out their own Passions. But if we examine the images of the novel, we begin to see that it falls into a broadly mythic pattern. On the most general level, the novel recapitulates the entire Bible from Genesis to the Revelation. The very first page acquaints us with the "Two Realms" between which Sinclair,

[8] I quote *Demian*, with slight modifications, according to the Bantam Modern Classic edition of the translation by Michael Roloff and Michael Lebeck (New York: Harper and Row, 1965). For a more general discussion see Theodore Ziolkowski, *The Novels of Hermann Hesse* (Princeton, N. J.: Princeton Univ. Press, 1965); and Mark Boulby, *Hermann Hesse: His Mind and Art* (Ithaca, N. Y.: Cornell Univ. Press, 1967).

as a ten-year-old boy, imagines that he is torn. At home, in
the harmony of his father's house, he has experienced a
"light" world of order and Christian goodness. But this harmony is achieved only by ignoring and denying the entire
"dark" world of sex, violence, and lust that Sinclair encounters whenever he goes down to the servants' quarters
or out onto the streets of his town. With the first stirrings
of puberty Sinclair begins to sense that this "dark" world,
rejected so disdainfully by his family, is no less a natural
part of life than the "light" world that they have contrived
to satisfy their Christian ethics. As Sinclair, tempted by the
"dark" world, moves away from the security of home, he
looks back at it longingly as at "a lost paradise." When he
is thrust out of this paradise of his childhood—it is no accident that this happens when he claims to have stolen some
apples—he realizes that "a locked gateway to Eden with its
pitilessly resplendent host of guardians" (p. 64) has sprung
up between himself and the innocence of his past. Sinclair's
expeditions into the "dark" world are explicitly related to
the parable of the Prodigal Son. When Demian enters into
Sinclair's life, he tells him that those who rebel against the
world of their fathers bear "the mark of Cain." In his greatest loneliness Sinclair feels himself akin to Jesus in
Gethsemane. Sinclair's subsequent struggle to win the blessing of a new deity—"a god that contains the devil and in
front of which you needn't close your eyes when the most
natural things in the world take place" (p. 51)—is related
in a chapter whose title refers to Jacob wrestling with the
angel. And scattered through the book are occasional free
quotations from the Bible.

If we turn to the end of the novel we find an equally unmistakable biblical allusion. As Sinclair stands on the battlefield in Flanders, he experiences the mortar shell that
wounds him as the vision of a great goddess in the sky,
crouching to give birth to a new humanity: "Suddenly she
cried out and from her forehead sprang stars, many thou-
sands of shining stars that leaped in marvelous arches and

semicircles across the black sky. One of these stars shot straight toward me with a clear ringing sound and it seemed to seek me out" (p. 139). Hesse is playing here with John's vision in Revelation 12:1-2:

And there appeared a great wonder in heaven: a woman clothed with the sun, and the moon under her feet, and upon her head a crown of twelve stars:
And she being with child cried, travailing in birth, and pained to be delivered.

Within this generally biblical framework, which begins with the Fall from Paradise and ends with the Revelation, Hesse has embedded a wealth of other mythic-religious symbols. The bird breaking its way out of an egg—an image of spiritual rebirth that recurs from the first page to the last —is borrowed from late Roman cultism by way of the cultural anthropologist J. J. Bachofen: the black-and-white egg represents the Manichaean world that is divided rigidly into good and evil, a world that must be shattered if a new and whole reality is to be created. Abraxas, the god embracing both poles of being, is a central being in Gnosticism— one of the various pre-Christian cultic deities sometimes related to Jesus. The figure of Frau Eva derives its mysterious ambivalence from a curious amalgam of elements borrowed from the biblical Eve (the mother of all those who are distinguished by the mark of Cain), the *magna mater* of pagan cults, and the *anima* of Jungian psychology. *Demian* is in one sense, in fact, an encyclopedia of comparative religion. Pistorius speaks to Sinclair of Zoroaster, reads to him from the Veda, and teaches him to utter the sacred Om. At school Sinclair meets Spiritists and Theosophists. Demian is surrounded by a host of religious seekers: astrologers and cabalists, devotees of Tolstoy's primitive Christianity, and adherents of obscure pagan cults. "Thus we became acquainted with the wonderful thousand-headed tangle of gods from prehistory to the dawn of the Christian conversion," Sinclair recalls (p. 123).

In this intensely religious book—its obsession with the exotic romance of history of religions reflects a vogue of the twenties—Christianity is reduced, or elevated, to a level with the other major religions of the world. "Each and every religion is beautiful," Pistorius tells Sinclair. "Religion is soul, no matter whether you take part in Christian communion or make a pilgrimage to Mecca" (p. 93). And Sinclair's development amounts to an elaborate allegory of man, beginning with the paradise of childhood, continuing with the fall into sin, and culminating with redemption in a realm that transcends conventional Christian assumptions regarding good and evil.

It is only within this mythically religious framework that we recognize the plausibility of Demian's function as a mediator set between Sinclair's initial fall and his final "redemption." The novel, as the subtitle indicates, is actually "The Story of Emil Sinclair's Youth." Why, then, is it named after Demian? The external facts of plot are of very little help here. But if we scrutinize his figure more carefully, we note a group of characteristics that constitute a surprising and yet unmistakable pattern. His most salient physical trait is the "brightness" that illumines his forehead. Through self-control and an uncanny skill in the psychological manipulation of others, students and teachers alike, he accomplishes various deeds that astonish the other boys. At first Sinclair tries to avoid him because he is "surrounded by too many legends and secrets" (p. 44). We are told of disputations in which Demian confounds his teachers with his questions and answers. When he talks to Sinclair, he tends to make his point by means of parables adapted freely from the Bible (e.g., the myth of Cain, or the story of the repentant thief). He is driven by his faith in the coming of a new spiritual kingdom. And toward the end of the book Demian has assembled around his person a circle of admirers, all of whom are striving to realize the spiritual kingdom that he foretells.

It seems clear, in view of these specific details and the

generally religious ambiance of the book, that we are dealing with another fictional transfiguration of Jesus, albeit a wholly ironic one. Demian has what amounts to a halo and performs what can be regarded as miracles. He is a "healer" by the sheer force of his personality. He disputes with teachers, preaches a coming kingdom, and instructs his disciples through parables. His death, finally, is clearly an act of self-sacrifice in the service of the millennium that he predicts. But the figure of this Jesus is seen in a wholly mythic way, as is made clear repeatedly from the prologue on, where Sinclair writes: "In each individual the spirit has become flesh, in each man the creation suffers, within each one a redeemer is nailed to the cross" (p. 4). We also learn from Sinclair that "the biblical account of the suffering and death of the Savior had made a deep impression on me since my earliest childhood" (p. 50). Later Pistorius tells Sinclair that "Christ is not a person for me but a hero, a myth, an extraordinary shadow image in which humanity has painted itself on the wall of eternity" (p. 94). And Demian explicitly puts Jesus on a level with Nietzsche, thus justifying the presentation of an essentially Nietzschean doctrine within a Christian structure: "What Nature wants of man stands indelibly written in the individual, in you, in me. It stood written in Jesus, it stood written in Nietzsche" (p. 116). In this novel, then, Jesus is explicitly seen as a mythic figure, divested of his specifically Christian associations and compared to the other great heroic figures of mankind. And in the person of Demian, the semi-mythic hero of the novel, the characteristics of Jesus are mythically intertwined with those of Nietzsche—much as in Peeperkorn the traits of Jesus and Bacchus are related. Demian, in other words, is a textbook case of the fictional transfiguration of the mythic Jesus.

It is wholly appropriate, therefore, that the novel contains its own theory of myth. Demian repeatedly insists that the stories of the Bible are accessible of different interpretations: "Most of the things we're taught I'm sure are quite right and true, but one can view all of them from quite a different angle than the teachers do—and most of the time they then make better sense" (p. 24). As an example he cites the story of Cain: "People with courage and character always seem sinister to the rest. It was a scandal that a breed of fearless and sinister people ran about freely, so they attached a nickname and myth to these people to get even with them . . . " (p. 25). The whole function of Pistorius as a character can be reduced, essentially, to his role as a historian of religion who articulates the mythic theory that Sinclair has hitherto understood only intuitively.

But Hesse's novel differs from the other works we have considered in a second important sense as well; it is not simply the view of Jesus as a mythic figure that distinguishes Demian from the transfigured heroes of the Christian socialist and the psychiatric novels: ultimately Demian is a Jesus-figure only in the consciousness of the narrator, Emil Sinclair. There is no suggestion whatsoever that he thinks of himself as Jesus or that he pursues his own Passion or *imitatio*. At the same time, the absence of structural parallels between the plot and the Gospels shows that Hesse as author is not imposing the Jesus pattern on the novel, as was the case in the earlier Christian socialist works. It is only in the mind of Sinclair that the transfiguration gradually takes place and that Demian assumes his mythic characteristics. In other words, Hesse has shifted his attention from Demian to Sinclair, from the hero to the consciousness of the narrator, or—in the terms of form criticism—from Jesus to the gospelist. It is not the ten-year-old Sinclair who regards Demian as a Jesus, but the mature Sinclair looking back at the experiences of his childhood and attempting to impose some order or pattern upon them. In the last analysis, then, Demian receives his mythic traits retrospectively in order to satisfy the exigencies of the narrator and his audience. The parallel to the form-critical view of the gospelist who endows Jesus with the traits required by the faith of his community is overwhelmingly precise. Again, Hesse has included in his novel the theory to bear out this interpretation. With reference to Frau Eva, namely, Sinclair specifically suggests that "she existed only as a metaphor of my inner self, a metaphor whose sole purpose was to lead me more deeply into myself" (p. 127). By analogy, Demian receives his transfigurational attributes metaphorically in order, retrospectively, to lend value to the experiences of Sinclair's own youth.

This view should help to explain a few further aspects of the novel. At one point in the book, when he feels deserted by Demian and unsure of himself, Sinclair writes a plea to his friend which he recites ritually: "A leader has left me. I am enveloped in darkness. I cannot take another step alone. Help me" (p. 110). After experiencing the consolation of his plea, Sinclair repeats it constantly: "I knew the little prayer by heart and often recited it to myself. It was with me every hour of the day. I began to understand what prayer is" (p. 110). In other words, having rejected the conventional Christianity of his parents, Sinclair becomes acquainted with *prayer* when he addresses his friend Demian. This point can be understood properly, I believe, only if we understand Demian as a transfiguration of Jesus. Finally, in the last sentence of the book the personal pronoun referring to Demian (in the German text) is suddenly and inexplicably capitalized—not just once, but twice for emphasis. When he peers deep into his soul, Sinclair writes, he can see his own image, "now completely resembling Him, Him, my Friend and my Leader." Like the prayer, this capitalization would be meaningless without the context of the ironic transfiguration. Now, a book about a Jesus-figure by a disciple is called a gospel. If *Demian* is indeed a gospel in form—albeit an ironic gospel in line with the mythic interpretation of Jesus and the teachings of form criticism concerning the role of the evangelist—then the tone of Hesse's novel, the visionary and messianic zeal that inflamed a generation of readers, becomes absolutely appropriate and in keeping with the basic impulse underlying the work. *Demian* reflects the prevailing popular view of Jesus in the second decade of the century just as accurately as *Emanuel Quint* had caught the mood some ten years earlier: psychiatry has given way to myth.

The vogue of the mythic interpretation lasted roughly until World War II. But just as the psychiatric Jesus had a late and brilliant revival in Kazantzakis' novel, the mythic Jesus has reappeared in Carlo Coccioli's fascinating *Manuel the Mexican* (*Manuel le Mexicain*, 1956). As the genre of fictional transfiguration develops and as its potentialities become greater, we find fewer and fewer examples as pure as the early Christian socialist works. Coccioli's novel may have been suggested at least in part by *The Greek Passion*, for it employs, though in a wholly different way, the identical framework fiction of a village Passion Play. It is related to the psychiatric works, in addition, by the implication that the hero is afflicted with a mild form of epilepsy, a motif that is not consistently developed. Furthermore, its Mexican setting links it to Graham Greene's *The Power and the Glory*; Coccioli has affirmed that he was first inspired to visit Mexico by reading *The Lawless Roads* (1939), the travel account in which Greene recorded the actual events that suggested the plot and incidents for his novel. But the syncretism of Christianity with Aztec mythology, coupled with the problematic role of the narrator, places Coccioli's novel unmistakably in the tradition of *Demian*.

Carlo Coccioli (born 1920) began his career by writing in his native Italian, but by the time he composed his Mexican novel he had switched to French. This situation—in which the Italian author filters the Mexican subject through the French language—reflects with astonishing aptness the author's detached attitude toward the Christianity that constitutes the principal theme in most of his novels. Coccioli was the grandson of a Freemason and the son of an atheist; his mother had to resort to stealth and have him confirmed secretly while his father was away on a trip.[9] Such a heritage and such beginnings were certainly not auspicious for the development of any youthful Christian devotion. Coccioli has told the story of his religious education in his *Journal* for the years 1955-56. His first serious exposure to Christianity, when he was eighteen, came at the hands of a Czech Jew, "who knew the Scriptures almost as well as he knew the works of Benedetto Croce" and who spoke to Coccioli of both with great passion (p. 213). The second stage came while Coccioli was at the University of Naples, where he studied Islam and published his first article—on the Christology of the Koran: "I knew almost nothing about Christ, but I was acquainted with everything that Mohammed knew about Christ" (p. 214). From this he moved gradually into the realm of Moslem mysticism and, eventually, to gnosticism. In Officers Training School, finally, Coccioli belonged to a small study group that read the New Testament under the guidance of one of his officers: "It gave me the chance to read St. Matthew and his Sermon on the Mount; I began to tell myself that Christ was not the Christ of the pious images, but that he was power, extreme revolt, and that he inflamed. He seared me" (p. 214).

This indirect approach to Jesus—first from the Jewish point of view, then from the Moslem point of view, and finally from a Christian point of view—virtually insured the emergence of a mythic view of Jesus. Coccioli came to the conclusion that "the visages of God are numerous; he hides himself everywhere; and there is no place where he is unable to take pleasure in revealing himself" (p. 214). In another place the mythic intent manifests itself even more clearly: "The civilization that I would consider perfect

---

[9] The criticism on Coccioli, apart from brief reviews, is quite sparse. See Thomas F. Staley, "Faith and the Absurd: The Post-Existential Vision of Carlo Coccioli," in *The Shapeless God: Essays on Modern Fiction*, ed. Harry J. Mooney, Jr., and Thomas F. Staley (Pittsburgh: Univ. of Pittsburgh Press, 1968), pp. 3-18. The most useful biographical source, from which I quote in my own translation, is Coccioli's *Journal* (. . . -1956) (Paris: La Table Ronde, 1957).

would have a Christian soul and a pagan body. The construction of my books cannot avoid reflecting vividly this dualism which, for me, is in no sense an opposition. It is an opposition—and sometimes even a frightful conflict—only to the extent that one does not succeed in comprehending the great wisdom of accepting Christ without renouncing the ancient Dionysos" (p. 104). This richly mythic conception of Jesus caused Coccioli to be unresponsive to Renan for precisely the reasons that Drews and Schweitzer, half a century earlier, had rejected the pallid Jesus of liberal theology. After reading the *Vie de Jésus*, Coccioli was able to esteem the work intellectually; but neither did he like it nor was he persuaded by it, for his faith refused to be directed by reason, as Renan would insist: "The litanies of the Virgin, whose source is not the intelligence that is subject to weakness and contamination, are more convincing for the meaning of Mary than all the logical arguments of Ernest Renan" (p. 298). It is precisely this powerful blend of faith and myth—which, as Coccioli concedes, loves the Church but not its priests—that motivates the strange hero of *Manuel the Mexican*.[10]

Manuel Orea Ayopac is the illegitimate son of María de Jesus and a young itinerant worker, José Manuel. After José gets María pregnant during the carnival festivities in her hometown of Tepoztlan, in the state of Morelos, she follows him, in a kind of flight into Egypt, to the South. But after José is murdered on the coffee-plantation where he has been working, María sets out for home. Along the way, around Christmas of 1933, her son Manuel is born. Manuel grows up in Tepoztlan under the influence of his great-uncle, Don Isidro Tlatelpa, a former bolshevik and a nonbeliever who is devoted, as a passionate Mexicanist, to the legends of the Aztec past. Up to this point Manuel has been a casual Christian with a detached curiosity about the seemingly remote Mexican past. But when he is seventeen, he

---

[10] I quote from the translation by Hans Koningsberger (New York: Simon and Schuster, 1958).

has a vision in church on Christmas night: the Lord Tepoz-teco appears before him in the guise of Christ and orders Manuel to go through Mexico preaching the unity, not the incompatibility, of past and present. Leaving home with the peddler Guadalupe, a former *cristero* who plays John the Baptist to Manuel's Jesus, the boy is introduced for the first time to the history of Christian Mexico. When he senses the beginnings of a homosexual attachment to the older man, Manuel sets off on his own to preach his mystical message concerning the unity of Mexican Time.

On the Friday preceding Palm Sunday in 1954 Manuel meets twelve men in the village of Tlaltenalco. Their village, in the Federal District of Mexico, holds an annual Passion Play at Easter, and Manuel agrees to play the role of Jesus. He is recognized, on this occasion, as the boy who recently had saved a village girl from a man attempting to rape her. On Holy Thursday, however, he is arrested: it is now claimed that he had in fact raped the girl himself. During these events Manuel's friend El Chato tries to defend him (like Peter in Gethsemane), but then runs away. The villagers, instead of turning Manuel over to the police, decide to take justice into their own hands. On Good Friday, therefore, he is taken out and crucified as planned. The tourists watching the procession are not aware that the crucifixion is in earnest; Manuel dies on the cross.

When the plot is recapitulated in this way, it is perfectly apparent that we are dealing with a fictional transfiguration that makes highly detailed use of the parallels between the plot and the Gospel. But the stark outline of the Gospels is complicated in at least three important ways. First, the narrative sequence is inverted. The novel begins with a preface recounting the events at Easter, 1954; at this point the incidents are confusing because we still know nothing of Manuel's background or of his mystical message of Mexican Time. In fact, the bulk of the novel can be viewed as a lengthy attempt to justify the otherwise unmotivated events of the prologue. The first half of the novel (chaps. 1-9), however, postpones the necessary exposition by recounting the story of Mary and Joseph. This section, in turn, is so picaresquely fanciful that the reader would hardly associate it with the Bible narrative if he had not been prepared for it by the initial Passion scene. (José runs away from home when he discovers that his mother is a prostitute; he himself is a homosexual and kills the foreman of the coffee-plantation where he works because both of them are vying for the affection of the owner; when he returns there with María, he is murdered in revenge by the family of the foreman.)

Only the second half of the book (chaps. 10-20) deals with Manuel. But—and this is the second factor that complicates the Gospel pattern—since his motivation is more mythic than psychological, it is easy to lose sight of the transfigurational pattern even though it is so explicit. Manuel is presented in the first five chapters of this section as a youth torn between men representing two wholly contradictory views of Mexico: his uncle Isidro, the Mexicanist, is obsessed with the Aztec past and its values, while the former *cristero* Guadalupe is concerned with Mexico only since its conversion to Christianity. But the bearded Lord who appears to Manuel at Christmas in 1950 proclaims: "I, the Lord Tepozteco, I am the Christ, I am their Christ, son of the purest of Virgins, Tonantzin, whose head is crowned with twelve stars . . . " (p. 259). This vision, which equates Jesus mythically with the Plumed Serpent and the Daughter of Zion with the Aztec goddess, initiates Manuel's mission: to proclaim the unity of the Aztec past and the Christian present in the unity of Mexican Time: "The present will truly be the son of the Past, and then Mexico will know a unique Time. . . . I command you to say this to the people; or will you be able, my dear boy, to make them believe in my word?"[11]

---

[11] Coccioli's mythic syncretism is by no means wholly fanciful. The Cora Indians of western Mexico still celebrate a peculiar Passion Play that blends Christianity with an ancient faith in Tayau, the sun

Like *Demian, Manuel the Mexican* contains its own theory of myth as a justification of its transfiguration of Jesus. As Manuel begins to understand his mission, he sees that "the Christ and the Tepozteco, the Past and the Present, the Virgin Mary and Tonantzin, Plutarco Elías Calles and the Archbishop, Don Isidro Tlatelpa and Mr. Guadalupe, all those contrasts resolve themselves into a unity—someone for whom Mexico is one" (p. 354). Paradoxically, the transfigured Jesus is invoked to preach a message that is as unconventional as the Nietzschean doctrine of Hesse's transfigured hero. As Manuel explains to the simple peasants: "God, the Unique One, has shown himself to the world as the son of a virgin. Thus, very far from our country, they have given to this son the name of Jesus Christ. Here in our own country this same son has received another name. The Virgin, the mother of unblemished purity, has, very far from our country, received the name Mary. Here in our country the same mother has received another name" (p. 13). If the novel has a basic flaw, it is that all too much of the dialogue reads like a lecture on comparative religion.

Manuel's mission is prompted by his analysis of the Mexican dilemma: its ambivalent sense of time has paralyzed the country and caused it to fall behind the Western world in its development. (In this analysis of the cultural malaise Coccioli comes close to Galdós.) "I live in anguish when I think above all of the great humiliation of Mexican Time, which presents itself to our comprehension with a Before and an After. We say, in the time of Moctezuma, in the time of Cortés. We say, before the Conquest, after the Conquest. We say, in the time of the gods, in the time of God. We say, formerly there was Quetzalcóatl and Tepoztecatl and Tepochtli. Now there is Our Lord Jesus Christ. Thus we speak, because our Time is divided, our heart is divided!

---

god. See Guillermo Aldana E., "Mesa del Nayar's Strange Holy Week," *National Geographic*, 139 (June, 1971), 780-95.

Our blood is divided! Our intellect is divided!" (p. 12). It is this division, embodied in the symbolic figures of Don Isidro and Mr. Guadalupe, that has torn Mexico apart: "We take the Before and we take the After and we put one up against the other, and he who adores the Before has contempt for the After, and he who respects the After mocks the Before" (p. 12). Manuel refutes this doctrine of "two Times" that are irremediably opposed: "I have come to announce that all that is a lie. I have come to state that Mexican Time is unique. . . . There is no opposition between the past and the present!" It is the irony of the plot that Manuel exemplifies this timeless identity of past and present by undergoing the crucifixion in the re-enactment of the ancient ritual, a strangely Mexican version of the Passion: "On the martyred shoulders of the Boy the red cape has been thrown. Red, because it must hide the blood spilled by those who suffer in their flesh the Mexican Passion" (p. 34). All the details of the *via dolorosa* have this weird ambivalence. For instance, the boy is escorted by twelve soldiers: "Their uniforms are not those of the Roman soldiers who led Jesus to Golgotha, but rather, apart from imported elements of the Technicolor kind, those which clothed the Spaniards who at the order of Cortés seized México-Tenochtitlán in order to sacrifice it on an altar stone as a propitiatory victim" (p. 36).

This brings us to Coccioli's third complication of the Gospel plot. For though all of this makes for excellent speculation on problems of comparative religion, it is quite implausible as psychological motivation. Since Manuel is not portrayed as a paranoid who actively pursues his own Passion, we are left with the implication that the astonishing parallels to the Gospel occur either by chance or by supernatural means. Now, since a sophisticated contemporary audience finds it difficult to accept either miracle or unlikely chance, Coccioli has introduced himself into his own novel as a narrator who anticipates all the objections of the reader: "Perhaps this story is absurd, but if one tried to attribute to it a logical meaning, our kind of logic, we would betray the truth—because in this story there is truth —a truth which might seem grotesque to some people, ignominious to others, and to some, full of grandeur. Oh, it's not a clear story; nothing, after all, is clear in life (in the intellectual meaning of the word); but the clarity of our story is certainly no less than that of the adventures which find a way of expression in the *Retablos* (the painted *ex voto* panels), something between the human and the divine" (p. 32).

His narrator does not merely comment like the narrator of *Emanuel Quint*; he has an active role in the story, like Emil Sinclair. The narrator, we learn, came to Mexico City at the end of April, 1953, to escape a dying love affair. Like Coccioli in his published *Journal*, the narrator is romantically, almost blindly, in love with Mexico, which he views as a bastion of primal human values in the face of an Americanized technological world. He indulges so frequently in ruminations consistent with a European intellectual that we are perhaps justified in assuming that many of the lofty speculations on syncretic myth are in fact his own, which he has imposed on the simple Manuel. Shortly after his arrival he meets Manuel, who at that point is spreading his gospel of Mexican Time in the capital. When Manuel accompanies him on a trip to Guatemala and back, the narrator allegedly learns the details on which his novel is based: "This story has very little fantasy. The writer cannot say more than he knows himself or than he can deduct from the facts he has come to know" (p. 214). After their return from Guatemala in November, 1953, the narrator writes the first draft of the first eighteen chapters—in some ten days, as we are told. Then he leaves Mexico City in January, 1954, just after Manuel himself has set out on what turns out to be his last missionary trip. The remainder of the story—the events leading up to Manuel's crucifixion—is related in letters that the narrator receives from friends in Mexico. The conclusion of the book, in the form of a letter recording

Manuel's death, brings the novel full circle (the prologue described the Passion scene up to the moment of death) and thereby gives it a cyclical structure that reflects the cyclical theme of annual re-enactment of the Passion. As the narrator finishes and revises his book in Florence toward the end of 1954, doubts continue to assail him: "I have just written that someone spoke to me of his 'meeting' with an Indian god; I ask myself if all this is not the height of absurdity, if all this is not a myth" (p. 311).

Just as unmistakably as Hesse, Coccioli has combined the mythic interpretation with the form-critical problem regarding the role of the gospelist. But the emphasis is somewhat different. In *Demian* there are virtually no conspicuous external parallels between the plot and the Gospels; Demian becomes a Jesus-figure almost solely in the consciousness of the narrator, Emil Sinclair; the narrator's role, therefore, amounts to persuading himself and the reader that the parallels are indeed present. In *Manuel the Mexican*, in contrast, the parallels are so blatant as to be almost unbelievable; as a result, the narrator has an ambivalent, twofold task. He must assure us, by a scrupulous account of his sources, by careful documentation, by including allegedly authentic letters, and so forth, that his story is indeed real and not merely "mythic" or fictitious. At the same time, he is confronted with very real doubts regarding his ability to make this story comprehensible and plausible to a sophisticated non-Mexican audience. And his entire story, all objectivity aside, is heavily colored by his own highly romantic view of Mexico and his own theory of myth. We have, in other words, a very precise analogue to the gospelist who had to make the leader of a minor Jewish sect historically real to his listeners and, at the same time, plausible as a divine figure. His portrayal, according to the insights of form criticism, was often colored by his own beliefs—in Coccioli's case, the love of Mexico and his mythic view. *Manuel the Mexican* is a fascinating attempt to write a fictional transfiguration of the mythic Jesus. If the attempt is not wholly successful as a novel, it is because the author has too often succumbed to the temptation to reduce psychological motivation to myth and to replace dialogue with lectures on comparative religion.

Both Hesse and Coccioli felt the need to enhance the plausibility of their mythic transfigurations by filtering the material through the consciousness of a narrator who either assumes responsibility for the parallels (Emil Sinclair) or disarms the reader's incredulity by anticipating objections (Coccioli). We must now consider a major novel that retains the mythic dimension without the benefit of a personal narrator. As a result, the myth seems to be imposed upon the story in a manner that challenges our credulity, making the novel as predictable and moralizing as William Faulkner suggests through his title: *A Fable* (1954).

Many critics have noted Faulkner's obsession with what has been termed his "Passion Week of the Heart": a repeated fictional re-enactment of the crucifixion that ends, however, without the redeeming Christian act of the resurrection.[12] From the early New Orleans sketches of 1925 that Faulkner called "Mirrors of Chartres Street" (1925)—"Out of Nazareth" and "The Kingdom of God"—through the Easter events of *The Sound and the Fury* (1929) to the ironically inverted *via dolorosa* of Joe Christmas in *Light in August* (1932), Faulkner has employed the Passion of Jesus, with notable frequency, in order to lend both structure and dignity to the thoroughly secularized plots of his stories and novels. This pronounced tendency culminates in *A Fable*, in which the New Testament parallels are so

[12] Hyatt H. Waggoner, "William Faulkner's Passion Week of the Heart," in *The Tragic Vision and the Christian Faith*, ed. Nathan A. Scott, Jr. (New York: Association Press, 1957), pp. 306-23. From the growing bibliography on *A Fable* I shall single out only the chapter in Dillistone's *The Novelist and the Passion Story*; and the useful résumé of criticism in Edmond L. Volpe, *A Reader's Guide to William Faulkner* (New York: Farrar, Straus, 1964).

highly contrived and the psychological motivation so implausibly weak that one would almost suspect, were the book the least bit playful in spirit, that Faulkner is parodying himself. (In a number of passages, certainly, he parodies his literary style, as when the French officers mouth oratorical profundities that are perfectly appropriate in the rhetoric of a Yoknapatawpha County judge, but faintly ridiculous in the speech of a graduate of St. Cyr.)

Faulkner has made it clear that he regards the stories of the Bible, both Old Testament and New, as myths that the writer may adapt for his own purposes. In an interview for *Paris Review* (Spring, 1956) he points out that Christianity is even more useful than other myths because "no one is without Christianity" in the broad sense of a "code of behavior by means of which he makes himself a better human being than his nature wants to be." He sees Christianity, then, less as a faith than as an ethical system, and the New Testament amounts to a mythical narrative in which the life of Jesus provides a "matchless example of suffering and sacrifice and the promise of hope"—a definition with which Arthur Drews or C. G. Jung would not find it difficult to agree.

Within *A Fable* this mythic understanding of the Bible is suggested in such passages as the one in which the author cites "Adam and Lilith and Paris and Helen and Pyramus and Thisbe and all the other recordless Romeos and their Juliets" as prototypes of "the tender legend" of human love (p. 153).[13] Not only is the Bible story put on the same level as classical and modern literary myth; Faulkner cunningly intensifies the mythic view by inserting the Lilith of Hebrew legend rather than the Eve of Genesis as Adam's companion. Faulkner goes on to define legend or myth as a kind of archetypal pattern that is simply "used" by the incumbent: "since, being immortal, the story, the legend, was not

[13] *A Fable* cited according to the Modern Library edition (New York: Random House, 1966).

to be owned by any one of the pairs who added to its shining and tragic increment, but only to be used, passed
through, by each in their doomed and homeless turn"
(p. 154). Precisely this same mythic quality attaches to the
hero of the novel, "the obscure corporal whose name few
knew and even they could not pronounce it" (p. 128).
Along with the twelve men in his squadron he was "an
enigma, since none of them seemed to have any history at
all beyond the day when they had appeared, materialised
seemingly out of nowhere and nothingness . . ." (p. 128).
This transfigured Jesus has no past and no future, but only
the eternal present of the mythic role that he assumes. Even
without a personal narrator as its mouthpiece, then, Faulkner's novel contains its own theory of myth—a hallmark of
the mythic transfigurations.

Even though to the other characters within the fiction
Faulkner's hero seems to have "materialised" mythically out
of nowhere, Faulkner has gone to great lengths to give him
enough of a biography to mark him unmistakably as a fictional transfiguration. From the time of his birth at Christmas in a Middle Eastern stable—his sister cannot remember "if we were driven from the inn itself or just turned
away or maybe perhaps it was our mother still who would
cut even that cord too with man" (p. 290)—to his execution
at age thirty-three, every important incident of his life is
made, by hook or by crook, to conform to the Gospel narrative. Sometimes the parallels, exceeding the limits of the
tolerable, become sheer travesty: when the corporal is shot
at the end, he falls in such a way that "a tangled mass of old
barbed wire" (p. 385) coils itself around his head in a modern equivalent of the crown of thorns. At other times the
parallel is perfectly plausible, but totally irrelevant to the
development of the plot and inserted gratuitously for the
sake of the myth. We hear, for instance, that the corporal
arranges a kind of wedding at Cana by taking money from
gambling soldiers and giving it to a young couple. We learn
also of deeds of healing, as when the corporal collects from

the troops of his division enough money to pay the surgeon's fee for a child going blind for lack of an operation.

It could be argued that these parallels serve to characterize the hero; but in fact they are not psychologically motivated or even fully compatible with his character as we get to know it later. Much of this background information comes to us indirectly through long flashbacks and digressions, for the novel is framed by the compact structure of the Passion Week itself: the action begins in the early morning of a Wednesday in late May, 1918, when thirteen soldiers of the French army are brought by truck to the town of Chaulnesmont for court martial. The conspicuous yet ironic parallel to the triumphal entry into Jerusalem tells us from the very first page what kind of a "fable" we are dealing with. The unnamed corporal—his name, Stephan, is mentioned only once, after his death (p. 399)—and his twelve men, it turns out, are accused of having instigated a pacifist "mutiny" that took place two days earlier. On the preceding Monday the enlisted men of an entire French division had refused to leave the trenches, and this act of insubordination set off a chain reaction that brought the entire western front to a cease-fire within three hours.

It is not until Thursday evening, and some three hundred pages later, that we become acquainted at first hand with the thirteen soldiers, who are anything but evangelical apostle-types (pp. 333-40). They watch while their guards bring in a long wooden mess table, which is placed in the center of the cell: " 'Going to fatten us up first, huh?' one of the prisoners said. The sergeant didn't answer; he was now working at his front teeth with a gold toothpick." When the food and wine has been brought in, the sergeant exhorts the prisoners: " 'All right, you bastards. Be pigs.' " We gradually become aware that this scene is Faulkner's thoroughly secularized version of the Last Supper. Sitting at the head of the table, the corporal fills the bowls and passes them along. In their nervousness and anxiety the men are too busy talking to eat, and finally the corporal admonishes them: " 'Eat. You'll spend the rest of the night wishing you did have something to clap your jaws on. Save the philosophy for then.' "

Shortly after this the guards come back into the cell to get one of the prisoners, named Polchek, the Judas-figure who betrayed the leader of the mutiny. As they take Polchek, another man stands up expectantly: his name turns out to be Pierre Bouc, and there is no record that he belongs to the corporal's squad. When the guards interrogate him, the corporal urges Bouc to tell them who he is: " 'No,' the man whispered. Then he said loudly: 'No!' He blundered up. 'I don't know them!' he said, blundering, stumbling, half-falling backward over the bench almost as though in flight until the sergeant checked him." After this Last Supper, which includes the ritual betrayal by Judas as well as the denial by Peter, the corporal himself is fetched by the guards.

To his great surprise, the corporal is led out of the jail and taken by the general in his automobile for a ride up to the ramparts of the old Roman citadel overlooking the city. This becomes the setting for a scene that turns out to be a curious amalgam of the Temptation, the trial by Pilate, and Gethsemane, including elements of each (pp. 340-54). The general, Supreme Commander of the Allied Forces, turns out through the wildest of improbabilities to be the corporal's father, having begotten him years earlier during a tour of duty in the Near East. (This relationship, upon which the meaning of the book depends, is mythically plausible perhaps, but it is fictionally and realistically highly unlikely.) The general first attempts to persuade the corporal to deny his followers in the mutiny, promising him wealth and power in return: "There is the earth. You will have half of it now." When this satanic temptation fails, the general tries to strike a Pilate-like bargain. He reveals to the corporal that Polchek had betrayed the plan for mutiny on Sunday, before it even had occurred, and that as a result of this information the generals on both sides had been able

174

to manipulate the cease-fire to their own advantage. The general offers to execute Polchek: "You will not only have your revenge and discharge the vengeance of the rest of those three thousand whom he betrayed, you will repossess the opprobrium from all that voice down there which cannot even go to bed because of the frantic need to anathemise you. Give me Polchek, and take freedom." When the corporal rejects this second compromise, the general finally offers to acknowledge the corporal as his own son. Their conversation concerning fear, death, and human dignity takes on overtones of Jesus' agony in the garden of Gethsemane. Here, however, two opposing points of view come into conflict. The corporal feels, somewhat romantically, that an act of sacrifice is necessary to save humanity. The general advances a more realistic point of view: "No no, it's not I but you who are afraid of man; not I but you who believe that nothing but a death can save him. I know better. I know that he has that in him which will enable him to outlast even his wars; that in him more durable than all his vices. . . ."

When the general in his various hypostases as a Satan-Pilate-God fails to convince the corporal of the inefficacy of his sacrifice, he returns the corporal to jail, where the latter is separated from his "disciples" and thrown into a cell with two common criminals, Lapin and Casse-tête. The following day, Friday, the three of them are executed by a firing squad of Senegalese troops (pp. 382-86.) They are tied, as though crucified, to "three freshly planted posts set in a symmetric row on the edge of a long pit." As they await their death, the corporal has a chance to console the repentant thief, Casse-tête. When he falls, the strand of barbed wire coils thorn-like around his head.

The analogies do not end even with the corporal's death. That same evening his body is claimed by two women named Marthe and Marya—they are his sisters in the novel, but they have no other function than the purely symbolic one of representing the Marys of the New Testament—who take it back to their farm near St. Mihiel, where they bury it in a dirt bank. Early on Sunday, during a pre-dawn artillery bombardment, the dirt bank is struck by shells. When the women go out to look for the fresh grave, "they found a few more shards and fragments of the coffin, but the body itself was gone" (p. 401). Some time after this secular entombment and resurrection, a squad of soldiers arrives in the vicinity to select a body to fill the tomb of the Unknown Soldier; Faulkner leaves us with the implication that it is the corporal's body that is taken to the symbolic grave in Paris. Several years later Polchek suffers, at least symbolically, the Judas-fate of suicide by hanging. As he leaves the house of the two sisters, whom he has visited—there is even a reference to the thirty coins—"he turned, framed for a moment in the door, his face livid and intolerable, with nothing left now but the insolence, the tall feather in the hat which he had never removed breaking into the line of the lintel as if he actually were hanging on a cord from it against the vacant shape of the spring darkness" (pp. 432-33).

The events of the Passion fill barely the last quarter of the long novel; the remainder is taken up by a variety of more or less tenuously related sub-plots—the background histories of various figures, including the corporal and the general; a long and independent novella set in the American South and involving a stolen race horse; and the cynical plot whereby the commanders of the Allied and the German military forces collaborate to sustain the war despite the spontaneous peace movement that arises among the enlisted men of both sides as a result of the corporal's mutiny. But the novel as a whole is organized in such a way as to highlight the Passion, which provides the framework for all the other action: the novel begins with the "triumphal entry" of the corporal and his twelve men into the city, and it ends shortly after the "resurrection" of his body. The highpoint of the novel comes with the long dialogue between the corporal and the Supreme Commander, between the transfigured Jesus and his father.

The mythic aspect of the novel is intensified by the fact that the Supreme Commander is surrounded by an aura of the Old Testament that is as unmistakable as the parallels to the New Testament in the life of the corporal. As a result, the central conflict in the novel—between the Supreme Commander of the Allied Forces and the common soldier who leads the revolt against his military authority—is at the same time a conflict between father and son, between God and Jesus. The confrontation, however, is an ironic inversion of Christian belief, for not only are the two positions of God and Jesus in fundamental opposition; both are ambivalent positions whose validity is relativized by the dialectics of the novel. The corporal, in his capacity as a common soldier, represents man's essential humanity and an idealistic faith in man's ability to transcend his rapaciousness. Yet his self-righteous insistence undeniably causes harm to some people: the commanding officer of his division, General Gragnon, is executed as a direct result of the corporal's refusal to compromise with the Supreme Commander. The latter, in contrast, more problematically aware of the dualism in the human character, probably comes closer to Faulkner's own view. He argues that the corporal's faith in "an esoteric realm of man's baseless hopes" is supported only by his "passion for unfact" (p. 348). As a realist, he knows that man's more spiritual impulses are inevitably coupled with guilt, rapacity, folly. Faulkner, in other words, has used the symbolic myth of God and Jesus as the vessel for thoroughly un-Christian arguments.

The author has left unresolved his own point of view in the face of such ambiguities. Characteristically, the realistic old general presides over the death of the corporal—God finally decides to sacrifice Jesus as a matter of expediency when his son refuses to compromise. This seems to be Faulkner's cynical comment on the victory of shrewd realism over idealism, of rapacity over humanity. Yet the novel ends, several years after the events of May, 1918, with the funeral, with full military honors, of the Supreme Commander. This could be Faulkner's acknowledgment that, after the demise of Christianity, man is now confronted with the death of God. Yet as pessimistic as the novel seems to be, Faulkner has put into the last major utterance of the general a paraphrase of his own acceptance speech for the Nobel Prize (1950), in which he attested his faith in mankind.

"I dont fear man. I do better: I respect and admire him. And pride: I am ten times prouder of that immortality which he does possess than ever he of that heavenly one of his delusion. Because man and his folly—"
"Will endure," the corporal said.
"They will do more," the old general said proudly. "They will prevail." (p. 354)

There are several other figures in the novel who exemplify basic human values just as clearly as the general and the corporal, thereby raising the plot to that level of universal validity that can be called myth or fable. Thus the English runner who uncovers the generals' plot to continue the war and who attempts to do something about it represents Man Seeking Faith. (Several critics have noted the importance of the symbol of running in this novel.) The Negro minister Sutterfield, who links the story of the race-horse with the main plot, has such an intact faith that he embodies Man Believing. These and others represent symbolic attitudes of which Faulkner along with his readers and critics may be aware. However, they are not filtered through the consciousness, either serious or ironic, of a personal narrator; nor are they evident to the characters within the fiction.

Only one figure seems to be consciously aware of the transfigurational parallels: the priest whom the general sends to the corporal's cell in a final effort to change his

mind. The priest, who sees and cites the parallels, is overcome by remorse and decides to kill himself when he leaves
the corporal. Faulkner jeopardizes the effect achieved by
the priest's death, however, when he uses it as an occasion
to slip in another Gospel detail that he was unable to use
elsewhere, in a manner so labored as to be preposterous. As
he leaves the jail, the priest borrows a soldier's bayonet
"thinking *It was a spear, so I should have taken the rifle too,*
and then no more: thinking *The left side, and I'm right
handed,* thinking *But at least He wasn't wearing an infan-
tryman's overcoat and a* Magazin du Louvre *shirt and so at
least I can do that,* opening the coat and throwing it back
and then opening the shirt until he could feel the blade's
cold minuscule point against his flesh. . . . *But He was not
standing either,* he thought *He was nailed there and He will
forgive me* and cast himself sideways and downward,
steadying the bayonet so that the end of the hilt should
strike the bricks first . . . " (p. 370).

It is precisely this sort of strained effort to introduce the
parallels—in this case, the lance wound—even when they
are totally irrelevant to the context that vitiates the power
of Faulkner's narrative and reduces it to an often tedious
allegory. As a passionate indictment of war, as a compelling
statement regarding the murky depths of human nature, as
a moving expression of the author's faith in man's capacity
to prevail, *A Fable* stands as a monument to Faulkner's
noble conception of the human condition in all its ambivalence. But in comparison with the experimental daring of
The Sound and the Fury, the subtle myth-making of *The
Bear,* or the ribaldly humorous reality of *The Reivers,* it is
very thin indeed as fiction. In fact, in comparison with the
finest fictional transfigurations it strikes us as a clumsy allegorical work. The author has strained our credulity, not
to mention our aesthetic sensibilities, by imposing the Gospel parallels obtrusively from without. The characters move
through the patterns of their myth almost by rote without
any compelling psychological motivation. And reading its

long perorations, we cannot but recall the early Christian socialist tracts and wonder if, in many cases, the fictional transfiguration is doomed to labor under the burden of preachiness inherited from the very Gospels that it sets out to re-enact.

These three mythic transfigurations reveal neither the similarity of form nor the identity of intent that permitted us so easily to group the Christian socialist novels and the psychiatric interpretations. Yet without insisting on any rigid categories, we can single out certain features that distinguish these three works from the others while relating them to one another. *Demian, Manuel the Mexican,* and *A Fable* have none of the impulse for social reform that dominated the earliest fictional transfigurations; and although they work with close parallels to the Gospel, they lack specifically those features that most appealed to the Christian socialists: e.g., the churchman as hero who comes into conflict with ecclesiastical authority. This omission is logical, of course, for the authors view Jesus as a myth rather than as a historical man with reformatory intent. By the same token, they eschew the analysis of the paranoid personality that fascinated Hauptmann and Kazantzakis; hence, the New Testament parallels are not motivated as the search of the demented hero for his own Passion; and all three works conspicuously lack the humor that qualified the skeptical view of the world in *Emanuel Quint* and *The Greek Passion.*

At the same time, two basic similarities underlie the three novels and permit us to view them together as a single category. First, all three novelists have a specifically mythic understanding of Christianity in general and Jesus in particular: Faulkner's definition of Jesus as a "matchless example" is quite close to Hesse's notion of "a hero, a myth, an extraordinary shadow image in which humanity has painted itself on the wall of eternity." And Faulkner's catalogue equating Adam and Lilith with Paris and Helen shows a

mythic view resembling Coccioli's Aztec-Christian syncretism. In addition, all three writers have included their
theory of myth within their novels, thus providing the reader with the necessary tools of understanding. Hesse sees
Demian as a culture-hero who is like Christ, Nietzsche, and
the other great mythic figures of mankind; Manuel is a
mythic amalgam of traits borrowed from Jesus and Tepoz-
teco; and Faulkner's corporal, without past or future, is presented as the personification of the longing for peace that
inspired the soldiers in the spring of 1918. Second, Demian,
Manuel, and the corporal are motivated neither by simple
reformatory zeal nor by a psychiatrically explicable psycho-
sis. Rather, their motivation is also mythic: that is, they
move with all the assurance of sleepwalkers, sublimely convinced of their righteousness, unswayed by rational argument, and acting out the motions of their legend, which in
Faulkner's words was not to be owned by any one of them,
"but only to be used, passed through, by each in their
doomed and homeless turn."

In the final analysis, Demian, Manuel, and the corporal
are not living, vital, knowable characters, but symbols created solely for the sake of their stories, to embody a specific
message: Hesse's vision of a new spiritual millennium; Coccioli's unity of past and present in Mexican Time; and
Faulkner's idealistic "passion for unfact." For this reason,
perhaps, the category of mythic transfiguration, for all the
brilliance of the various attempts, is destined to remain un-
successful by the test of aesthetic plausibility. In any case,
it rapidly gave way before the greater realism of the Marxist Comrade Jesus, and it invited the inevitable parody of
the Fifth Gospels.

6. Comrade Jesus

CRITICS HAVE long exercised their exegetical ingenuity on the mythic patterns underlying John Steinbeck's fiction. Apart from the Arthurian cycle and the Faust legend, it has been particularly the Bible, both Old Testament and New, that has shaped his works. In the early novel *To a God Unknown* (1933) Joseph and his brethren prefigure the story of Joseph Wayne, who leaves his Vermont home to make his fortune in California and then summons his brothers to join him in establishing a family community in the new land. As the title suggests, *East of Eden* (1952) is based on the myth of Cain and Abel, which is re-enacted by two successive generations of the Trask family (Charles and Adam; Cal and Aron). *The Winter of Our Discontent* (1961), which opens on Good Friday in 1960, invokes the Passion, the Descent into Hell, and the Resurrection—though more symbolically than structurally—as the background for a modern morality tale that takes place on Long Island.

It is hardly a surprise, then, to find a mythic biblical pattern underlying Steinbeck's finest novel, *The Grapes of Wrath* (1939). Here, in fact, the mythic pattern plays a more important structural role than is usually the case in Steinbeck since otherwise the novel has little form-giving plot as such, but simply records a representative epic of the thirties in the flight of the Joad family from the desolate fields of Oklahoma to what they vainly hope may turn out to be the Promised Land in California. The title alerts the reader to the biblical dimension, for the words from Julia Ward Howe's "Battle Hymn of the Republic" refer to the "great winepress of the wrath of God" described in Revelation 14:19. It has been generally recognized that the three principal sections of the novel—the drought in Oklahoma (chaps. 1-10), the journey along Route 66 (chaps.

182

11-18), and the events in California (chaps. 19-30)—correspond to the oppression of the Hebrews in Egypt, the Exodus, and the arrival in Canaan, the land of milk and honey.[1] It has been pointed out in addition that many of the modern details have exact counterparts in the biblical narrative: the flight of the Okies takes them through the desert, where many perish; the fried dough on which the impoverished wanderers subsist is a depression equivalent of the unleavened bread of the Hebrews; the laws that govern the roadside camps are mosaically strict and autonomous.[2] Indeed, biblical interpretations have been proposed for the name Joad itself: it can be taken as a reference to the trials of Job, or it can be read as an allusion to the people of Judah.[3]

Embedded within this major framework and emerging most strongly at the end, there is a minor pattern that is of more immediate relevance in our context. For whether we regard the Joads as the family of Job or the people of Judah, the fact that twelve of them set out with the former revivalist preacher Jim Casy prepares us for New Testament parallels as well.[4] The spiritual leader of the migrant workers has been endowed with characteristics that clearly identify him as a transfiguration of Jesus—note his initials—and he is himself self-consciously aware of the parallels. Early in the novel, when Jim Casy first meets the Joads, he is asked to say grace. Warning them that he is no longer a preacher, Casy agrees to say a word of thanks. He prefaces his remarks with the statement that he has been out in the hills—" 'almost you might say like Jesus went into the

---

[1] Peter Lisca, *The Wide World of John Steinbeck* (New Brunswick, N. J.: Rutgers Univ. Press, 1958).

[2] Joseph Fontenrose, *John Steinbeck: An Introduction and Interpretation* (New York: Barnes and Noble, 1963), pp. 75-76.

[3] Ibid., p. 75 (Judah); Lester Jay Marks, *Thematic Design in the Novels of John Steinbeck* (The Hague: Mouton, 1969), p. 79 (Job).

[4] Fontenrose, Marks, and Martin Staples Shockley, "Christian Symbolism in *The Grapes of Wrath*," *College English*, 18 (1956), 87-90.

wilderness to think His way out of a mess of troubles' "
(p. 109).[5] Casy explains that Jesus sought out the wilderness as a place of spiritual renewal when he became exhausted with the trials of the world: " 'I ain't sayin' I'm like
Jesus,' the preacher went on. 'But I got tired like Him, an'
I got mixed up like Him, an' I went into the wilderness like
Him, without no campin' stuff' " (p. 110). Let us state explicitly that we are dealing here neither with the hallucinations of a paranoid hero nor with the mystical identification
of a narrator who believes in the transfiguration of his hero.
For all the naive simplicity of the language, we are confronted with a far more sophisticated consciousness than we
have had before. Jim Casy specifically denies any identity
with Jesus, and yet he is aware of certain parallels between
his own life and that of Jesus. We shall return to the implications of this more detached, even ironic consciousness.
For the moment it suffices to note that Casy's—that is to say,
Steinbeck's—famous theory of the "oversoul" was the direct
product of his Jesus-like sojourn in the wilderness: " 'I got
thinkin' how we was holy when we was one thing, an' man-
kin' was holy when it was one thing' " (p. 110).

This minister of a new spiritual doctrine, who has the
initials of Jesus Christ and who receives his inspiration in
the wilderness, sets out for California with twelve Joads.
(To be sure, not all twelve of them arrive in "the golden
land"; but as in the case of the revelers in the Peeperkorn
scene of *The Magic Mountain*, they survive long enough to
fulfill their symbolic role as disciples and hence to fortify
the fictional transfiguration of Jim Casy.) Although Casy is
cast in his role within the first chapters of the novel, it is
only toward the end that the New Testament parallels begin to outweigh those from the Old Testament and to determine the course of the action. Symbolically this is absolutely
appropriate: the new Messiah arises out of the Chosen Peo-

[5] *The Grapes of Wrath* cited according to the Modern Library
edition (New York [1941]).

ple only after they have fallen into despair in the Promised
Land.

Shortly after their arrival in California Tom Joad gets
involved in a brawl with a police deputy. Since Tom has
only recently been released from prison and is still on
parole, Casy surrenders to the police to protect Tom. When
they meet again, months later, Casy has been radically po-
liticized by his experiences in jail: he has become a union
organizer and is picketing a peach orchard where the Joads
are working along with other strike-breakers. In jail, as he
tries to explain to Tom, he finally learned what he had
sought to discover in the wilderness: the message of human
solidarity. While he is outlining the theory of labor organization to Tom, they are interrupted by some noises outside.
Stepping out of the tent to investigate, they are seized almost immediately by some of the men who have been
threatening to beat the union organizers and to run them
out of the area. When Casy is caught in the crossbeam of
the flashlights there is an unmistakable suggestion of the
nimbus: "'That's him. That shiny bastard,'" one of the men
shouts. Then:

> A short heavy man stepped into the light. He carried
> a new white pick handle.
> Casy went on, "You don' know what you're a-doin'!"
> The heavy man swung with the pick handle. Casy
> dodged down into the swing. The heavy club crashed
> into the side of his head with a dull crunch of bone,
> and Casy fell sideways out of the light.
> "Jesus, George, I think you killed him."
> "Put the light on him," said George. "Serve the son-
> of-a-bitch right." The flashlight beam dropped,
> searched and found Casy's crushed head. (p. 527)

When Tom later tells his mother about Casy's death, his re-
phrasing of Jesus' words from the cross—"You don' know
what you're a-doin'"—is repeated twice for emphasis
(p. 535). As a result, the reader is sure not to miss the bib-

lical allusion even though the witnesses of the action, Tom and the labor goons, are unaware of their significance.

In Steinbeck's version several motifs from the Passion occur out of their normal Gospel order, producing a curious amalgam of crucifixion and Gethsemane. It is only after Casy's death and his paraphrase of the words from the cross that Tom Joad seizes the club and, in imitation of the disciple Peter in the garden, strikes the assailant: "The first time he knew he had missed and struck a shoulder, but the second time his crushing blow found his head, and as the heavy man sank down, three more blows found his head" (p. 527). Like Peter, Tom manages to escape the circle of searchers and makes his way back to the safety of the workers' camp: "At last the roosters crowed, far away, and gradually the window lightened" (p. 530). It is only after the cock's crow that Tom finds it necessary to deny Jim Casy. Indeed, in order to protect Tom from the searching police, the entire Joad family must lie and, within a few days, pack up and leave the camp. Finally, to avoid exposing his family to further risk, Tom decides to abandon them altogether. By this time, as he explains to Ma Joad, he has become wholly the disciple of Casy and, like the disciple Peter, intends to devote his life to spreading the word. His words of farewell to his mother unconsciously paraphrase Matthew 18:20: "For where two or three are gathered together in my name, there am I in the midst of them." And the passage ends with an allusion to Jesus' appearance to the disciples. It will not matter if he is killed, Tom says:

> "Then I'll be all aroun' in the dark. I'll be ever'where
> —wherever you look. Wherever they's a fight so hungry
> people can eat, I'll be there. Wherever they's a cop
> beatin' up a guy, I'll be there. If Casy knowed, why,
> I'll be in the way guys yell when they're mad an'—I'll
> be in the way kids laugh when they're hungry an' they
> know supper's ready. An' when our folks eat the stuff
> they raise an' live in the houses they build—why, I'll be

there. See? God, I'm talkin' like Casy. Comes of thinkin' about him so much. Seems like I can see him sometimes." (p. 572)

It is highly doubtful that the migrant workers' camps heard much rhetoric of this quality. It is symptomatic, therefore, that Tom Joad attributes his highflown speech to Casy himself—almost like Peter citing Jesus—and that the entire speech is based, in turn, on a thought borrowed directly from the Gospels.

It seems clear that Jim Casy is a transfigured Jesus whose message of human solidarity and agrarian socialism, discovered in the wilderness and perfected in a California jail, leads him to a violent death at the hands of the political and economic establishment whose interests he threatens. Among his followers he wins a Peter-like disciple in the person of Tom Joad, who strikes down his assailant, hears cocks crow, and for a time must deny his teacher before he too sets out to preach his message across the land. Like *The Magic Mountain*, Steinbeck's novel exploits the fictional transfiguration not for its entire structure, but only for one major scene. But the scene represents the thematic climax of the entire work, for Casy's self-sacrificial death in the service of his fellow man constitutes the only faint ray of hope in this otherwise bleak world of the oppressed Okies.

Steinbeck received the conventional Western biblical heritage at home in Salinas, California, and in the Episcopal Sunday school that he attended as a boy. There is strong indirect evidence, however, that his understanding of Judaeo-Christian tradition and imagery was crucially affected by the mythic interpretations that were current in the twenties and thirties. Even though he does not mention Jung by name, the reflections on marine biology that Steinbeck published in *Sea of Cortez* (1941) repeatedly refer to myth in the vocabulary of analytical psychology. Speaking of one sea legend, he writes that "the ocean, deep and black in the depths, is like the low dark levels of our minds in which the dream symbols incubate and sometimes rise up to sight like the Old Man of the Sea." The frequent aquatic images that rise up in the individual unconscious indicate to Steinbeck the existence of "a group psyche-memory which is the foundation of the whole unconscious." He concludes that "the harvest of symbols in our minds seems to have been planted in the soft rich soil of our prehumanity."[6]

In *Sea of Cortez* Steinbeck restricts himself to remarks on aquatic symbols. As a theory of myth, however, it is close to several of the mythic interpretations of Jesus that regard his figure as a recurrent archetype that received its classic expression in the Bible. Consistently enough, Steinbeck includes in his novel a crucial passage that seems to suggest precisely such an interpretation of Jesus. Early in their acquaintance Casy is explaining to Tom Joad why he gave up the ministry.

> "I says, 'What's this call, this sperit?' An' I says, 'It's love. I love people so much I'm fit to bust, sometimes.' An' I says, 'Don't you love Jesus?' Well, I thought an' thought, an' finally I says, 'No, I don't know nobody name' Jesus. I know a bunch of stories, but I only love people.'" (p. 32)

Jesus, in other words, is reduced to "a bunch of stories," a mythic expression of the immense human love that Casy feels for his fellow man. And it soon occurs to Casy, in addition, that God and Jesus are nothing but relative labels for the oversoul of the group-animal.

> "I figgered about the Holy Sperit and the Jesus road. I figgered, 'Why do we got to hang it on God or Jesus? Maybe,' I figgered, 'maybe it's all men an' all women we love; maybe that's the Holy Sperit—the human sperit— the whole shebang. Maybe all men got one big soul ever'body's a part of.'" (pp. 32-33)

[6] John Steinbeck and Edward F. Ricketts, *Sea of Cortez: A Leisurely Journal of Travel and Research* (New York: Viking, 1941), pp. 30-34.

Clearly, Steinbeck shares the mythic theory that Jesus is nothing but the projection of a deep cultic longing, and he even manages to include this theory of myth in the very novel that incorporates it. To this extent *The Grapes of Wrath* resembles the mythic transfigurations that we considered in the preceding chapter. That Steinbeck was consciously exploiting the mythic potentialities is suggested by the journal he wrote while composing *East of Eden.* "This one story," he noted with reference to the Genesis account of Cain and Abel, "is the basis of all human neurosis—and if you take the fall along with it, you have the total of the psychic troubles that can happen to a human." Steinbeck sees in the Bible the enduring mythic expression, as it were, of basic human problems: "It is using the Biblical story as a measure of ourselves."[7]

At the same time, myth is not the central impulse of the novel, as it was in *Demian* or *Manuel the Mexican. The Grapes of Wrath* is perhaps the classic American novel of social protest. Steinbeck is infuriated by the avarice that deposes the sharecroppers from their lands in the dustbowl so that the big landowners can make even more money; he is outraged at the hunger and poverty that exist among the migrants in the face of so much prosperity in California; he is scandalized by the inhuman devices employed by the fruitgrowers to keep down the price of labor among the starving Okies. His answer to these problems, in contrast to the moral reform proposed in the Christian socialist novels, is essentially political: his transfigured hero, Jim Casy, gives up the ministry to become a union organizer; and Tom Joad decides at the end of the novel to devote his life to the cause of labor. They are opposed by the forces of economic and political oppression, not by a dogmatic Church.

For all its political impact, however, *The Grapes of Wrath* advances no formalized political or social philos-

[7] John Steinbeck, *Journal of a Novel: The East of Eden Letters* (New York: Viking, 1969), pp. 104-105.

ophy. Jim Casy is called a "red son-of-a-bitch" (p. 527), but only by the management goons. In his simple human love and agrarian socialism Casy is no more communist than is the "bolshevik" Manolios in *The Greek Passion*. Yet this impulse toward political reform puts Steinbeck's novel into a category with other contemporary works evincing a more pronounced political message. Ever since liberal theology Jesus had been endowed with political meaning by various groups. Eliza Lynn Linton's Joshua Davidson was a "communist" in the less programmatic sense of the 1870's. During the nineties Jesus was called "the Social Democrat par excellence" and "the first socialist," and around the turn of the century Kalthoff was arguing that Jesus was nothing but the mythic projection of the longing for social and political reform among the downtrodden masses of Rome. By 1922, when Upton Sinclair wrote the appendix to his "Tale of the Second Coming," Jesus was regarded as "the world's greatest revolutionary martyr, the founder of the world's first proletarian party." It seems perfectly consistent with this tradition that the transfigured Jesus should make his appearance in the thirties as a card-carrying Party member. At the same time, the designation "Comrade Jesus"—initially suggested by the fact that two of the heroes in this chapter are in fact members of the Party—achieves its ultimate justification because all these men move beyond rigid Party dogma and discipline to encounter their fellow man in the broadest sense as "comrades" or "companions."

This is evident in *The Grapes of Wrath*, for Jim Casy, the labor organizer, remains a proto-communist with no Party allegiances. A few years earlier, in the novel *In Dubious Battle* (1936), Steinbeck had explored the possibilities of a communist hero and found him wanting. In that novel, which is also set in a California fruit-pickers' camp, the strike-leader is a Party organizer; but his activities are unmasked as motivated by a cold attachment to Marxist principle and a willingness to exploit people as a means to the end—qualities that have nothing in common with the basic

190

humanism of Jim Casy and Tom Joad. It is only a small step from labor organizer to Party functionary, however: the transfigured heroes of Ignazio Silone's *Bread and Wine* (1936) as well as Arthur Koestler's *Darkness at Noon* (1940) are both men whose long-standing devotion to the Party is only beginning to give way in the face of considerations of a more purely human nature. But before we examine those works, we should mention two factors that will help to put this Comrade Jesus into perspective.

The authors of these works, like their heroes, are often men who began with a strong religious impulse and sound religious upbringing: Steinbeck came from a devoutly religious family and attended Sunday school regularly; Silone was a faithful Catholic until he joined the socialist youth movement; and the fact that Koestler was national president of the Austrian Zionist fraternities during his student years suggests at least an awareness of his Jewish heritage. These writers, in other words, did not come to Marxism out of an intellectual and spiritual vacuum; rather, it can be assumed in every case that they were familiar with the Judaeo-Christian tradition and with the experience of institutionalized religion. To the extent that they are concerned with social, rather than psychological and mythic, problems, they betray a Christian socialist origin. (Indeed, it is perhaps worth noting that these Comrade Jesuses emerge specifically in those countries—Italy, England, and the United States—that had a strong Christian socialist tradition and where, at the same time, the psychiatric and mythic theories seem to have made least headway.) But unlike the writers of Christian socialism, they rapidly became disenchanted with the capacity of religion and the Church to solve the huge social problems of the twentieth century. However, instead of simply discarding the impulses that led them originally to institutionalized religion, they shifted their longing for order to a new monolithic system: the Party. The point is important, for only if we understand that the enthusiasm for the Party was often nothing but a transfer of allegiance from religion to politics can we comprehend the frequent conversions to Marxism during the twenties and thirties as well as the logic underlying the comparison of Party and Church. It rests upon the assumption that the religious and the political institution share both a similar organization and a similar goal—indeed, that they satisfy a similar spiritual need.

The analogy is developed elaborately in Richard Crossman's classic anthology of ex-communists, *The God That Failed* (1949). The title is significant because it hints at the close association between politics and religion that existed in the minds of many communists. In his introduction Crossman argues that one of the principal attractions of the Party was precisely its dogmatism and its claim on absolute spiritual loyalty at the expense of personal freedom: "The Communist novice, subjecting his soul to the canon law of the Kremlin, felt something of the release which Catholicism also brings to the intellectual, wearied and worried by the privilege of freedom."[8] Crossman goes so far as to suggest that this longing for a new political order to replace the outmoded religious one may account for the fact that communism has had notably more success in Catholic than in Protestant countries.

However that may be, both Koestler and Silone in their contributions to the volume stress the parallels between Party and Church, arguing that the appeal of communism lay in the sacrifices it demanded and not in the promises it made. Koestler begins his discussion by talking about the act of virtually religious faith that motivates the believing communist: "A faith is not acquired by reasoning. One does not fall in love with a woman, or enter the womb of a church, as a result of logical persuasion" (p. 15). And in a similar vein Silone speaks of his life as a communist in Fascist Italy: "One had to change one's name, abandon every former link with family and friends, and live a false

[8] Richard Crossman, ed., *The God That Failed* (New York: Harper, 1949), pp. 6-7.

life to remove any suspicion of conspiratorial activity. The Party became family, school, church, barracks; the world that lay beyond it was to be destroyed and built anew. The psychological mechanism whereby each single militant becomes progressively identified with the collective organization is the same as that used in certain religious orders and military colleges, with almost identical results" (p. 99). Let us seize this point before it slips away. For both Koestler and Silone the Party becomes a surrogate for the Church, a new channel for the religious impulse that is strong in both writers. As a result, it is absolutely appropriate that churchly or religious images insinuate themselves as the precise analogy for political situations.

Koestler and Silone are anything but unique, of course, in their association of Church and Party. In *The Magic Mountain* (1924) Thomas Mann embodied the paradoxical analogy in the demonic figure of Leo Naphta, the Jew turned Jesuit, who is devoutly committed to a doctrine of terrorism and communism. In Ernest Hemingway's *For Whom The Bell Tolls* (1940) religious images—"crusade," "communion," "religious experience," the music of Bach, Chartres Cathedral—crowd into Robert Jordan's mind when he recalls "the puritanical, religious communism of Velazquez 63, the Madrid palace that had been turned into the International Brigade headquarters in the capital. At Velazquez 63 it was like being a member of a religious order. . . ." And the recent European dialogue between Marxists and Christians has increasingly emphasized the view of Marxism as a religion rather than as a philosophy. Some critics have even argued that the *Manifesto* can be properly understood only if it is seen in the literary tradition of the gospel. In any case, the analogy of Church and Party has become so widespread that it now amounts to an intellectual commonplace. Certainly the modern reader is prepared to accept religious imagery in a political context.

At the same time, the historically trained mind of the Marxist causes him to see the central figure of the Church,

Jesus, in a new and different light. We find in the novels of Silone and Koestler precisely the same situation as in *The Grapes of Wrath*: it is neither the hallucination of the hero nor the consciousness of the narrator that produces the parallels between the hero and Jesus. Instead it is history that has created the analogy by thrusting the hero—a labor organizer in a repressive environment, a Party agent in a hostile country—into a position vis-à-vis society and authority that is analogous to the position that Jesus occupied in the Jerusalem of his day. There is no sense whatsoever of mystical identification or paranoid *imitatio*: the analogy is produced neither by psychiatry nor by faith, but by historical awareness. This suggests, in turn, that the analogy must be largely ironic. This is notably the case in the novels of Silone and Koestler, where we are dealing with sophisticated heroes who, for all their loss of religious faith, are aware of the similarity between their predicament and that of Jesus and who often have a Gospel passage in mind to illustrate their analogy. To this extent they are the direct literary descendants of the polished intellectuals and churchmen of Fogazzaro's *The Saint*. Yet there is at least a rudimentary form of this awareness even in the mind of Jim Casy, who makes an almost pedantically precise distinction between identity and analogy: " 'I ain't sayin' I'm like Jesus,' the preacher went on. 'But I got tired like Him, an' I got mixed up like Him, an' I went into the wilderness like Him, without no campin' stuff.' " (The point needs to be made since, in general, the dimension of irony is lacking in the rhetoric of *The Grapes of Wrath*.)

If we approach *Bread and Wine* directly from a reading of *The Saint*, it is difficult to avoid the impression that Silone was consciously trying to rewrite Fogazzaro's novel for a new generation. This impression becomes more persuasive if we recall that *The Saint*, an immense *succès de scandale* in its own day, was long regarded as the most important Italian novel since *I Promessi Sposi*. And Silone (born

194

1900) is notoriously unexperimental in his novels, preferring to emulate the standard models of nineteenth-century Italian fictions. Granted, the theme of ecclesiastical reform has been secularized: Silone is interested in political and social revolution. But the parallels between the two works are striking nevertheless.[9] The action of *Bread and Wine* takes place in 1935, when the revolutionist Pietro Spina has just returned illegally to Fascist Italy after several years of political exile in various countries. To conceal himself from the authorities he dons clerical garb and takes the name Don Paolo Spada. (The name Spina—"thorn"—carries inevitable associations with Jesus, and the decision to become Spada—"sword"—may suggest a certain longing to change one's destiny, to move to the attack.) As in *The Saint*, then, we again have a man of Jesus' age during his years of mission—Pietro Spina, like Piero Maironi, is in his early thirties—who gives up his name to assume a new identity as a priest. Both heroes come from wealthy families, but were orphaned in their childhood. Both men, when they go into hiding in clerical disguise in remote mountain villages, become renowned for "miracles" of healing that they are alleged to perform and, over all their objections, are regarded as the reincarnation of Jesus by the simple peasants. Just as Piero Maironi was torn between his nunlike wife, who dies, and the passionately competent Jeanne Dessalle, Pietro Spina is aided by the lusty Bianchina and

[9] Silone's novel was first published in 1936 in German and English translations; the Italian text appeared in Switzerland in 1937. I refer throughout to the revised edition of 1955 that Silone, to distinguish it from the original *Pane e vino* of 1936-37, called *Vino e pane* (Milan: Mondadori, 1955). I decided to use the later version for two reasons: it presumably represents the author's own wishes regarding the final authorized edition, and what the revision has lost in specific (often dated) topicality, it has gained in tautness of form and generality of theme. Both versions have been separately translated into English under the title *Bread and Wine*: the first by Gwenda David and Eric Mosbacher (London: Methuen, 1936); the revised edition by Harvey Fergusson II (New York: Atheneum, 1962). I cite Fergusson's translation according to the Signet Classic reprint.

revered by the other-worldly Cristina, who gives up her life for him. Both men eventually leave their mountain retreats to go to Rome, where they meet clandestinely with groups interested in their teaching: Benedetto addresses the Catholic laymen in a secret place nicknamed the Catacombs, while Pietro Spina's communist cell actually assembles in the sewers of the city. In both novels, finally, the action is introduced by an elderly John the Baptist figure who has helped to shape the hero's ideas; in fact, Silone even hints at some kind of intellectual continuity by giving Pietro Spina's mentor the name that Fogazzaro's hero assumes, Don Benedetto; moreover, both Silone's Don Benedetto and Fogazzaro's Giovanni Selva are under attack by the Church for their liberal ideas.

Now that we understand that the Party is in one sense a surrogate for the Church, we can see that there is also a clear parallel in theme between *The Saint* and *Bread and Wine*. Fogazzaro's novel was put on the *Index* primarily because the author used it as a vehicle through which to popularize his ideas regarding necessary reforms and modernizations within the Catholic Church. By analogy, R.W.B. Lewis has pointed out, the main theme of all Silone's books is to justify and make sense of his decision, after almost ten years as a loyal and active communist (1921-31), to leave the Party.[10] Pietro Spina's position vis-à-vis the Party therefore becomes almost precisely analogous to Piero Maironi's position with regard to the Church. (The fact that Fogazzaro and his hero ultimately submit to the discipline of the institution while Silone and his fictional counterpart remain firm in their decision to leave the Party tells us much about the character of the authors, but does not invalidate the basic analogy.)

[10] R.W.B. Lewis, *The Picaresque Saint*, p. 135; Lewis's chapter on Silone is unusually informative and suggestive. See also Robert MacAfee Brown, "Ignazio Silone and the Pseudonyms of God," in *The Shapeless God*, ed. Harry J. Mooney and Thomas F. Staley (Pittsburgh: Univ. of Pittsburgh Press, 1968), pp. 19-40, and Nathan A. Scott, Jr., *Rehearsals of Discomposure: Alienation and Reconciliation in Modern Literature* (New York: King's Crown Press, 1952), pp. 66-111.

Silone repeatedly exploits the analogy between Church and Party in the course of the novel, most elaborately perhaps in the recollections of Pietro Spina's friend, Luigi Murica, who recalls the romantic allure of his early political activities: "In the group we read poorly printed newspapers and pamphlets preaching hate of tyranny and announcing as a certainty, as inevitable and not far off, the advent of the revolution which was to establish fraternity and justice among men. It was sort of a weekly dream, secret and forbidden, in which we communicated and which made us forget our daily misery. It was like the rites of a hidden religion" (p. 239). In view of the pointed analogies in vocabulary and organization to the early Christian community, it is appropriate and even inevitable that the ideal leader of the communist movement should turn out to be none other than Jesus. A friend reminds Pietro Spina of a dream that he used to describe to his friends: "You spoke in terms of your home town: to make a soviet of the Fucino Valley and to nominate Jesus president of the soviet" (p. 180).

The analogy between Church and Party established in such passages as these is anything but gratuitous. In fact, it helps to explain the motivation of character because Pietro Spina's decision to leave the Church anticipates his subsequent dissatisfaction with the Party: "He had left the Church not because he no longer believed in the dogmas or the efficiency of the sacraments but because it had seemed to him that the Church was identified with the corrupt, wicked and cruel society which it should have been fighting. When he became a socialist, that was all that drove him. He was not yet a Marxist" (p. 95). In effect, he exchanged one form of order for another. For the community whose rule he now accepts has also become a "synagogue" —that is, an institution existing more for the sake of its own dogma than for the people it was intended to help: "Has not the organization ended up by extinguishing in me all moral values, which are held in contempt as petit bourgeois prejudices, and has not the organization itself become the supreme value? Have I then not fled the opportunism of a decadent church to fall into the Machiavellianism of a sect?" (p. 96). Later, when Pietro Spina thinks of leaving the Party, his friend Romeo says that it would be like abandoning the idea: " 'That's false thinking,' said Pietro. 'It'd be like putting the Church before Christ' " (p. 183).

The fact that Christian imagery comes so easily and naturally to Pietro Spina's mind tells us, indirectly, a great deal about the background of this communist who at one time had the ambition "to be a saint" and who still, at least in the Italian text, quotes the New Testament in the Latin he learned as a seminarian. The same tension between Church and Party also justifies the leitmotif of weaving, which is introduced in the first paragraph as Don Benedetto's sister Marta sits at her loom: "The shuttle jumped back and forth in the warp of black and red wool, from left to right and from right to left . . . " (p. 11). The analogy is most clearly rendered through the fact that Pietro Spina, the communist revolutionist, disguises himself as a Catholic priest. Through this symbolic gesture the red and the black are interwoven just as inextricably as in Marta's fabric.

After fifteen years as a loyal Party member Pietro Spina has become just as sick of the abstractions of political theory as he had, years before, of the sterile dogma of the Church. (In this he reflects Silone's own disenchantment with the futile dialectics that he witnessed in 1927 when he represented the Italian Communists at the Moscow Congress.) At the beginning of the novel he is still carrying around some notes on the agrarian revolution—material that could incriminate him if found on his person. Yet he finds himself unable to read them: "It was as if they were written in Chinese. Actually, theory had always bored him" (p. 47). He has returned to Italy, he says, "for air." While he was living abroad and at a distance, Italy "slowly became an abstraction for me and an incubus. I really needed to feel my feet on the ground once more" (p. 40). This Antaean quality distinguishes him from the great revolutionaries—Mazzini, Lenin, Trotsky—who were able to thrive and advance their cause even in exile. Pietro Spina longs above all to live "with my head freed from all abstractions" (p. 84). His return to Italy is therefore a desperate attempt to return to reality and to get away from the "professionalism" that marked the Party (p. 96). This down-to-earth quality that incapacitates Pietro Spina as a theoretician makes him all the more sensitive to human problems of right or wrong. He comes to realize increasingly that "morality can live and flourish only in practical life. . . . The evil to be fought is not that sad abstraction which is called the devil; the evil is everything which prevents millions of men from acting like human beings" (p. 264).

If the great evil that Pietro Spina detects first in the Church and then in the Party is abstraction, its opposite is human commitment. In the novel the supreme symbol of this solidarity is neither the Christian mass nor the meeting of the Party cell, but the sharing of bread and wine in the simple act of human companionship, an idea of community that is not at all remote from the central thought of *The Grapes of Wrath*. This secularized rite of communion through which men commit themselves as human beings to one another occurs often in the course of the novel, but the crucial passage comes close to the end when Pietro Spina shares his last meal with the family of Luigi Murica and explains the sharing of bread and wine as a symbol of human solidarity and unity: " 'The bread is made from many ears of grain,' said Pietro. 'Therefore it signifies unity. The wine is made from many grapes, and therefore it, too, signifies unity. A unity of similar things, equal and united. Therefore it means truth and brotherhood, too; these are things which go well together' " (p. 270). This sense of companionship, as opposed to the arid formalism of the Party, is the true meaning of communism for the people. Speaking of the peasants in *Bread and Wine*, Silone remarks: "To them, Socialism just meant being together" (p. 149).

It is no accident that a writer who is so keenly aware of

the analogy obtaining between Church and Party and who wants to return behind the abstraction of both to purely human relationships should detect in the life of his hero distinct parallels to the life of Jesus. In the note "To the Reader," which is prefaced to his dramatization of the novel, Silone makes it clear that the fictional transfiguration of Pietro Spina was the result of analysis, not chance.[11] An author who begins by depicting contemporary society, he writes, is gradually compelled to search into its structure: "The most notable thing about this society is its antiquity." The conspicuously new element in the present is the proletarian—a figure not unknown to antiquity, but considered not to be proper material for history, thought, or art: "If the condition of this personage appears to us moderns the closest to human truth, it is because between the ancients and us there has come Jesus Christ." What Silone calls the "Christian revolution" has enabled us to see the classical human relationships in a new light: "The rediscovery of a Christian heritage in the revolution of our time remains the most important gain that has been made in these last years for the conscience of our generation." Modern socialism, he concludes, "has gone beyond the narrow boundaries of the bourgeois spirit and has rediscovered its Christian ancestry." (Here we have again a clear analogy of Church and Party.) But this Christian heritage cannot be assumed easily or lightly: "In the sacred history of man on earth, it is still, alas, Good Friday. Men who 'hunger and thirst after righteousness' are still derided, persecuted, put to death." It is neither psychiatric insight nor mythic consciousness that establishes this parallel, but history itself: "The revolution of our epoch, promoted by politicians and economists, thus takes on the form of a 'sacred mystery,' with the very fate of man on earth for its theme."

This conception of the modern condition as a "sacred mystery" legitimizes Silone's fictional transfiguration and

[11] Ignazio Silone, *And He Hid Himself*, trans. Darini Tranquilli (New York: Harper, 1945).

makes of it more than a literary technique brilliantly employed. As we have seen, Silone has at least two valid reasons for making a Jesus-figure of his hero: given the analogy of Church and Party, Spina's criticism of communism and his turn to a less abstract and more human relationship is equivalent to Jesus' criticism of the Pharisees and his teaching of brotherly love; furthermore, as a man who "hungers and thirsts after righteousness" in the Fascist Italy of 1935, Pietro Spina is exposed to all the dangers that threatened Jesus in a Roman-dominated Jerusalem. As a result, the parallels between the modern action and the events of the Gospels do not seem at all contrived in *Bread and Wine*. Pietro Spina's arrival is proclaimed at the beginning by Don Benedetto; he works "miracles" in the provinces before he enters upon his public ministry in Rome; he explains his faith in a new kingdom on earth in the form of parables that can be understood by the peasants and workers; he partakes of a Last Supper of bread and wine before he is betrayed by a Judas figure.

Silone as author takes it upon himself to alert us, on the first page of the novel, to the ritual quality of life, which re-enacts the ancient mysteries in eternal patterns of repetition. As Don Benedetto and his sister sit on their terrace in the April afternoon, Silone describes the scene: "Along the little provincial road, which was as stony and as hard to travel as the bed of a dried-up stream, there came a young farm girl mounted on a small donkey, with a child in her arms. . . . Life as seen from the priest's garden resembled a monotonous old pantomime" (p. 12). And a few pages later it is pointed out that "on almost every hill was a small village that looked like a crèche" (p. 16). (Both of these passages prepare us for the symbolic rebirth of Pietro Spina in the following chapter, when he has returned from Belgian exile to Italy.) In addition, the simple people of the novel, like the villagers in *The Saint*, come to believe rather naively that Pietro Spina is a miracle-worker. The rumor rapidly spreads among the peasants of Pietrasecca that Don

Paolo Spada is more than a priest or doctor—that he is even a saint. Bianchina, whom he had "saved" on her deathbed, seeks him out and attaches herself to him as a devoted servant because she thinks that "he might be Jesus in person" (p. 85). She satisfies her curiosity by inspecting his hands: "There was no trace of the stigmata. No sign of the crucifixion. He was not Jesus. He was a saint, but not Jesus" (p. 87). It is this same Bianchina who later, half-seriously, announces herself in her capacity as Don Paolo's messenger as "Ecce ancilla Domini" (p. 193). This kind of prefigural thinking seems to be familiar to the people of Silone's Abruzzo mountains. R.W.B. Lewis reminds us that the Abruzzese peasants like to recount biblical anecdotes in which the characters turn out to be recognizable as local figures.

In general, however, it is neither the other characters in their simple faith nor Silone as author who creates and points out the parallels between the action and the Gospel, but rather the alert, seminary-trained characters who note with a certain ironic detachment that history has forced them into a Gospel-like role. This accounts for the frequent play with biblical allusions. When Pietro Spina's former classmate, Nunzio Sacca, is secretly summoned to treat him, Pietro tells the frightened doctor: " 'Physician, heal thyself. [Pietro actually cites the Latin of the Vulgate.] I assure you that I'm better off than you. You may not believe me, but it wasn't I who called you' " (p. 40). Nothing could be further from Pietro's mind, of course, than any sense of *imitatio*: he has no wish to identify himself with or to imitate Jesus. But his lively mind, schooled on the Bible, seizes with ironic delight on certain phrases and situations. When the doctor urges Spina to leave Italy, Pietro refuses.

"In that case," said the doctor, "the affair is no concern of mine. I wash my hands of the whole business."
"I like hearing you express yourself in Biblical metaphors," said Pietro ironically. "I see that some of that priestly education has stayed with you." (p. 41)

While Pietro is hiding in a stall at the beginning of the novel, the Gospel analogy also strikes him: "'I feel as if I were in a crèche,' he told Cardile. But for the comparison with the crèche to be complete, he needed a cow on one side and a donkey on another. In his case they weren't lacking, but they were down in the stall" (p. 45). Frequent remarks of this sort reveal both the historical sophistication and ironic sensibility with which Pietro Spina observes his own situation.

Spina is not the only figure in the book who is aware of the parallels. Don Benedetto is urged to sign a declaration of submission to the government and the present policies of the Church to save himself from exile: "My dear Don Angelo,' he answered, 'can you imagine John the Baptist offering a concordat to Herod to escape decapitation? Can you imagine Jesus offering a concordat to Pontius Pilate to avoid being crucified?'" (p. 224). And a short time later, in a conversation with Pietro Spina, Don Benedetto cites John the Baptist to express his feelings about the present "generation of vipers" (p. 231). Don Benedetto's ironic awareness of his role as John to Pietro Spina's Jesus is given an additional poignancy by the fact that he ultimately suffers the fate of the Baptist, being killed at the hands of the Fascists.

When Pietro Spina is vaguely ashamed and annoyed at the necessity of assuming a disguise and changing his name, Don Benedetto reminds him that "the Scriptures are full of clandestine life," citing the flight into Egypt and the occasions when Jesus hid himself from the Judaeans: "'This would not be the first time that the Eternal Father felt obligated to hide Himself and take a pseudonym'" (p. 230). This "religious apologia for the clandestine life made Pietro more serene and illuminated his face with childlike joy." When Pietro Spina is subsequently exposed, it is implied that his betrayer is the priest Don Piccirilli, to whom Don Benedetto had once tellingly remarked: "It is the spirit of Judas Iscariot which poisons men's relationships" (p. 27).

Pietro Spina learns of his betrayal while he is sharing bread and wine with the parents of Luigi Murica, in a scene that bears unmistakable resemblances to the Last Supper. At the end of *Bread and Wine* he simply disappears, having avoided his "crucifixion" by striking off across the mountains in a blizzard. His postfigurative role is completed, however, in the sequel *The Seed Beneath the Snow* (1950). In this novel, which takes place in the four months immediately following Pietro Spina's disappearance, it turns out that he has not gone across the mountains into Switzerland, but that he has returned to his hometown, where he is hidden by his grandmother and other friends. This novel presents us with an entirely new cast of characters, and Pietro Spina is just barely the central figure. At the end, however, he achieves the self-sacrifice and execution that he requires to fulfill his role. When his friend, the half-mad Infante, kills his own father, Pietro Spina sends him away and, not unlike Jim Casy, surrenders to the police: "Handcuffed between two policemen, Pietro was taken to prison. He walked silently and briskly."

Like most of Silone's fiction, *Bread and Wine* is highly episodic in its organization—the original version of 1936 even more than the revised edition of 1955—with no strong continuity of plot. As a result, it depends for its coherence largely upon certain groups of images, which are therefore thrust into even greater prominence in the narrative: the motif of weaving; the motif of the wolves that eventually kill Cristina as she attempts to follow Pietro Spina into the mountains; and above all the pervasive theme of bread and wine. Most importantly, the work is held together by the parallels to the Gospel. In fact, these parallels are not at all conspicuous, scattered as they are throughout the episodic work. But we realize to what a decisive extent the Gospel structure provides the essential framework for the novel if we glance at Silone's dramatization of his novel, *And He Hid Himself*, where even the title refers explicitly to Jesus (John 12:36) and not loosely to the sacrament of the

Eucharist. First of all, the dialogue of the play makes far more frequent and explicit allusion to the Gospel. Second, the scenic representation reflects the allusions. The play opens with the stable scene and its many references to the nativity; Act III is set in a garden (Gethsemane), while in the background one sees a mountain with three crosses "as in images of Calvary," clearly foreshadowing the crucifixion. Act IV, finally, takes place in a room dominated by a large black wooden crucifix and ends with a symbolic evocation of the Last Supper as Pietro Spina shares bread and wine with his friends. In general, the play has stripped down the plot of the novel in such a way that secondary scenes and narrative lines have vanished, exposing the fictional transfiguration in much greater prominence and revealing Pietro Spina's destiny as a "sacred mystery."

The close correspondences between Silone's novel and *The Saint* can be attributed in part to the fact that both works go back to a common source in the Gospels. Yet numerous other similarities in detail—e.g., the parallels between Giovanni Selva and Don Benedetto, or the hero torn between the spirituality of virginal faith and the sensuality of womanly passion—force us to recognize, in conclusion, that the differences between the Christian socialist and the Marxist transfigurations lie not so much in plot and organization as in theme and consciousness.

At least three factors justify us in using the term Comrade Jesus to define the hero of *Bread and Wine*. First, the analogy of Church and Party suggests that Pietro Spina stands in the same critical relationship to the Party as did Jesus to the institutionalized religion of his day: both seek human commitment rather than dogma and abstraction. Second, Silone's historical consciousness understands that the revolutionary hero of the present must inevitably re-enact the "sacred mystery" of the New Testament: "In the sacred history of man on earth, it is still, alas, Good Friday." Finally, the Marxist hero of the present has such a sense of ironic detachment that, without a trace of paranoia or mysticism, he can appreciate the parallels between his own life, into which he has been hurled by history, and the "sacred mystery" of the Passion, which continues to be the pattern for life on earth. This thinking in analogies, this historical consciousness, and this sense of ironic detachment— these same three features permit us to see in the hero of Arthur Koestler's *Darkness at Noon* another hypostasis of Comrade Jesus.

At first glance few novels might seem more dissimilar than Silone's rambling narrative of a revolutionary turned priest and Koestler's compact account of the hearings of the Party functionary N. S. Rubashov. Whereas Pietro Spina's adventures lead him from the Italian mountains to the slums of Rome, Rubashov is limited to the interrogation room of his prison and the cell where he is confined between the three hearings. The sprawling multiplicity of characters from every level of Italian society with whom Spina comes in contact is reduced to the two men who interrogate Rubashov, the warden who brings him his occasional meal, the eye that peers through the judas window of his cell, and the sparse figures of his memory. Yet for all the formal differences between the epic richness of the one and the Aristotelian economy of the other, there are undeniable similarities between *Bread and Wine* and *Darkness at Noon* —beginning, one might note, with the vaguely biblical allusions in the titles of these works devoted to communism or, more specifically, to defection from the Party.

Both novels, in fact, can be regarded as fictional anticipations of the *apologiae* that the two writers subsequently contributed to *The God That Failed*. But whereas Silone's novel is a largely autobiographical account of the reasons for his own defection, Koestler's book is an attempt to explain to the non-communist world the mentality that produced the spectacle of the Moscow Trials.[12] Specifically

[12] Peter Alfred Huber, *Arthur Koestler: Das literarische Werk* (Zürich: Fretz und Wasmuth, 1962), p. 14.

Rubashov is forced to the conclusion, in the course of his interrogation, that certain seemingly minor swervings from strict Marxist ideology have made him at least theoretically capable and guilty of the various crimes of which he stands accused. As a result, to maintain Party unity he "confesses" and consents to his punishment. At the same time, his initial doubts show that Rubashov is subject to precisely the same kind of skepticism that plagued Pietro Spina and ultimately led to his defection.

In the world of *Bread and Wine* the Gospel parallels are natural and very much in place: the analogy rises smoothly to the minds of the simple religious peasants or the seminary-trained skeptics in a land whose Church still officially underwrites the policy of the Fascist government. In Koestler's Russia the situation is totally different. The government is monolithically and officially atheistic, and the portrait of "No. 1" glowers down from walls where formerly the icons of Christ were suspended. The only believing Christian in the entire work is the porter Wassilij, whose Marxist daughter has thrown away his Bible "for educational reasons." Otherwise, the figures have either lost their faith, or they are so young that they have been raised without faith. For the prosecutor Gletkin, Jesus Christ is nothing but a fairy-tale figure that he vaguely recalls from the mutterings of the village priest. For his older and more sophisticated colleague Ivanov, Christianity is a familiar myth with which he plays ironically. "I would like to write a Passion play in which God and the Devil dispute for the soul of Saint Rubashov," he muses (p. 149).[13] And in another place he contrasts Judas favorably with such traitors as Gandhi and Tolstoy: "Gandhi's inner voice has done more to prevent the liberation of India than the British guns. To sell oneself for thirty pieces of silver is an honest

---

[13] *Darkness at Noon* cited according to the Modern Library edition (New York, n.d.). Koestler's German text was lost; hence the English translation by Daphne Hardy, published in England in 1940, must be regarded as the original edition.

transaction; but to sell oneself to one's own conscience is to abandon mankind. History is *a priori* amoral; it has no conscience" (p. 153). He is even capable of quoting Jesus in order to ward off the temptation represented by Rubashov's arguments: "'*Apage Satanas!*' repeated Ivanov and poured himself out another glass. 'In old days, temptation was of carnal nature. Now it takes the form of pure reason'" (p. 149). In an atheistic dictatorship, where even a metaphor mixing state and religion can be a crime, it is no accident that Ivanov is eventually liquidated for false thinking.

Within this context of political repression Rubashov repeatedly finds himself thinking of the Party if not in churchly, then at least in more generally religious, terms: "The Party's warm, breathing body appeared to him to be covered with sores—festering sores, bleeding stigmata. When and where in history had there ever been such defective saints?" (pp. 57-58). One of Rubashov's favorite images, which occurs several times in the course of the novel, stems from the comparison of post-revolutionary Russian history to the great Exodus: "What happened to these masses, to this people? For forty years it had been driven through the desert, with threats and promises, with imaginary terrors and imaginary rewards. But where was the Promised Land?" (p. 266).

These analogies are not incidental or peripheral. The imagery that suggests itself to Rubashov points to the underlying pattern of thought that has led to his arrest. "I don't approve of mixing ideologies," Ivanov tells him, arguing that the only two possible conceptions of human ethics are radically opposed: "One of them is Christian and humane, declares the individual to be sacrosanct, and that the rules of arithmetic are not to be applied to human units. The other starts from the basic principle that a collective aim justifies all means, and not only allows, but demands that the individual should in every way be subordinated and sacrificed to the community . . ." (pp. 156-57). Ivanov is expressing precisely the inhuman dedication to Party unity at the expense of individual liberty that shocked Silone at the Moscow Congress of 1927 and gradually drove him out of the Party. And although Rubashov has not yet reached the point of Pietro Spina, his "mixed ideology," which permits "Christian and humane" sentiments to weaken his Marxism, clearly contributes to his downfall. Like Pietro Spina, Rubashov has begun to criticize communism as an institution.

Rubashov is in jail because he has been accused of an attempt on the life of "No. 1"—a charge that not only he but also his prosecutors know to be patently absurd. In a deeper sense, however, Rubashov comes to realize that he is indeed guilty in principle: for a man who even in theory concedes the fallibility of the State is capable of acting against it. When Rubashov has finally been brought to the point of acknowledging this theoretical guilt, he hopes that he can once again be a useful member of the Party. But the Party expects a final sacrifice from him: to function as a scapegoat. " 'Your task is simple,' " Gletkin tells him after he has "confessed" to all the crimes of which he has been accused: " 'to gild the Right, to blacken the Wrong.' " Rubashov is expected to make the masses understand, in the simplest language, that opposition is a crime and that the leaders of the opposition are criminals: " 'If you begin to talk of your complicated motives, you will only create confusion amongst them' " (pp. 237-38). Although Rubashov recognizes the absurdity of the charges and although he has come to question the logical consistency of Marxist reasoning, he agrees to sign the statement: "Premises of unimpeachable truth had led to a result which was completely absurd; Ivanov's and Gletkin's irrefutable deductions had taken him straight into the weird and ghostly game of the public trial. Perhaps it was not suitable for a man to think every thought to its logical conclusion" (p. 258).

This softening of Rubashov's rigorous Marxism parallels Pietro Spina's disenchantment with abstraction: and the religious imagery to which both men cling expresses their shift from sterile dogma to a more human commitment. At the same time, when he agrees to an act of ritual self-sacrifice for the sake of the masses, Rubashov is clearly aware of the parallel to the life of Jesus that history has forced upon him: "That the whole thing came to this—to punish him, not for deeds he had committed, but for those he had neglected to commit? 'One can only be crucified in the name of one's own faith,' had said comfortable Herr von Z . . . " (p. 219).

Because of his tendency to think in analogies, which constantly supplies religious imagery for political circumstances, and because this general tendency is forced into a more specific channel by his historical consciousness, which supplies parallels between his own situation and that of Jesus, Rubashov constantly entertains such parallels with ironic satisfaction. Two hours after his arrest, for instance, Rubashov lies in his cell, smoking and looking at his feet: "He slowly moved his toes in the sock and a verse occurred to him which compared the feet of Christ to a white roebuck in a thornbush" (p. 13). It is a sign of Rubashov's ironic detachment that the biblical associations frequently occur to him through the mediation of art. As he attempts to envisage the prisoner in the neighboring cell, who implores for communication by tapping through the walls, Rubashov thinks: "Perhaps he was kneeling on the bunk with his hands folded—like the prisoner in No. 407 had folded them to receive his piece of bread. And now at last Rubashov knew of what experience this gesture had reminded him—the imploring gesture of the meagre, stretched-out hands. *Pietà* . . . " (p. 31). This association leads, in turn, to the recollection of a meeting with a Party agent in a German art musuem. Sitting on a plush sofa opposite an early German ink drawing of the *pietà*, Rubashov had had to reject the pleas for help from a young German agent and, in fact, send him to his death. The religious *topos* therefore becomes a recurrent image in Rubashov's mind for his own defection from the Party line: his "mixed ideology" that inserts the human element into Marxist dogma.

Much later in the book, when Rubashov is confronted with the informer who has betrayed him, Rubashov's ironic appreciation of the situation is made explicit: "Again the young man's gaze sought Rubashov's face with a forlorn and almost tender expression. Rubashov had the absurd notion that he was about to come over from the wall and kiss him on the forehead" (p. 203). In addition, quotations or paraphrases from the Bible smuggle their way almost unwittingly into Rubashov's thought and speech: "Did the righteous man perhaps carry the heaviest debt when weighed by this other measure? Was his debt, perhaps, counted double—for the others knew not what they did? . . . " (p. 56). Or later, after Rubashov has confessed to the first of the seven false charges that have been brought against him: "He had believed that he had drunk the cup of humiliation to the dregs" (p. 213).

In a novel with the compact organization of *Darkness at Noon* we do not expect to find the same parallels of plot that occur in the more episodic *Bread and Wine*. The parallels exist for the most part in the ironic awareness of the sophisticated hero and his former colleague Ivanov. Yet Koestler as author has also done his part to bring out the transfiguration. The title, of course, refers to the darkness that covered Jerusalem at the time of Jesus' crucifixion: "Now from the sixth hour there was darkness over all the land unto the ninth hour" (Matt: 27:45; also Mark and Luke). Just before Rubashov is fetched for his execution, he reflects that the Party had reached its present nadir because it neglected ethics for the sake of reason: "Perhaps now would come the time of great darkness. Perhaps later, much later, the new movement would arise—with new flags, a new spirit knowing of both: of economic fatality *and* the 'oceanic sense' " (p. 260). The title, then, suggests both the analogy of Church and State and the historical consciousness that Rubashov is fulfilling a role that corresponds to that of Jesus. In Silone's terms, he is re-enacting the "sacred mystery" of the revolution. In addition, Rubashov's career at least delicately recapitulates certain parallels. As secretary of the trade delegation he has twelve assistants; his missions to the various foreign outposts of the Party are missions of doctrinal preaching. He is ultimately betrayed by a former friend whom he likens, in his imagination, to Judas; he is interrogated by a Pilate-like Ivanov, who attempts to bargain with him for his life; finally, like Jesus, he accepts punishment for crimes that he did not commit in order to benefit the faith of the masses. He dies with the knowledge that his execution presages a new "darkness at noon."

After the understatement of the plot-parallels and the subtlety of Rubashov's ironic consciousness, the episode of the porter Wassilij—inserted just a few pages from the end —strikes us as a gesture of compromise, Koestler's last-minute reminder to the obtuse reader that his hero is, after all, a fictional transfiguration of Jesus. In these few pages— the only scene that takes place outside the prison—the old porter Wassilij listens to his daughter read a newspaper account of Rubashov's public trial. Wassilij is still a devout Christian; and although his daughter has removed his Bible, he still knows many passages by heart; in addition, he had formerly known Rubashov. A fugue-like counterpart arises as Wassilij supplies appropriate quotations for the proceedings in the courtroom.

"It is typical of the correct procedure of revolutionary justice that the President immediately granted this wish and, with a shrug of contempt, gave the order for the hearing to be interrupted for five minutes."

The porter Wassilij lay on his back and thought of the time when Rubashov had been conducted in triumph through the meetings, after his rescue from the foreigners; and of how he had stood leaning on his crutches up on the platform under the red flags and decorations, and, smiling, had rubbed his glasses on his sleeve, while the cheerings and shoutings never ceased.

*"And the soldiers led him away, into the hall called
Praetorium; and they called together the whole band.
And they clothed him with purple and they smote him
on the head with a reed and did spit upon him; and
bowing their knees worshipped him."* (p. 246)

Wassilij's daughter shows him a resolution demanding that
the traitors be mercilessly exterminated and insists that he
sign it:

> He squinted over to the paper, which lay spread next
> to the Primus stove. Then he turned his head away
> quickly.
> *"And he said: I tell thee, Peter, the cock shall not
> crow this day before that thou shalt thrice deny that
> thou knowest me. . . . "* (p. 247)

When Wassilij signs the resolution, he contributes to the
fictional transfiguration by assuming the role of Peter. But
at the same time, in all his human weakness he foreshadows
the "new movement" and "new spirit" that Rubashov anticipates after the "darkness at noon." Acting out of fear though
he does, he at least does not share the virtually mechanical
faith in pure reason and Party logic that motivates his
daughter. At some time in the future, Koestler seems to imply or at least hope, this spark of human decency will incite
a new race of Peters to create a new state just as the biblical
Peter created a new Church. So the book ends with the
same kind of analogical thinking with which it began.

For all the similarities—in analogical thinking, in historical consciousness, in ironic awareness—that unite the
two books, *Bread and Wine* and *Darkness at Noon* are ultimately distinguished by one fundamental difference. Silone
was attempting to justify his departure from the Party,
while Koestler was trying to explain the motivations for
such an absurd happening as the Moscow Trials. Pietro
Spina generates an immense faith in the human individual
that sustains him when he loses the intellectual support that

originally had led him from the Church to the Party: he now believes in the companionship of bread and wine. Rubashov, in contrast, is still a faithful Party member who wishes to continue serving the Party—whose death, in fact, is an ultimate gesture of faith in the Party. In his final speech to the court he says: "There is nothing for which one could die, if one died without having repented and unreconciled with the Party and the Movement" (p. 251). If we think in analogies, we understand that this last sacrifice for the Party is in fact motivated by the same impulse that motivated so many sacrifices for the Church. As Koestler put it ten years later in *The Age of Longing* (1951): "As religious convictions have been replaced by social idolatry while man's instinctive horror of apostasy remained the same, we are all bound to perish as victims of our secular loyalties."

If we limit the category "Comrade Jesus" to include only those fictional transfigurations that are somehow Party-oriented, then Graham Greene's "whiskey priest" does not belong, strictly speaking, in the company of the proto-communist Jim Casy, the communist Rubashov, or the post-communist Pietro Spina. Yet Greene (born 1904) cannot deny his membership in the generation of Steinbeck, Silone, and Koestler; and his obligatory though perfunctory flirtation with communism before he was converted to Catholicism in 1926 provides him with essentially the same intellectual background. As a result, although its hero is a priest rather than a Party agent, *The Power and the Glory* (1940) can be grasped most readily within the intellectual framework that characterizes the other works we have discussed in this chapter.

R.W.B. Lewis has observed that Greene's whiskey priest is, "if not the twin, at least a brother of Pietro Spina": both men represent the last voice of truth in a totalitarian society, and their flight from oppression—the one in Fascist Italy, the other in the Marxist state of Tabasco in Mexico—

takes the form of an episodic series of encounters.[14] At the same time, Lewis's aperçu can be qualified with the observation that Greene's novel, if we disregard the secondary episodes and concentrate on the central theme, boils down to a plot as dramatically compact in its organization as *Darkness at Noon*. The three confrontations between the idealistic police officer, who for all his good intentions manages to stifle life, and the drunken priest, who in all his degeneracy succeeds in embodying the power and the glory of the human condition, have all the inevitability of a Greek tragedy and all the elegance of a *pas de deux*.

Greene is familiar, like Silone and Koestler, with the analogical thinking that sets up parallels between Church and State: in the 1962 introduction to his novel he speaks of "the totalitarian states, whether of the right or of the left, with which the Church of Rome is often compared."[15] But within the novel this analogy does not play a central role: analogical thinking, after all, is useful only to the extent that the Comrade Jesus stands in the same critical relationship to the Party as Jesus to the organized Church. Here, in contrast, the priest is the sole representative of the Church in a state that has officially abolished religion. Curiously, however, Greene makes use of the analogy in a different way, for his antagonist, the police lieutenant, is specifically described as having priest-like characteristics: "There was something of a priest in his intent observant walk—a theologian going back over the errors of the past to destroy them again" (p. 32). And by candlelight his lodging "looked as comfortless as a prison or a monastic cell." In Greene's hands the conventional analogy assumes a new and more complex function: it helps to emphasize the ironic ambiva-

[14] *The Picaresque Saint*, p. 249. See also Francis L. Kunkel, *The Labyrinthine Ways of Graham Greene* (New York: Sheed and Ward, 1959); A. A. DeVitis, *Graham Greene* (New York: Twayne, 1964); and John Atkins, *Graham Greene* (London: Calder and Boyars, 1966).

[15] *The Power and the Glory* cited according to the Compass Book edition (New York: Viking, 1958); here, p. 5.

lence in the characters of the slovenly priest and the hard but idealistic representative of the state. The black-and-white characterization of Silone and Koestler is missing here; protagonist and antagonist are complementary figures.

If the analogical pattern is not so conspicuous, the historical consciousness emerges quite explicitly in Greene's thought. History, in fact, provided Greene with his story. In the winter of 1937-38 Greene made a trip to Mexico to gather material for a study of the religious persecution, which had reached its height in the states of Tabasco and Chiapas. (This is the Mexico of which the *cristero* Guadalupe tells Manuel in Coccioli's novel.) His account of that journey in *The Lawless Roads* (1939) anticipates virtually every scene and character of his novel—from the "fanged mestizo," who becomes the Judas of his persecuted cleric, to the priests themselves, whose lives constituted the model for Greene's unnamed "whiskey priest." We read of a priest who has been hiding for years in the swamps, one step ahead of the police. And Greene dwells at some length on the story of Father Miguel Pro, who, executed by the government of President Calles in November, 1927, subsequently became a kind of folk hero and furnished other details for Greene's hero. In short, Greene did not transpose the events of the Passion from the Gospel into modern society; history supplied the parallels, and he had only to draw the consequences. He does this within the novel in two separate places. A sub-plot seemingly contrived expressly for this purpose tells of a mother who reads to her three children from an inspirational work smuggled in every month from Mexico City; it deals with a devout young Mexican boy who remains true to his faith despite the persecution. Twice within this sub-plot there is reference to a children's play based on the persecution of the early Christians:

> " 'It was he,' " she said, " 'who obtained permission to perform a little one-act play founded on . . . ' "

"I know, I know," the boy said. "The catacombs."

The mother, compressing her lips, continued:
"'... the persecution of the Early Christians.'"
(p. 67)

It is against this background of primitive Christianity that we witness the persecution of the transfigured hero by the fanatical police lieutenant through the desolate world of Greene's novel. The key word in *The Power and the Glory* is "abandoned": along with such synonyms as "left," "deserted," "vacant," it sets the emotional tone for the entire narrative. The geographical isolation of the remote state of Tabasco is symptomatic of the loneliness of men "in the whole abandoned star." Now the two principal characters react to this "abandonment" in wholly different ways. For the lieutenant, the priest-like adherent of the new Marxist society, this "vacant universe" represents a challenge and an opportunity to construct a new world. For the sake of the Mexican children, to whom he is attached with an almost pederastic affection, he is prepared to sacrifice everything; he would ruthlessly exploit any means to achieve his end: "He was quite prepared to make a massacre for their sakes—first the Church and then the foreigner and then the politician—even his own chief would one day have to go. He wanted to begin the world again with them, in a desert" (p. 77). His monomaniacal pursuit of the priest, the last vestige of the detested Church in the entire state, has something inhumanly implacable about it. As a pure tool of the state he resembles no one so much as Koestler's prosecutor, Gletkin; both men are repeatedly characterized by the creaking leather of their gun holsters.

For most people, however, this sense of abandonment—by man, by God, by the world—has produced the very opposite of the lieutenant's confident optimism: they have given way to "despair—the unforgivable sin" (p. 66, p. 83). Again we are reminded of Koestler, who noted that men require a framework, a support for their faith, whether in the

217

form of the Church or the Party. Tabasco is in a state of despair precisely because most of its citizens, abandoned by their Church and not yet absorbed by the Party, have nothing to which to cling. Hence like the porter Wassilij they read the tattered little devotional volumes smuggled in from other provinces. And hence they cling so pathetically to the whiskey priest, an ecclesiastical scandal, a man who has broken his vows of chastity: "He was the only priest most of them had ever known—they took their standard of the priesthood from him" (p. 91). For all his human frailty, the priest is sustained by the knowledge that he alone must bear the awesome burden of the Church against the entire state.

The action of the novel revolves around three encounters between the priest and the lieutenant, twice when the officer does not recognize his prey and the last time when he arrests and executes him. This action (Part II and Part III) is narrated from the point of view of the whiskey priest himself. Parts I and IV, in contrast, constitute a framework in which we witness the priest and the action from a variety of external points of view: Mr. Tench the dentist; the lieutenant; the little boy who listens to his mother read the clandestine stories; the married priest José; Captain Fellows and the little girl Coral. Whereas Part I shows us these characters in their despair and abandonment, in Part IV we see the impact of the priest's death on many of these same figures. Only with respect to this framework can it be said that the novel is a series of picaresque encounters; the eight central chapters have all the taut economy of an Aristotelian drama. In Part II the priest is in desperate flight, fearful of betrayal, toward the border of a neighboring province. Having resigned himself to the realization that he can no longer help his people, that indeed his presence brings punishment upon those who are suspected of aiding him, he has decided to give up what Silone's Don Benedetto called "the clandestine life" and to seek refuge. Twice he narrowly escapes the lieutenant: once when the police search a village where he is hiding and a second time when he is fortuitously arrested for possession of alcohol. But at the beginning of Part III the priest has crossed the border and is recovering from his tribulations in the home of a North American landowner. After a few days of rest he plans to go to the nearby town of Las Casas, where he can once again begin a normal priestly life. But on the day he sets out he is lured back across the border into Tabasco— to administer Extreme Unction to a dying outlaw—where he is captured by his relentless pursuer, who takes him back to town for trial and execution.

It is largely the priest's own ironic awareness that perceives what Silone would call the "sacred mystery" of this plot. When we meet the priest, he has been in flight and hiding for years. Starving, ravished by drink, fear, and conscience, he is a far cry from the sophisticated Pietro Spina and Rubashov. Yet his education and training in a North American missionary seminary have provided him with a detached awareness of his own state that is wholly lacking in the other characters. Years of fear have even honed his originally somewhat fatuous sense of humor into a keen blade of irony. In one flashback, for instance, he recalls a dinner given in honor of the tenth anniversary of his ordination: "He sat in the middle of the table with—who was it on his right hand? There were twelve dishes—he had said something about the Apostles, too, which was not thought to be in the best of taste" (pp. 124-25). Now that his Passion has become earnest, he no longer takes the same pleasure in such jokes.

In the course of the novel several more or less incidental New Testament motifs crop up seemingly at random. When the priest has said mass in the village and then takes cover as the police invade the village at dawn, the cock crows. It is perfectly clear that the cock is a response to the priest's own fear of betrayal and denial by the villagers: "Again the cock crew. If they were so careful, they must know beyond the shadow of a doubt that he was here. It *was* the end." In general, however, there are two main areas in which his ironic consciousness is constantly at work. The first is the Judas-motif that arises from the priest's obsession with betrayal. The first suggestion comes early in Part II when the yellow-toothed mestizo attaches himself to the fleeing priest as a guide: "He knew. He was in the presence of Judas" (p. 123). From this point on the Judas-motif recurs constantly, and in every case it exists solely in the priest's own consciousness. A few pages later, for instance, he sees "the yellow malarial eyes of the mestizo watching him. Christ would not have found Judas sleeping in the garden: Judas could watch more than one hour" (p. 124). When the half-breed stumbles in the false dawn, "a small coal of cruel satisfaction glowed at the back of the priest's mind—this was Judas sick and unsteady and scared in the dark" (p. 133).

The second area of ironic awareness revolves around the criminal James Calver, who is wanted in the United States for bank robbery and homicide. We first hear of Calver when the lieutenant pins his "Wanted" notice on his office wall, facing the only photograph he has of the detested priest, an old newspaper photograph of a first communion party: "On the wall of the office the gangster still stared stubbornly in profile toward the first communion party: somebody had inked the priest's head round to detach him from the girls' and the women's faces: the unbearable grin peeked out of a halo" (p. 78). This motif of the two photographs, repeated frequently throughout the novel, must transmit almost more meaning than it can bear. First, we note that the photograph of the priest has been defaced in such a way as to make it resemble a picture of Jesus with nimbus; this helps to strengthen the transfiguration theme. Second, although the priest (like the lieutenant) remains nameless throughout the novel, the American gangster oddly has a name whose initials remind us of Jesus Christ and whose surname unmistakably suggests the Calvary toward which he will eventually lead the priest. Finally, it is only the fortuitous circumstance that the two pictures are juxtaposed on the office wall, where the priest sees them, that contributes to the sense of responsibility the priest feels for this criminal he has never met: "the two faces—his own and the gunman's—were hanging together on the police-station wall, as if they were brothers in a family portrait gallery. You didn't put temptation in a brother's way" (p. 211). Only this curious subliminal feeling of responsibility makes the priest, already safely across the border, susceptible to the importuning of the mestizo Judas, who slyly entices him back into Tabasco to administer the last rites to the dying gangster. In the New Testament symbolism of the novel, then, it is Judas again who leads Jesus to his Calvary.

The parallels do not stop here. When the priest finally reaches the gunman, he urges him with specific reference to the good thief on the cross at Golgotha (hence perhaps the name Calver?) to seek repentance: "You believed once. Try and understand—this is your chance. At the last moment. Like the thief" (p. 254). When the priest is returned to the town for trial, the lieutenant seeks out the renegade priest José and offers him an opportunity to hear his colleague's confession with impunity. But, like Peter, Padre José denies the priest and refuses to go to him, denying him his final consolation. The priest's last night in jail turns into his Gethsemane: "This night was slower than the last he spent in prison because he was alone. Only the brandy, which he finished about two in the morning, gave him any sleep at all. He felt sick with fear, his stomach ached, and his mouth was dry with the drink. He began to talk aloud to himself because he couldn't stand the silence any more" (p. 282). In the modern secularization of what Silone called the "sacred mystery," of course, we do not find the dignity conventionally associated with the cross in Christian thought. Greene's whiskey priest, like Faulkner's corporal, is executed by firing squad; Rubashov is liquidated with a bullet in the back of the neck.

Greene's priest dies afflicted by the despair and abandonment that eats away at the entire state: "He felt only an immense disappointment because he had to go to God empty-handed, with nothing done at all. It seemed to him at that moment that it would have been quite easy to have been a saint. It would only have needed a little self-restraint and a little courage" (p. 284). However, he dies with the feeling that he has "missed happiness by seconds at an appointed place." But although the individual is denied any consolation in Greene's abandoned world, the author seems to suggest that humanity as a whole will endure through its power and glory. This sense is achieved in the final scene of the novel, which—extending the technique of the transfiguration—functions virtually as a resurrection. We see the little boy Juan, in whose imagination fiction and reality come together as he realizes that the priest his family once sheltered was in fact a hero like the other martyrs of the Church whose lives are recorded in the forbidden little books. When he hears of the priest's death, he understands that he had "had a hero in the house, though it had only been for twenty-four hours. And he was the last" (p. 298). As he lies in bed, "resentful" and "deceived" because the heroic has been removed from his otherwise ordinary life, there is a knock at the door. At first the boy refuses to let the tall, pale stranger in, but the visitor explains with a frightened smile that he is a priest.

"You?" the boy exclaimed.

"Yes," he said gently. "My name is Father—" But the boy had already swung the door open and put his lips to his hand before the other could give himself a name. (p. 301)

In a higher sense Greene's whiskey priest, whose only "miracles" amount to a few card tricks that he used to perform at parish entertainments, is also a Comrade Jesus. He meets Jim Casy, Pietro Spina, and Rubashov on the common ground of a humanity that transcends all institutional dogma, whether of Church or Party. This lapsed priest, who has succumbed to fornication, drink, and the sins of pride and despair, has nevertheless devoted the last eight years of his life to the service of his fellow man and specifically *without* the support of the Church, which has withdrawn from Tabasco into safer refuges. It is in the last analysis as a man, as a comrade, that he says mass for the villagers or prisoners in the jail; and it is as Comrade Jesus that he eschews the security of the Church to give up his life for the sake of the criminal James Calver.

It is noteworthy that all four of the novels we have considered in this chapter have New Testament titles, but all of them refer to symbolic qualities or circumstances rather than to the person of Jesus (as was the case, for instance, in the Christian socialist transfigurations). This fact suggests at least two implications. First, it reflects the total secularization not just of the figure of Jesus, but of the Christian "message." "The grapes of wrath" refer quite specifically to the California grapes and the righteous anger of the exploited migrants; "bread and wine" has been taken away from the Church as a sacrament and handed over to the people as a purely human rite of companionship; "darkness at noon" adumbrates the darkest period in the history of Russian communism. And "the power and the glory" describes, not at all ironically, the enduring qualities in mankind and, specifically, in the lapsed whiskey priest. Second, these biblical allusions alert the reader to the symbolic or allegorical dimension of the works—a dimension that needs some signaling since it does not consist in the often heavy-handed construction of plot parallels that is so often found in earlier, less sophisticated, transfigurations. Here, as we have noted, the transfiguration takes place primarily in the ironic awareness of the hero, who is detached and intelligent enough to recognize the parallels into which he has been thrust by history.

Both the sense of history and the keen awareness of social reality distinguish these novels from the headier abstractions of the mythic transfigurations, while the hero's ironic consciousness separates him from the paranoid Jesuses. The fictional transfiguration, as a genre, has grown far more sophisticated since the earliest Christian socialist work: it now operates with understatement instead of clumsy allegory and it has become a vehicle for broader human concerns.

7. The Fifth Gospels

THE FOUR GROUPS of novels that we have considered up to this point share at least two features that relate them thematically and structurally. They all explicitly advance or implicitly express a moral conviction of some sort; this means in turn that the transfigured hero is taken seriously and thrust into the center of the narrative as the mouthpiece of the author's theme. This was evident in the case of the Christian socialists, where the hero acted as the advocate of ecclesiastical or social reform. Similarly, for the Marxist-oriented writers—in many senses the linear descendants of the Christian socialists—it is Comrade Jesus, the sincere spokesman of a new humanity, who holds the often loosely picaresque narrative together largely through the force of his own personality. For writers with psychiatric interest the transfigured hero is central because he becomes the object of an almost clinical scrutiny; at the same time, for all their paranoia both Quint and Manolios are humanly attractive men who embody a singularly pure Christianity. In the mythic transfigurations, finally, the role of the transfigured hero is somewhat reduced as the narrator moves into the foreground (Hesse, Coccioli) or as other mythic figures assume an equal significance (e.g., Faulkner's supreme commander). Yet the Jesus-figure still occupies the thematic center of the narrative, representing in Hesse's words "an extraordinary shadow image in which humanity has painted itself on the wall of eternity."

At no point up to now have their transfigurations suggested that these authors have anything but the highest regard for the figure of Jesus. Whether they view him as historically real or as the mythic projection of an ideal vision, whether they believe in him as Christians or admire him as humanists, these writers invariably display a respect for the man who supplied the figural pattern for their modern heroes. And it is precisely because of this esteem that

225

they invoke the form of the fictional transfiguration: they want to exploit certain associations that accrue to the figure of Jesus.

The last generation to share these assumptions was born around 1900 and its members—Steinbeck, Silone, Koestler, Greene—produced their transfigurations around 1940. (*The Greek Passion* and *A Fable* appeared a decade later, of course; but both Kazantzakis and Faulkner were born before the turn of the century, and their works were actually carry-overs of the older psychiatric and mythic views of Jesus.) When we turn to the next distinct generation of writers—those born in the late twenties and early thirties—the whole pattern changes. Lars Görling's transfigured hero is an incompetent young social worker incapable of helping his wards; Günter Grass portrays his Jesus-figure as a gangling schoolboy with an enlarged Adam's apple who performs legendary feats of masturbation, while Gore Vidal shows us a religious charlatan whose charisma is exploited by unscrupulous publicity agents. John Barth, finally, has reincarnated Jesus in the person of a faun-like undergraduate sired through artificial insemination by a giant computer. An unlikely lot of saviors indeed!

It is easy to speculate on the reasons underlying this shift in attitude. It is in part the inevitable concomitant of a theological movement that has attained public prominence by proclaiming the death of God; for if God is dead, then it follows that Jesus might be reduced proportionately in his role—either to a charlatan, say, or a misguided idealist.[1] It could also be suggested that an age grown skeptical of heroic action was ultimately bound to reduce Jesus, too, to the status of anti-hero. But such speculations, as fascinating as they may be to cultural historians and critics of society, are not germane to our considerations. We found it necessary, in earlier chapters, to discuss at least briefly the Christian socialist, the psychiatric, the mythic, and the Marxist

[1] E.g., Neill Q. Hamilton, *Jesus for a No-God World* (Philadelphia: Westminster Press, 1969).

views of Jesus because the earlier fictional transfigurations were for the most part a projection of certain current and well-defined attitudes toward Jesus. But this last group of novels is not unified by any common view of Jesus or any positive response to society. If they do indeed constitute a group, it is for negative reasons: moral neutralism has replaced any positive theme; and in structure a serious treatment has given way to parody. These factors, however, can easily be ascertained without any reference to the *Zeitgeist*; they are evident in the attitudes and works of the writers of this generation.

Earlier generations were born into a religious faith that they subsequently had to modify or even discard as a result of serious intellectual struggle—the cases of Fogazzaro, Hauptmann, Hesse, and Silone spring to mind as representative of their groups. But whatever the outcome of their *crise de conscience* might be, the inherited religious background remained with them as a common cultural possession long after faith had evaporated. In *Darkness at Noon* Koestler indicates how the generation gap can be reflected through attitudes toward religion: both Rubashov and Ivanov have lost their faith or, rather, substituted Marxism for the Church. But the faith they once shared provides them with an ironic sense that sets them apart from the young Gletkin, who recalls random stories of Jesus as one might recall the fairy tales of his childhood. That Rubashov and Ivanov perish at Gletkin's hands can be read as, among other things, Koestler's comment on the fate of religion in modern society.

Gletkin, in any case, is more representative than Rubashov and Ivanov of the writers born after World War I, who constitute to a great extent a post-religious generation. Many of them were raised without religious faith; and if they began with faith, it was usually not so deep-rooted that their discarding it was traumatic. In a 1952 lecture Gore Vidal (born 1925) stated his own lack of belief in the conventional religious certainties: "I accept the universe as im-

227

personal, a great *is* which contains us all living or dead."[2] It is not the loss of faith that distinguishes this attitude from earlier agnostics or atheists, but rather the casual indifference with which the entire matter is handled. We find here none of the self-righteous chest-thumping of those late nineteenth-century theologians of Ibsen and Hauptmann who have given up their faith, nor even the wistful irony of the Christians-turned-Marxist of the thirties. Günter Grass (born 1927) is typical of the new breed. A Catholic who lapsed into non-belief, Grass remarked to an interviewer with a nonchalance unimaginable in earlier times: "Questions of religion simply do not disquiet me."[3] The moral neutralism stemming from their loss of faith distinguishes this generation from its predecessors—most notably from the Marxists of the thirties, who always knew precisely where they stood and where their values were situated. Thus Todd Andrews, the hero of John Barth's early novel *The Floating Opera* (1956), remarks that "Nothing has intrinsic value." Though these writers may have arrived at this neutral stance independently, it has become the hallmark of the generation. In an interview John Barth (born 1930) recalls: "I thought that I had invented nihilism in 1953"[4]; but subsequent experiences made it clear to him that his attitude was representative rather than exceptional. The individual cases of Vidal, Grass, and Barth bear out the generalization of Ihab Hassan, who suggests that what he calls "the existential novel" is devoid of any presuppositions concerning formerly accepted values, traditions, or beliefs.[5]

When such writers approach the New Testament, it is

[2] Quoted from unpublished manuscripts by Ray Lewis White, *Gore Vidal* (New York: Twayne, 1968), p. 35.

[3] Interview with Geno Hartlaub in the Hamburg *Sonntagsblatt*, January 1, 1967; quoted in Wilhelm Johannes Schwarz, *Der Erzähler Günter Grass* (Bern und München: Francke, 1969), p. 129.

[4] John J. Enck, "John Barth: An Interview," *Wisconsin Studies in Contemporary Literature*, 6 (1965), 3-14.

[5] Ihab Hassan, "The Existential Novel," *The Massachusetts Review*, 3 (1961-62), 795-97.

with the detachment of the non-believer who sees the story
with wholly neutral eyes. This is apparent in the case of
Pier Paolo Pasolini's award-winning film of *The Gospel According to Saint Matthew* (1964). Pasolini (born 1922), a
Marxist and self-styled atheist, stumbled onto the story of
Jesus by the purest chance, as he confided to an interviewer.[6] Finding himself stranded in Assisi with several
hours to pass—Pope John was in town and traffic had come
to a standstill—Pasolini had no reading matter at hand in
his hotel but the New Testament. Like Gletkin, he had only
the vaguest childhood memories of Jesus; but he became so
enchanted with the aesthetic beauty of Matthew's story that
he resolved on the spot to film it. The result, produced on
a low budget with a cast of Italian communists, is a highly
faithful and starkly realistic rendering of the text that exploits all the social criticism implicit in the Gospels. At the
same time, since Pasolini, the Marxist and atheist, treats the
story as pure fairy tale and feels no need to rationalize the
narrative, he unhesitatingly includes all the miracles: his
Jesus walks on the waters, heals the lame, feeds the multitudes, causes the fig tree to wither, and so forth.

Pasolini's literal rendition of the Gospel is only in apparent conflict with two other recent works inspired by the
New Testament. The sensationally successful rock opera
Jesus Christ Superstar (1970), by Andrew Lloyd Webber
and Tim Rice, features a problematic Judas who becomes
disenchanted with Jesus precisely because Jesus begins to
believe the myth that has grown up about him. In his opening song, which establishes the tone of the whole work,
Judas warns his friend that the people will destroy him
when they discover that he is simply a man, rather than the
new Messiah. And in their musical *Godspell* (1971), John-
Michael Tebelak and Stephen Schwartz present a red-nosed
Jesus dressed in a Superman sweatshirt, leading his troupe

[6] Interview with Gunnar D. Kumlien in *Commonweal*, 82 (July 2,
1965), 471-72.

of circus clowns through a routine of songs, soft-shoe dances, and pantomime based on the Gospel according to St. Matthew. *Godspell* was no doubt influenced by the notion of "Christ the Harlequin" and "Christianity as Comedy" advanced by Harvey Cox in his "Theological Essay on Festivity and Fantasy" entitled *The Feast of Fools* (Cambridge, Mass.: Harvard University Press, 1969). But in a television interview (on the NBC "Today" show of July 8, 1971) Tebelak conceded frankly that he became interested in the subject matter as a dramatic adaptation of myth. All three works, then—the Marxist film, the British rock opera, and the American musical show—are informed by the same detached and morally neutral attitude that regards the story of Jesus as pure myth, available for aesthetic exploitation in a variety of forms. (This fact does not preclude the audience from responding to the works in a genuinely religious manner.)

Now it is probably a safe generalization to say that most of the writers of this generation read Joyce before Jesus. Gore Vidal sharpened his pen on the postfiguration of a classical myth in *The Judgment of Paris* (1952) before undertaking his fictional transfiguration of Jesus. Similarly, John Barth had employed the general myth of the wandering hero in *The Sot-Weed Factor* (1960) before he arrived at the more specific form of the transfiguration. This means that a high degree of literary sophistication is added to the moral neutralism. Hesse and Faulkner had to learn to look at the inherited religious material from the more recently acquired mythic point of view; contemporary writers, in contrast, inherit the mythic point of view—from Joyce, from Thomas Mann, and from other writers and thinkers of the "modern" generation—and then cast around for suitable subject matter. This kind of aesthetic detachment leads very easily to parody. Gore Vidal used the Gospel as the basis for a well-known *Esquire* (April, 1967) piece on the Kennedys entitled "The Holy Family: The Gospel according to Arthur, Paul, Pierre, and William and several minor

230

apostles."[7] It is therefore hardly surprising to find a strong strain of parody in his fictional transfiguration. John Barth readily concedes that his novel contains elements of farce and parody: "This frees the writer's hands to do things with language and plot that would be unacceptable in anything realistic."[8] And Barth's closest counterpart in Germany, Günter Grass, would surely accept that statement: it was Grass, after all, who completely inverted the hallowed form of the *Bildungsroman* as the vehicle for Oskar Matzerath, the dwarfish anti-hero of *The Tin Drum* (1959). Vidal, Grass, Barth, and their contemporaries strike us as the spiritual heirs of Thomas Mann's Adrian Leverkühn, who, before he forsook theology for music, confessed that all things struck him as a parody of themselves. These sophisticated talents of the twentieth century with their jaded sensibilities, who know everything and have lost all naïveté, must agree with this modern Faustian view that all the devices of art "are suitable today only for parody."

Barth's experimentation with the myth of the wandering hero in *The Sot-Weed Factor* stimulated his curiosity: "From 1960 on I became enormously interested in this pattern and the great amount of learned commentary on it and decided that it would be a good skeleton for a large, comic novel."[9] In other words, he began with the general mythic pattern and only subsequently decided to fill it in with specific details borrowed from the New Testament: "One of the things that interested me particularly when I began writing was the way many heroes and prophets manage the discovery of their nature and destiny." This led to the Gospels, in which Jesus acts to fulfill the prophecy—"as if he knew the script in advance!" In preparation for writing his novel Barth spent several years taking notes on the hero-myth and re-reading Homer, Vergil, and the Gospels. It is

[7] Reprinted in Vidal's *Reflections Upon a Sinking Ship* (Boston: Little, Brown, 1969), pp. 160-82.

[8] Phyllis Meras, "Interview with John Barth," *New York Times Book Review*, August 22, 1966, p. 22.

[9] Interview with Phyllis Meras.

this conscious exploitation of myth and the Gospels that distinguishes these writers from earlier generations. As Robert Scholes has remarked in connection with Barth, "the really perceptive writer is not merely conscious that he is using mythic materials: he is conscious that he is using them consciously."[10] And this consciousness, in turn, produces the parodistic emphasis that is so conspicuous in the novels of this generation. As a result of the writers' moral neutralism and lack of religious faith the Gospel story has become pure myth to be exploited at will.

Novelists, then, have continued to seize upon the myth of Jesus as a pattern or structure for their fiction: it is still the greatest story ever told, or at least the most familiar one, and thus provides a common basis for parody that not even such well-known but more literary myths as those of Faust and Ulysses afford. But if their moral neutralism prevents writers from focusing on the figure of Jesus for the reasons that obsessed earlier ages—social, psychiatric, mythic— then they must find a new point of view to justify their interest. And here we note a common structural feature that tends to compensate for the absence of any central point of view in these recent fictional transfigurations. We have already observed that many writers tend to reduce the role of the hero through parody since he is not ennobled by being the bearer of a moral message. But in most cases they offset this reduction of emphasis by introducing the figure of a narrator who, moving into the foreground, occupies more and more of our attention.

Görling and Grass are obsessed primarily with the mentality of the narrator, who turns out to have betrayed the transfigured hero. This has two implications. It means that the narrator regards himself as a Judas-figure. And it means that the authors' attention is shifted from the hero (whose role has in any case been reduced in importance and dig-

[10] Robert Scholes, *The Fabulators* (New York: Oxford Univ. Press, 1967), p. 171.

nity through the parody) to the problematics of the narrating Judas. (In the vocabulary of form criticism we can say that they are shifting their interest from the savior to the evangelist.) Borrowing a term from the book that Hauptmann contemplated but never wrote, we might call narratives of this type the *Evangelium Judae*.

The other two authors are interested less in the consciousness of the narrator than in the process through which the materials of a gospel come to be formed in the community surrounding the transfigured hero and through which the document itself comes to be produced. Vidal traces the transmogrifications of a legend that gradually assumes a form wholly different from the facts as they are known to reliable eyewitnesses. And Barth carries the whole operation *ad absurdum* by producing a narrative allegedly assembled by a computer from tapes recorded by the modern "savior" himself. To the extent that both novels seek to re-create, albeit in wholly different settings, the process described by form criticism, they can be described as *analogues* to the Gospels.

For the sake of convenience we might designate both types—the *Evangelium Judae* and the analogue—as Fifth Gospels, for this common denominator suggests the formal as well as the thematic considerations that motivate the generation. All four novels that we shall consider exploit the form of the Gospels as explicitly as parody requires: three allegedly represent first-person accounts concerning a transfigured hero by "disciples" who have witnessed at first hand his deeds and destiny, while Barth's analogue purports to be a "gospel" actually compiled at the instigation of a "disciple" from first-person records of the "savior" himself. But they are all "fifth," or supernumerary, gospels to the extent that the neutral point of view locates them palpably outside the framework of any ethical system conventionally associated with the four Gospels of the New Testament. (I am using the term, obviously, in a sense wholly unlike that of Renan, who set out to write a serious fifth Gospel—that is, a modern retelling of the Gospels—in his *Life of Jesus.*)

The technique of the Fifth Gospel was anticipated to a certain extent in *Demian* and *Manuel the Mexican*: both are first-person narratives, written after the death of the hero, by personal narrators who participated in or at least witnessed much of the action. But neither of those novels revealed any trace of the obsession with betrayal that characterizes the *Evangelium Judae*. We see the difference clearly if we consider *491* (1962) by the Swedish writer Lars Görling (1931-66)—a novel whose notoriety was considerably enhanced by the fact that the film version was seized by U. S. Customs authorities on the grounds that it was obscene.[11] The novel is allegedly the first-person account, by a young man named Nils Nisseman, of certain events that took place from March to May of 1953—that is, some eight years before the time of writing. At age sixteen Nisse was picked up by the police in Stockholm for breaking and entering. But he was saved from prison by the Juvenile Welfare Board, which wished to use him in a control group for a series of psychological tests. Accordingly, he was sent to live with six other boys, as unsavory a lot of "disciples" as we shall encounter, in an eight-room apartment in a condemned building taken over by the Welfare Board.[12]

The Assistant Supervisor in charge of this unattractive lot of car thieves, smugglers, and pimps is a twenty-three-year-

[11] Görling has written another novel entitled *Triptyk* (1961), poems, a volume of short stories (1964), as well as several radio and TV plays. In Sweden he is known as one of the more articulate critics of the welfare state and its society. See Peter Werner, "Lars Görling och samhället," *Bonniers Litterära Magasin* (May-June, 1967), pp. 335-46.

[12] *491* cited here according to the translation by Anselm Hollo (1966; rpt. New York: Grove-Evergreen, 1967).

old student who is marked as a transfigured Jesus from the
moment we hear his name: Krister. When Nisse first meets
him, he is working at carpentry, building a coffin-like box
in which to sleep. This strange box is the first suggestion of
the tendency toward isolation from reality that ultimately
brings about Krister's betrayal and downfall. A second indication is the almost Marian mother-cult that he celebrates.
Since Krister's father died when he was only two, he is
deeply attached to the memory of his mother: he has assembled all her belongings, including her piano, in a carefully
locked room in the apartment, and he retires there from
time to time when reality becomes too oppressive. This unlikely Jesus dreams of "a kind of Judgment Day ahead of
time: not that anyone should be judged, only that all would
suddenly *see*! Suddenly see and understand and be unable
to dodge things" (p. 86). This liberal attitude of "tout com-
prendre est tout pardonner," which permits the individual
to withdraw to the sleeping-box or iconic room if the world
obtrudes too much, eventually comes into conflict with the
hardnosed realism of Nisse: for it is Krister's blind idealism
that prevents him from seeing reality as it is and from pro-
tecting his wards in a world where, for instance, the Supervisor of the Juvenile Welfare Board exploits his position to
indulge his taste for pederasty.

At first the seven little hustlers live peacefully side-by-
side with Krister, who is blissfully oblivious of the fact that
they are going about their business of car theft, burglary,
smuggling, and pimping as though he did not exist. There
are even hints that they regard him as a kind of Christ-
figure. When the pastor visits the welfare home at Easter,
he speaks of

". . . Jesus Christ, Who suffered for our sake, and died
for our sake, that He is risen. Hallelujah."

We were all looking at Krister.

"Yes, Jesus lives, my young friends, and He is right here
in our midst. Here and now." (p. 112)

It is on this occasion that the trouble between Krister and Nisse begins, for Nisse steals the pastor's tape recorder and pawns it. When the theft is discovered, Krister reports the facts to the Supervisor, who uses his influence to prevent prosecution. Meanwhile Nisse, unaware of these developments, has found out that the Supervisor is homosexual. When he approaches him in his office with a blackmail attempt, the Supervisor assaults Nisse sexually and then insures his silence by threatening to send Nisse back to jail for the theft of the tape recorder. Up to this point Nisse has accepted Krister's proclamations of liberal relativism with a sometimes contemptuous, sometimes amused, tolerance. But now he becomes infuriated because Krister has not lived up to his principle of seeing without judging: not only did he *judge* Nisse by reporting him to the Supervisor; he refused to *see* that the Supervisor was using his power to corrupt the boys and to indulge his own vices. Nisse explodes in a tirade of fury and hatred: "You sold me out! You Judas! You, whom I trusted! You betrayed me! You weren't half as big as I thought, much smaller than you want us to believe! Not half as big as you should have been! Easy to be brave when you let others bear the burden!" (p. 160).

At this point Nisse makes up his mind to shatter Krister's beliefs: "To force him to see everything the way it really was! To smash all his dreams! To make him experience things the way we did!" (p. 237). His procedure is suggested by the passage in Matthew (18:21-22) from which the title is adapted: "Then came Peter to him, and said, Lord, how oft shall my brother sin against me, and I forgive him? till seven times? Jesus saith unto him, I say not unto thee, Until seven times: but, Until seventy times seven." Nisse sets out, savagely and systematically, to sin against Krister until he faces reality—to commit the magical four hundred and ninety-first sin that will destroy his liberal tolerance. This theme justifies the catalogue of crime and vice that assured the novel its *succès de scandale* in Europe and the United States.

At first Nisse contents himself with encouraging the other boys to step up the pace of their normal criminal routine: they steal cars and auto parts; they attempt unsuccessfully to smuggle whiskey; they bring the streetwalker Steva home to live in their apartment. When all of this makes no impression on Krister, who is so fully obsessed with his own thoughts that he does not even realize that a prostitute is living in the house, Nisse contrives more radical plots. In an effort to force him to acknowledge what is going on, he begins selling Krister's own possessions. Initially he restricts himself to books and small objects that can be easily pawned; but when that gets no reaction, he arranges to dispose of Krister's most precious belongings—all the rugs and furniture in the locked room, including the piano. Even this flagrant injury cannot make Krister face reality. Instead of getting furious, instead of turning Nisse over to the police, he seeks out his betrayer in the public gardens of Stockholm (an inverted Gethsemane!) and cajoles him to reveal where he sold the goods so that he can buy them back again.

Beside himself with rage at such craven blindness, Nisse plots the final blow. When Krister finds that he lacks several hundred kronor, Nisse suggests that he might borrow the necessary sum from Steva. Naïvely he does so, and when Steva brings him the money the following morning, he is genuinely shocked to learn that she has spent the night earning it through prostitution. One of the other boys, not realizing that the whole affair was plotted by Nisse as an act of revenge, summons the police and accuses Krister of pandering and contributing to the delinquency of minors. When the police arrive, another of the boys, the Mongolian idiot Genghis, attacks one of them like Peter in the garden: "And before anyone had grasped what it was all about he had jumped the cop standing next to Krister and bit him hard on his ear" (p. 281). Krister, horrified as he begins to grasp the full extent of Nisse's betrayal, leaps out of the kitchen window and is killed when he lands headfirst on the stones of the courtyard below. Nisse's "gospel" concludes with the laconic note: "I got what was coming to me, for everything. But no one tried to even blame me for his death."

This novel represents the transfiguration of a sardonically inverted Jesus: a Jesus whose teaching infuriates his sneering disciples and does not save them from indignities and assault; a Jesus who inadvertently becomes pimp to an already depraved Magdalene; a Jesus who assiduously and blindly courts his own Judas; a Jesus who commits suicide when, after forgiving his offenders seventy times seven, he at last realizes that his entire belief has been rendered ineffectual. (Görling's novel constitutes an attack on the Swedish welfare state.) The novel is a gospel in a more specific sense as well, for this account is written after all by the very disciple who betrayed the transfigured hero. This brings us to the inevitable ambiguity of the *Evangelium Judae*: we can never be sure how much the trivialization of the hero has been affected by the narrator's own need to justify himself. Much of the fascination of the form stems from this very tension between Judas and Jesus—a Judas who feels that he can win our sympathy and attention only to the extent that he succeeds in ridiculing the character and aspirations of his Jesus.

If the *Evangelium Judae* is defined as the first-person account of a transfigured hero, even though he is reduced to parody, by the disciple who betrays him and is responsible for his death, then Günter Grass's *Cat and Mouse* (1961) clearly belongs to the same category.[13] There are other con-

---

[13] Grass's story has excited much critical comment. Apart from the general studies by Schwarz, Kurt Lothar Tank—*Günter Grass* (Berlin: Colloquium, 1965)—and W. Gordon Cunliffe—*Günter Grass* (New York: Twayne, 1969)—I have found the following articles most helpful: Karl H. Ruhleder, "A Pattern of Messianic Thought in Günter Grass' *Cat and Mouse*," *The German Quarterly*, 39 (1964), 599-612; Erhart M. Friedrichsmeyer, "Aspects of Myth, Parody and

spicuous parallels as well between Grass's novel and *491*—not to mention the similar scandal that attended both the publication and the filming of Grass's work. Both books, unlike any of the other fictional transfigurations, deal with teenage gangs: in *Cat and Mouse* the plot revolves around the activities of a group of high school boys in Danzig from September, 1939, until June of 1944. Also, the events are narrated in the first person by one of the participants looking back at the action from a later period. In *Cat and Mouse*, however, the present time of the narrator, Pilenz, moves so conspicuously into the foreground that we can accurately speak of two levels of action or two interwoven plots. (In *491* the narrator's present time was nothing but a narrative device to offer a certain detachment from the events described.) Several critics have noted that this shift in narrative point of view sharply distinguishes *Cat and Mouse* from Grass's *The Tin Drum* (1959), where the story is told through the consciousness of the central narrator, Oskar Matzerath, who is the observer rather than the observed.

At the time of writing, 1959, the thirty-three-year-old Pilenz has a job as secretary and social worker in a Catholic settlement house where, as he confesses, he "just can't let magic alone" (p. 73).[14] His reading matter alone characterizes him as a problematic religious nature: the Gnostics, the *Confessions* of St. Augustine, Léon Bloy (militant Catholic reform), Heinrich Böll (contemporary Catholic moral conscience), and Friedrich Heer (Catholic criticism and cultural history).

From relatively few hints we learn much that helps us to

Obscenity in Günter Grass' *Die Blechtrommel* and *Katz und Maus*," *Germanic Review*, 40 (1965), 240-47; James C. Bruce, "The Equivocating Narrator in Günter Grass's *Katz und Maus*," *Monatshefte für deutschen Unterricht*, 58 (1966), 139-49; and Robert H. Spaethling, "Günter Grass: *Cat and Mouse*," *Monatshefte*, 62 (1970), 141-53.

[14] *Cat and Mouse* cited here according to the Signet reprint of the translation by Ralph Manheim (New York: Harcourt, Brace & World, 1963).

understand Pilenz' role as narrator. He is, for one thing, a man of intellectual inclinations who is able to isolate and compare general patterns underlying historically distinct periods: he spends his time, he tells us, "trying to discover early Communism in Nazareth or late Christianity in Ukrainian kolkhozes" (p. 99). It is important to bear this in mind, for Pilenz' awareness of the transfiguration of his hero and his consciousness of the mythic pattern of action is ultimately a retrospective consciousness applied by the mature and reflective narrator to his youth. This interval of fifteen years separating him from the events that he narrates, coupled with his religious preoccupations, is necessary to account for the "gloomy conscience" that haunts him and drives him to do poorly paid social work. With his parish priest he spends "whole nights discussing the blood of Christ, the Trinity, and the sacrament of penance" (p. 73). This obsession with penance and guilt recurs thematically throughout his book. In fact, it gradually becomes clear that the very act of writing is an exercise in absolution through exorcism, for it was his priest, Father Alban, who encouraged him initially to put down his recollections: "'Just sit yourself down, my dear Pilenz, and start writing. . . . If you won't take up the fiddle, you can get it off your chest by writing—the good Lord knew what He was doing when He gave you talent'" (p. 90).

Now precisely what is it, we wonder, that this "gloomy conscience" is supposed to get off its chest? "I should at last be delivered from these all-night discussions with Father Alban, from trying to determine, in the course of endless investigations, to what extent blasphemy can take the place of prayer. I should be able to believe, to believe something, no matter what, perhaps even to believe in the resurrection of the flesh" (p. 99). These reflections on blasphemy and resurrection turn out to be anything but vague: they are highly precise anticipations of the central problems of the story. But the matter is complicated by the fact that Pilenz' "gloomy conscience" prevents him from telling his story outright. In *491* Nils Nisseman recounts his betrayal of Krister with a cold disdain for the reader and his moral approval: he would not deign to deceive us; his whole aim, after all, is to unmask the harshness of reality. Pilenz, in contrast, cannot bring himself to admit the extent of his guilt. As a result, it is only indirectly—through the language and the imagery of the story he tells—that we gradually discover the reasons for the overwhelming sense of guilt that torments him. This is the less obvious but probably central theme of the novel.

On a second and more overt level the story deals with Pilenz' boyhood friend, Joachim Mahlke, and their adventures in school and vacation. The narrative time-sequence begins in September, 1939, when the Polish mine sweeper *Rybitwa* is sunk in the harbor of Danzig during the first encounters of the war. That winter Mahlke learns how to swim, and the following summer (1940) the boys venture out to the *Rybitwa*, where Mahlke soon astonishes them with his feats of diving and the treasures that he brings up from the sunken ship. This goes on for two more summers. In the summer of 1942 Mahlke discovers the radio shack of the *Rybitwa* in a tower that juts up above the water level, and he installs a secret room there for himself. At about the same time, he is expelled from school for stealing an Iron Cross from an officer who has lectured at the school. That winter Mahlke is drafted for the Work Brigade, and Pilenz sees no more of him during the entire year of 1943. By the spring of 1944, however, Mahlke has entered the regular military, where he has rapidly advanced from gunner to tank commander, winning the Iron Cross for distinguished service on the Russian front. That June Pilenz finally sees him again when Mahlke comes home on leave and is denied permission to speak at the school from which he had been expelled two years earlier. Depressed by this refusal to acknowledge his achievements, Mahlke decides to desert.

Pilenz rows him out to the *Rybitwa*, where Mahlke intends to hide out for a time. But when Mahlke fails to come up after several days, Pilenz assumes that he is dead.

The basic plot does not in itself suggest the reasons for Pilenz' sense of guilt. We begin to grasp it only when we realize that Pilenz, the mature narrator, regards Mahlke as a Jesus-figure. The matter is complicated by the fact that Mahlke's classmates jestingly call him "the Redeemer" because of his strange appearance. At one point a classmate draws a picture of Mahlke on the blackboard: "The eyes, piercing points under sorrowfully uplifted eyebrows. The neck sinuous, half in profile, with a monstrous Adam's apple. And behind the head and sorrowful features a halo: a perfect likeness of Mahlke the Redeemer. The effect was immediate" (p. 35). (This drawing suggests the photograph of Greene's whiskey priest, which has been encircled in such a way as to suggest a nimbus.) Later Pilenz sees Mahlke at mass: "His hair was still parted in the middle and still held in place with the usual sugar water; but he wore it a good inch longer. Stiff and candied, it fell over his two ears like the two sides of a steep-pointed roof: he would have made a satisfactory Jesus the way he held up his joined hands on a level with his forehead" (p. 83). Near the end the Redeemer's hairdo is gone, shorn off by the army barber: "But the countenance was still that of a redeemer: the eagle on your inflexibly vertical cap spread its wings over your brow like the dove of the Holy Ghost" (p. 105).

But what was merely a mildly blasphemous joke for the irreverent schoolboys is taken quite seriously by the older Pilenz with his religious obessions. Though it is sometimes difficult to ascertain what the boys believed and what the thirty-three-year-old Pilenz has added, it becomes clear that Mahlke's entire story, in Pilenz' imagination, takes on many aspects of the Jesus myth. Very early, for instance, in a curiously insistent form, it is established that Mahlke knows his father only indirectly, from an old picture:

Mahlke was an only child.
Mahlke was half an orphan.
Mahlke's father was dead. (p. 12)

Again, the narrator's insistence that Mahlke lived on Oster-
zeile and not Westerzeile draws our attention to the otherwise unremarkable street name, which has implications suggesting both the East and Easter. Mahlke's feats of
swimming and diving are regarded as "miracles" and
"legendary" by his classmates, who follow him like a group
of disciples. And Pilenz occasionally compares his friend to
a fish, the unmistakable iconographic symbol for Jesus.

The most compelling parallels occur close to the end.
When Mahlke comes back from the war with his Knight's
Cross, he wants to speak at the school, but he is denied the
right to address his admirers, who nevertheless flock
around him to get his autograph. (Jesus is challenged regarding the rights of the Temple by the Scribes and
Pharisees, but the faithful appeal to him and try to touch
him in the hope of miracles.) After this humiliation Mahlke
lies in wait at night in the Baumbachallee for the principal,
Dr. Klohse, and slaps him. Now it is hard to understand
why Grass should describe this scene (night, garden,
anguish) and stress the time as being Thursday (the first
occasion in the entire novel when the day of the week is
specified for anything) unless he wanted to arouse associations with the Garden of Gethsemane—but a weirdly inverted Gethsemane in which Jesus, driven by his anguish,
does not restrain his followers from fighting but, indeed,
attacks his enemy himself. On the following morning there
are echoes of the Last Supper when Mahlke attends a mass
at which Pilenz serves as altar boy. When the priest utters
the words "*Ecce Agnus Dei*" (p. 113) the text continues:
"Of those taking communion, Mahlke was the first to kneel,"
suggesting an unmistakable connection between Mahlke
and the Lamb of God.

That same morning—a gloomy, cloudy Friday—Mahlke

makes his last trip out to the sunken mine sweeper, which turns out in a parodistic sense to be his *via dolorosa*. Mahlke, at this time already A.W.O.L. and in hiding, has had nothing to eat but gooseberries, and these have caused him to double up on the beach with cramps: "When I pulled up on the beach, Mahlke lay writhing in the sand, uniform and all. I had to kick him to make him get up. He shivered, sweated, dug both fists into the pit of his stomach; but even today I can't make myself believe in that bellyache in spite of unripe gooseberries on an empty stomach" (p. 120). For the first time Mahlke is unable to swim out to the *Rybitwa*: Pilenz rows him out, and presently, with a supply of canned pork, Mahlke dives down into the ship, never to be seen again. "Ever since that Friday I've known what silence is," Pilenz observes (p. 125). The following day he goes back to the beach to see if Mahlke has come up, but there is no sign. Fifteen years later, still searching for Mahlke, he has him paged at a meeting of war veterans who hold the Knight's Cross: "But you didn't show up. You didn't surface." Here, in the very last words of the story, we find again the curious incantational tones that characterized the last lines of *Demian*. Whether or not Mahlke, objectively considered, is a transfiguration of Jesus, in the mind and imagination of Pilenz, with his craving for "magic" and his religious obsessions, he has assumed that function.

Now Mahlke, in his own consciousness, is neither ironically nor paranoiacally a Jesus-figure: he neither pursues his own Passion or smilingly notes the parallels into which circumstances have forced him. But he does have one personal obsession that lends itself to and strengthens our view of him as a transfigured hero: his cult of the Virgin. Mahlke doesn't believe in God: "He's just a swindle to stultify the people" (p. 112). But his feeling for the Virgin amounts to an obsession: "The only thing I believe in is the Virgin Mary. That's why I'm never going to get married" (p. 112). Even the priest is worried about Mahlke's excessive zeal: "It had seemed to him for some time that regardless of what

principal agents in this operation are the narrator himself, a self-styled "contented relativist" (p. 123) who does not believe in Cave, but who is willing to play apostle to his Jesus by supplying the intellectual and philosophical basis for his single-minded teaching; Cave's personal adviser Iris Mortimer, whom the legend subsequently transforms marianically into Cave's mother; and the brilliant publicity agent Paul Himmell, who—in a bitter parody of his name-sake, the Apostle Paul—is the organizational genius who creates an institution, Cavesway, from Cave's casual utter-ances. It is also Paul Himmell who ultimately realizes that every great religion needs to be based upon a suitable sym-bolic act. As a result, he arranges to have Cave killed and his ashes spread across the United States from a jet so that his death, like the crucifixion, will formalize the new re-ligion. The three years between Cave's appearance and his murder correspond to the life of Jesus from the Baptism to the Passion, and the parallels are sufficient to permit Vidal's modern analogue to develop in full parodistic richness.

The narrator is ideally suited for his job. As a writer of independent means, he has been working for years on a book about the Emperor Julian and early Christianity and is constantly ready with analogies. When he first hears of John Cave he reflects ironically that the name has "a pair of initials calculated to amaze the innocent" (p. 29). And when he learns of Paul's plot to kill Cave, he expresses no surprise: "Where else could it lead? The same thing hap-pened to Jesus, you know. They kept pushing him to claim the kingdom. Finally, they pushed too hard and he was killed. It was the killing which perpetuated the legend" (p. 214). But for the most part the narrator's analogies deal not so much with Jesus and Cave specifically as with the history of Christianity and Cavesword generally. Speaking of the advantages of modern communication, he recalls that "it took three centuries for Christianity to infect the world. It was to take Cave only three years to conquer Europe and the Americas" (p. 184). During the first two years of op-

position, when the Cavites were forced to barricade themselves in a Cavite Center on Park Avenue, he felt "the sort
of security and serenity which monks must have known in
their monasteries" (p. 188). The special Congressional
hearing, which ended by proclaiming Cavesword as the
national religion, "prepared the way politically, to draw the
obvious parallel, for a new Constantine" (p. 190). In retrospect, finally, he realizes that he acted out a "mythic role"
in his relation to Cave (p. 19). At the same time, his sense
of irony and instinctive resistance to Cave's teaching of
death qualify his every utterance: when he calls himself a
"disciple," one always hears the ironic quotation marks
(e.g., p. 66).

When Luther loses the power struggle within the organization after Cave's death—his heresy is later known as
"lutherism"—he flees to Luxor in Upper Egypt. It is here,
just after the turn of the twenty-first century, that he sets
down his memoirs. At the same time, he learns from two
missionary "Communicators" of Cavesword about subsequent developments, and this counterpoint of the two temporal levels permits the irony of contrast between truth and
fiction, between Luther's anti-gospel and the accepted legend. Cave's death had led to the Council of Dallas, during
which the official doctrine of the Cavites was promulgated
in a series of edicts. During the first years the spread of
Cavesway produced a series of bloody persecutions and
counter-actions by the Christian Churches, which regarded
Cave as the Antichrist. Gradually, however, the movement
established itself throughout the western hemisphere with
a dogma and hierarchy as rigid as that of the medieval
Church. (The Resident of Dallas is the analogical equivalent to the Pope, and the hierarchy spreads downward from
that position to the so-called Communicators in the field,
the missionary priests.) Like the early Church, which
adapted the pagan holidays to its own use, the Cavite movement has accommodated its procedures to local customs.
Christmas has become Cavesday. And Easter, as Luther

learns to his astonishment, is now known as Irisday, in com-
memoration of Iris Mortimer. An entire iconology has
sprung up around Cave and Iris. And an analogy to the
Marian controversy has even arise among the "Communicators who deprecate our allegiance to the Mother, not
realizing that it enhances rather than detracts from Cave"
(p. 203).

Even during his lifetime Cave had allowed none of his
words to be transcribed since he felt that without his presence they would be meaningless. As a result, his sayings
were recorded only in paraphrases—"which gave a curious
protean flavor to his doctrine, since the recorded style was
never consistent, changing always with each paraphraser
just as the original meaning was invariably altered by each
separate listener as he adapted the incantation to his private needs" (p. 145). (We think, of course, of the process
through which the Gospelists adapted the logia to the needs
of their individual communities.) Luther, as the intellectual
and writer of the early group of disciples surrounding
Cave, had composed the authentic "Testament of Cavesword." This affords the basis for parody on two levels.
First, it becomes evident that Eugene Luther was not so
much a secretary as a ghostwriter for Cave. In fact, he was
responsible for most of the applications of Cavesword beyond the simple basic claim—which he does not even accept!—that death is good. Second, just before his death
Luther learns that his name has gradually been erased
from the history of the movement by revisionist historians,
and the authorship of his "Testament" has been assigned to
another member of the group. In terms of the analogy, it is
as though we knew St. Luke (an analogy suggested by the
narrator's name) only through the Acts of the Apostles
while the Gospel that he wrote had been assigned to another author altogether.

Vidal's novel clearly moves beyond Fifth Gospels of the
sort written by Görling and Grass. On one level—the events
of the fifties recalled in the long flashbacks—the novel is in-

deed quite close to the *Evangelium Judae*: from the first, Eugene Luther is a skeptic who does not like John Cave and who argues, as a true humanist, for life in opposition to Cave's doctrine of death. However, Luther does not have a bad conscience about the affair at all; although he "betrayed" Cave intellectually, he was not responsible for his death. As a result, he is not truly a Judas figure. On another level, the book is not simply the parody of a gospel: in fact, it is an analogue to the entire New Testament, including specifically the Acts of the Apostles and Paul's Epistles. In all of this parody, however—Jesus is reduced to a television demagogue, Paul to an unscrupulous publicity genius, and Luke to a morally neutral intellectual who gives his services not out of conviction, but sheer playfulness—there is little sense that Christianity itself is being attacked or ridiculed. There is so little of the substance or meaning of Christianity here that nothing is left but pure form: the form of the Gospel and the relationship between characters and between books of the New Testament. Filtered through the moral neutralism of Gore Vidal, the fictional transfiguration has become aesthetic play. As Vidal's narrator remarks of himself, "Neither Christianity nor Marxism nor the ugly certainties of the mental therapists had ever engaged my loyalty or suspended my judgment" (p. 79). In the face of such relativism, what can the Gospels represent but pure form? And if the Gospels, in turn, are regarded as pure form, the fictional transfiguration can become nothing but parody.

At this point we can ascertain the similarity between *Messiah* and *Giles Goat-Boy*. Like Vidal's novel, Barth's "Revised New Syllabus" goes far beyond the parody of a single Gospel. Barth originally set out, as he remarked in his interview with John Enck, to write "a comic Old Testament," "a souped-up Bible." In the course of writing, this original intention was modified to take in the New Testament as well. Like Vidal, Barth is not in the least concerned with the

problematics of theme or content: he exploits the Bible for
the sheer aesthetic fun of structural parody. But in distinction to Vidal, Barth has not written a kind of religious *1984*
by extrapolating with parodistic logic from present reality.
In *Giles Goat-Boy* the author has created "an entirely hypothetical world" of the sort that he admires in the fiction of
Borges—"a coherent alternative to this world complete in
every respect from its algebra to its fire."[16] The hypothetical
world of *Giles Goat-Boy* is "a university that *is* the world—
not one that is just *like* the world." It is not simply a simile,
but "a simile turned into a metaphor." For this reason, I believe, the term *analogue* is more precise than the word *allegory*, which Barth himself somewhat apologetically has
used to describe his works: "Maybe *allegory's* not the word
I should have used," he remarked to John Enck with reference to *The Sot-Weed Factor*. For the term *allegory* has
been pre-empted by literary history and criticism to designate a special literary form. The more neutral word
analogue simply defines the relationship between two texts.

It would be foolhardy to attempt here to recapitulate or
even to suggest the vast neo-baroque splendor of Barth's
zany cosmos. In brief, he depicts a university-world, controlled by the tyrannical computer WESCAC, whose institutional history reflects the history of Western civilization
and whose present state mirrors the recent world situation:
during Campus Riot II the Bonifacists of Siegfrieder College
exterminated millions of Moishians; though the Boundary
Dispute between East Campus and West Campus is at present no more than a Quiet Riot, there is general apprehension lest Campus Riot III break out at any moment. We
shall restrict ourselves to a single aspect, the biblical, of the
complex fiction that also contains elaborate analogies to
such other myths as those of Oedipus, Don Quixote, and the
Divine Comedy.

[16] John Barth, "The Literature of Exhaustion," *Atlantic Monthly*,
1967; rpt. in *The American Novel since World War II*, ed. Marcus
Klein (Greenwich, Conn.: Fawcett, 1969), pp. 267-79.

Barth began with the general idea of creating a hypothetical world; but in order to bring action into this fictional analogue he required a hero (as he told Phyllis Meras) who would "take on heroic proportions in the course of adventures at this universal university." We noted earlier that Barth, becoming interested in the mythic pattern of the wanderer after critics drew his attention to its presence in *The Sot-Weed Factor*, concluded that it would be "a good skeleton for a large, comic novel." He wanted to begin "by satirizing the basic myth and then, hopefully, escalate the satire into something larger, darker, and more compassionate." Barth decided to construct the figure of his hero in such a way that he would fulfill "all the prerequisites of hero-hood" listed in the studies of myth and folklore: the mystery of parentage, the irregularity of birth, the injury to his leg, being raised by a foster-parent in a foster-home, and so forth. Since all of these characteristics show up in the myths of Oedipus and Jesus—according to an ancient legend Jesus, like Oedipus, also had a limp—there is a certain amount of mythic syncretism in the novel: notably in Barth's witty re-creation of *Oedipus Rex* in the incapsulated "Tragedy of Taliped Decanus."

Barth needed more than a general mythic pattern, however: he wanted also to parody the phenomenon that we know under the label of figural thinking. He had noted in his study of myth that many heroes manipulate or "manage" the discovery of their nature and destiny: "The Gospel writers often say of Jesus, for example, 'He did this in order that the prophecy would be fulfilled.' As if he knew the script in advance!" Jesus provided the perfect model for this kind of conscious postfigurative behavior. But since we are dealing here with a metaphor and not a simile, with an *analogue* rather than an *allegory*, we no longer find the simple one-to-one relationship that determined the parallels in most earlier transfigurations. In the other works the lives of Emanuel Quint or Pietro Spina could be prefigured by the life of Jesus because Jesus and Christianity belong to the cultural and historical reality of the fictional world portrayed. The autonomous and self-contained university-world of *Giles Goat-Boy*, in contrast, has its own history and culture and knows nothing of a man named Jesus. The life of George Giles is prefigured not by Jesus but by the deeds of Enos Enoch, the "Shepherd Emeritus." Giles stands in the same relationship to Enos Enoch, in other words, as do other transfigured heroes to Jesus. Barth has included within his fictional world not only the parodied hero, but also the myth that the hero imitates. But the matter is more complicated, for the figure of Enos Enoch is clearly created in analogy to Jesus. George Giles is therefore a transfiguration of Jesus twice-removed: he imitates Enos Enoch, whose life parallels—strictly in the terms of the university-world—the life of Jesus.

Barth's trick for representing Christianity through analogy is very simple: he merely translates everything with unrelenting consistency into the language of Academia, beginning with his subtitle, "The Revised New Syllabus." God becomes the all-powerful Founder whose Final Examination relegates one forever to Commencement Gate or the Dean o' Flunks. School children are taught "the moral principles of Moishe's Code and the Seminar-on-the-Hill" (p. 55).[17] Enos Enoch is said to have "enrolled in the manual-training course taught by His mother's humble husband . . . " (p. 398). Later, "John the Bursar had been necessary to declare Enos Enoch's matriculation and administer to him the rites of enrollment . . . " (p. 511). Similarly, the most famous precepts and prayers are cited in analogy: "Many are Registered but few are Qualified" (p. 251); "Unto the Chancellor that which is the Chancellor's; unto the Founder that which is the Founder's" (p. 326). There is even the Grand Tutor's Petition, which begins:

> Our Founder, Who are omniscient,
> Commencèd be Thy name.

[17] *Giles Goat-Boy or, The Revised New Syllabus* (Garden City, N. Y.: Doubleday, 1966).

Thy College come; Thy Assignments done
On Campus as beyond the Gate. (p. 363)

The absolute and often predictable consistency with which
the analogy is pursued is amusing at first, but becomes tir-
ing after some seven hundred pages. Though Barth is
operating at an incomparably higher level of sophistication,
his compulsion to spell out every analogy is reminiscent at
times of the early Christian socialists, who felt impelled to
stress every parallel between the plot and the Bible. Perhaps this is inevitable: Barth's use of the analogue is as
radically new today as, a century ago, the simple straightforward transfiguration was. Perhaps this kind of composi-
tional redundancy will be unnecessary when readers become more accustomed to dealing with such "hypothetical
worlds" as those created by Barth, Borges, and others.[18]
In any case, the total playfulness and moral neutralism with
which Barth constructs his analogue removes any sense of
the heretical or blasphemous.

Barth's university-world contains its own history and traditions. Hence Enos Enoch, already in his own time, had
been aware of the mythic *figura* that it was his duty to follow. George Giles's John the Baptist, Max Spielmann, explains it to him in detail: "The fact was, he declared, Enos
Enoch like other Grand Tutors had had His advising as it
were in advance, and did what He did in many cases precisely because He knew it to be prescribed that 'A Grand
Tutor shall do such-and-so.' It was not the fulfillment of
predictions that made Enos Enoch Grand Tutor; it was the

[18] Leonard B. Meyer, *Music, the Arts, and Ideas: Patterns and
Predictions in Twentieth-Century Culture* (Chicago: Univ. of Chicago Press, 1967), pp. 116-22. Meyer argues that, in the arts, a new
style almost invariably involves a considerable amount of "composi-
tional redundancy" and repetition until it has established itself as
familiar. Meyer's discussion helps to account for the "redundant" or
excessively allegorical form of the early Christian socialist transfigurations as well as of the most recent parodies; for both types exploit
techniques that are for the moment essentially new and unfamiliar.

prior condition of Grand Tutorhood that led Him to search out the predictions and see to it they were fulfilled" (p. 111). Since the entire plot of the novel is activated when Giles sets out consciously to fulfill the predictions of Enos Enoch, what we are dealing with is in fact an elaborate parody not only of the Gospel itself, but also of the technique of postfigurative action. It is in his capacity as John the Baptist that Max Spielmann proclaims that Giles had "met nearly all the prerequisites of herohood, as far as could be judged . . . " (p. 108). Max's obsession with such hero-traits as mystery of parentage or irregularity of birth reflects Barth's own interest in myth. Like earlier writers, he has included his own theory of myth in his novel; but this theory itself becomes material for parody.

Barth has exercised considerable ingenuity to construct parallels between the life of George Giles and that of Enos Enoch. As a matter of fact, almost everything that we learn about Enos Enoch is revealed indirectly when Giles fulfills a prediction or re-enacts a deed. It is as though we knew the Old Testament only through references in the Gospels. The Virgin Birth, for instance, is parodied in one of the most memorable scenes in the book. Giles's mother, Miss Virginia Hector (note the name), who repeatedly assures people that she has never *gone all the way* with anyone, is seduced and raped by the giant computer WESCAC, which has been injected with its self-programmed Grand-tutorial Ideal, Laboratory Eugenical Specimen (known by the acronym GILES). To escape the persecution of the Chancellor of the University, who attempts to have the child destroyed, Giles is taken away secretly and raised, in the disguise of a goat, on the New Tammany College Farms by Maximilian Spielmann, "the great Mathematical Psycho-Proctologist." The goat-motif is a parodistic inversion of the Lamb of God: Giles is "Enos Enoch with balls" (p. 191). Giles's mission—to re-program the cybernetic monster WESCAC and thus to redeem the university—is inspired explicitly by Enos Enoch's teachings. After one of his setbacks, for instance, Giles reflects: "Whatever fugitive notion I'd had earlier concerning this item of my Assignment gave way before a true inspiration: Had not Enos Enoch and a hundred other wayfaring dons of fact and fiction taught, by their own example, that the Way to Commencement Gate led through Nether Campus? Was not my answer, *Failure is Passage*, but an epigrammatic form of that same truth?" (p. 625).

Although it is easy to lose sight of the basic pattern in the seven hundred pages of Barth's novel, George Giles's life is clearly marked by the circumstances and deeds associated with the life of Jesus: the Virgin Birth, the threatened slaughter of the innocents, the confirmation by a John-the-Baptist figure. He confounds the Pharisaical members of the university, gathers disciples ("protégés"), and is tempted by the dream of power. He is even accompanied by the Magdalene-figure, in the person of Anastasia, so beloved by the Christian socialist novelists; in Barth's inversion of the Gospel, however, the goat-like Jesus actually couples with the big-hearted harlot in order to achieve cognition and salvation.

The ordeal through which George is supposed to redeem the university is the descent into the belly of WESCAC. After the first two attempts his Grand Tutorship is denied. On the first occasion he is rejected because in answer to the sphinx-like questions he advances the simple fundamentalist doctrine that there is a rigid moral distinction between good and evil or, in the terms of the novel, "passage" and "failure." On the second occasion he moves to the opposite extreme and offers Enos Enoch's formula that "failure is passage"—an answer that is likewise rejected by the computer. It is only on the third descent, when he couples with Anastasia in the computer's belly, that Giles finally learns the truth: "Pass All/ Fail All"—human reality encompasses all aspects of being, all of which must be accepted. (This union of all possibilities reflects the moral neutralism that characterizes Barth's generation.) It is only after achieving

this revelation with the aid of Anastasia that Giles is prepared to save the university by driving out his adversary,
Harold Bray.

Bray embodies a crass, loudmouthed opportunism that
regards any means as justifiable for the sake of the end. In
the so-called "Founder's Hill Affair" Giles, supported by his
new-found doctrine, manages to drive Bray off the campus:
he flies away in a manner reminiscent of that other false
prophet, Simon Magus. Though subsequently accused of
"Grand-Tutorcide," Giles is not punished; but he is still denied his Grand-tutorship through the connivance of a
Pilate-like Chancellor whose "fastidious official neutrality"
(p. 705) keeps the affair out of the disciplinary committee.
In fact, the Chancellor's admiration for Pilate—"that Re-
musian vice-administrator of the Moishian quads in terms
gone by, who had winked at Enos Enoch's lynching"
(p. 683)—is specifically mentioned. However, his tutor Max
Spielmann, paying the penalty of John the Baptist, is
"Shafted" on Founder's Hill near the end of the book.

In the baroque wealth of the novel there are more allusions than one can enumerate. At the same time, the novel
does not depict the single episode that, more than any
other, distinguishes the life of Jesus: the Passion. The novel
ends, in fact, at the beginning of Jesus' years of ministry,
around the time of the death of John the Baptist. At the
time George is only twenty-one years old. In the "Cover-
Letter to the Editors and Publisher" and in the "Post-tape,"
however, we learn in brief certain other circumstances regarding George Giles and the recording of his "gospel." For
the twelve years following Max Spielmann's "Shafting"
George was busy recording his autobiography onto tapes
in WESCAC's storage, and during that period he worked
on the campus in the humble capacity of undergraduate
adviser. The analogy to Jesus' mission, which was unacceptable to the ecclesiastical authorities, is obvious. He became
"some sort of *professor extraordinarius* . . . whose reputation rested on his success in preparing students to pass their

final examinations. His pedagogical method had been unorthodox, and so like many radicals he had worked against vehement opposition, and actual persecution" (p. xxvi). Finally, when he had reached the age of thirty-three and a third, his tenure was revoked on charges of moral turpitude. After leaving the campus for a short time, he "returned clandestinely . . . to confer with his protégés, and then disappeared for good" (p. xxvi)—an analogy to the death, resurrection, and ascension. These sections of the novel sometimes seem to be nothing but an elaboration of the old academic joke about Jesus, who, according to campus wits, could never have gotten tenure because, although he was a great teacher, he never published. In Barth's version the "editor" of the manuscript objects that the story of Professor Giles was predictably like so many other academic stories: "What academic department has not its Grand Old Man who packs the lecture-halls term after term but never publishes a word in his field?" (p. xxvi).

To the extent that the manuscript—the section we have been discussing—is called "R.N.S.: The Revised New Syllabus of George Giles Our Grand Tutor . . . " the book is clearly a parody of the New Testament. *Time*'s reviewer called it a Black Bible, and Robert Scholes "a sacred book to end all sacred books." This basic Gospel structure is not vitiated by the inversion of sequence: it is only toward the end of the book, for instance, that Giles learns of his "nativity"—the identity of his mother and her impregnation by the computer. The basic mythic plot, in other words, is enhanced by a certain tension of dramatic suspense. In addition, the Passion itself is relegated casually to prefatory and concluding material. But what really distinguishes this "gospel" from the other Fifth Gospels is the fact that it is allegedly the first-person record by the transfigured hero himself and not by a third-person disciple figure.

We can disregard the rather playful framework devices that belong to the *novel* as distinguished from the encapsulated "Revised New Syllabus": the publisher's disclaimer, the editorial comments, and most of Barth's own "cover-letter." The manuscript itself has allegedly been compiled by the computer WESCAC from the various materials at its disposal: the reminiscences of Giles's pupils (the most precise equivalent of the Gospels), which are filled with discrepancies, irrelevancies, and contradictions; and the original material read onto the tape by George Giles himself—lecture notes, conferences with his "protégés," and so forth: "The machine declared itself able and ready (with the aid of 'analogue facilities' and a sophistication dismaying at least to a poor humanist like myself) to assemble, collate, and edit this material, interpolate all verifiable data from other sources such as the memoirs then in hand, recompose the whole into a coherent narrative from the Grand Tutor's point of view, and 'read it out' in an elegant form on its automatic printers!" (p. xxvii). The "Revised New Syllabus," in other words, is the parodistic analogue of the Bible scholar's dream—or nightmare! It amounts to a diplomatic edition of the harmonized Gospels, enriched with relevant historical materials from such extraneous sources as Philo or Josephus, and retold in the first-person of Jesus himself.

It would be difficult to go beyond Barth and still retain any recognizable semblance of the fictional transfiguration. He has parodied not only the Gospels (in the story of Enos Enoch), but also the whole relationship between Old Testament and New, as well as the entire tradition of "higher criticism" of the Bible. At the same time it is plain that Barth, for all his authorial exuberance, remains instinctively true to the two basic criteria that characterize the other Fifth Gospels. The moral neutralism of a generation that refuses to propound absolutes is expressed within the text by Giles's discovery that "Pass All" is equivalent to "Fail All." And the tendency toward parody, already inherent in the technique of the analogue, is intensified almost exponentially by the ingenious device of having the story programmed by that ultimate "objective" narrator of contemporary society, a computer.[19]

The fictional possibilities that remain once this extreme of parody has been attained are suggested by two recent novels. Neither constitutes a true transfiguration, but both display the trivialization of a Jesus-figure that has gradually been liberated from any meaning whatsoever. In *Why Is A Crooked Letter* (1969) Harry Pesin introduces us to a young commercial photographer named Jesus Christopher. On the advice of his father, a publicity agent, he shortens his name to Jesus Christ and rapidly wins fame in the hip world of contemporary Manhattan as a "transcendental photographer." In fact, Jesus specializes in erotic pictures: photographs of himself in bed with his girl friend, a series on the sex life of animals, and so forth. The novel makes no attempt to establish parallels between the modern action and the Gospels (though there are allusions to the archetypal myth of the quest). For all its fashionably intellectual pretensions, the book uses the name merely to trigger a sequence of situations and jokes that depend almost wholly on the overworked principle of incongruity.

E. M. Nathanson's *The Latecomers* (1970) resembles an improbable combination of Coccioli's *Manuel the Mexican*, Vidal's *Messiah*, and Görling's *491*, reduced stylistically and intellectually to the level of a television scenario. The basic framework is created by the techniques of parody. Several cynical promoters, including a demented evangelist and a

---

[19] Both of these tendencies are conspicuous also in Ken Kesey's novel, *One Flew Over the Cuckoo's Nest* (1962), which shares many of the characteristics of the fictional transfiguration. It is the story, told in the first person by one of the "disciples," of a convict who sets out to save the patients in a mental hospital from the Big Nurse and who ends up being "crucified" on the cross-shaped table used for electro-shock therapy. The parallels in the plot (e.g., a fishing expedition with twelve inmates, the hero's friendship with a prostitute, a doctor who "washes his hands of the whole deal") are supported by occasional references to the New Testament. But since the transfigurational parallels begin to emerge only in the last quarter of the book, it cannot be regarded as a consistently structured Fifth Gospel.

Las Vegas gambler, have built an elaborate biblical Disney-
land in the desert near Los Angeles: The Valley of His Passion Park, Inc. Ostensibly a religious establishment featuring a daily Passion Play, it is in fact a cover operation for
a casino that is to be housed in the "living parable" of
Sodom and Gomorrah. The action is precipitated by the
actor hired to play the role of Jesus. His real name is unknown since his mother, a one-time dance-band vocalist,
was so drunk at the time of his conception that she does not
remember who his father was. (This, I suppose, is the ultimate degradation of the motif of illegitimate birth introduced sixty years earlier by Hauptmann.) Under the name
Adam Straight he has achieved nation-wide fame as the
hero of a television series. Around age thirty, however,
while touring in Vietnam with a USO show, he had a revelation and began to identify himself with Jesus. Taken along
in a helicopter gunship that opened fire on a peaceful village, he suddenly decided that it was his mission to die for
humanity; all he lacked was a suitable occasion. (The fixa-
tion and death-wish are half-heartedly justified by an implausible confusion of paranoid and mythic motivation.)

Changing his name to Jesse Quest, he involves himself for
a time in civil rights and peace movements. These incidents,
as well as his mystical experiences during a pilgrimage to
the Holy Land, are recounted retrospectively by means of
the encapsulated "gospel" in which he has recorded his
own life. In order to "cleanse the temple," to destroy the
blasphemous Valley of His Passion Park by a huge scandal,
Jesse arranges to have himself crucified on the park's
Golgotha by a gang of teenage hoods. The novel, which is
presented in the form of a mystery solved by a newspaper
reporter and a corrupt sheriff's officer, actually begins with
the crucifixion. Gradually the two strands of plot are un-
raveled: the parodistic warp of the religious park used as
a cover for a criminal operation and the mythic-psychiatric
woof of Jesse Quest's Jesus-fixation. Now since Quest is already dead when the action begins, we do not come to

know him directly, but only in fragmentary flashbacks, through his own "Gospel" and the sketchy recollections of a few casual acquaintances. But this poses a serious technical problem that contributes to the failure of the novel: there is no fixed point of view with which the transfiguration can be identified. Since Quest never appears in person, the narrative cannot focus on the hero and present his paranoia plausibly, as is necessary in the psychological novels. And in the absence of a first-person narrator who can assume the burden of plausibility, the point of view shifts from one figure to another. The author clearly sacrifices character for the sake of plot. As a result, Quest never dominates the action sufficiently to stamp the book as a successful fictional transfiguration; and the techniques, having no real function, are reduced to mere manner. The novel ends predictably: Jesse's only real friend, a rather simpleminded former priest who actually believes in his mission, sets fire to Sodom and Gomorrah and burns the whole establishment to the ground in a holocaust that reminds us of the wide-screen finale of the film produced from Nathanson's earlier novel, *The Dirty Dozen*.

What distinguishes these two novels from the Fifth Gospels is not so much that they are conceived without reverence as that they are executed without subtlety or art. In the one case the name Jesus Christ, abstracted from any kerygmatic meaning or Gospel form, is exploited for sheer shock effect in a currently chic novel of sex and cerebration. In the other, various transfigurational devices are manipulated, with no aesthetic or psychological consistency, for the easy sensationalism of the pseudo-relevant bestseller.

Cultural prognosis is a notoriously hazardous undertaking. But if, for the purpose of discussion, we accept the "sequence of modes" that Northrop Frye outlines in his *Anatomy of Criticism*, then the "ironic" adaptations of the "sacred book"—the Fifth Gospels in our sense of the word— ought to be succeeded by a return to myth. I have no idea what aesthetic form the new myth may assume, unless we choose to regard such popularizations of the Gospels as

Jesus Christ Superstar and *Godspell* as its harbingers. But the recent "Jesus Revolution," so widely proclaimed by *Time* (June 21, 1971) and other witnesses of mass culture, surely signals a new impulse in our society. Essentially, the Jesus Revolution of the early seventies can be seen as yet another outburst of the revivalism that has periodically punctuated the rhythm of American society ever since the Great Awakening of the 1730's. The vocabulary may be contemporary, but the spirit is the same one that moved the mid-eighteenth-century followers of the Reverend George Whitefield to roll on the floor in ecstasy and that inspired the reformers of the nineties to walk "In His Steps." The current generation of "Jesus People"—disenchanted successively with a computerized society, politics, Oriental religions, sexual licentiousness, and drugs—is now "turning on to Jesus." Proclaiming "Jesus Power," many self-styled Jesus Freaks have reverted to a kind of primitive communalism in "Jesus Houses," from which they go forth to pass out "Jesus Propaganda," including bumper stickers and lapel buttons, on street corners. (In Los Angeles one group has founded a so-called Gospel nightclub called "His Place.") As a reaction against sectarianism, the ecumenical thrust of the movement has been greeted by liberal members of the established Churches. Simple joy in the celebration of the man Jesus and his teachings is a healthy antidote to the sometimes dour and sterile ritualism of institutionalized Christianity. Indeed, some of the Street Christians seem to have rediscovered the primal mythic ritual that Silone called "companionship." But what is good for the individual or even society is not necessarily beneficial for art. Glossalalia is no substitute for aesthetic form, nor mindless rapture for calm understanding. Before Hauptmann, Kazantzakis, and Silone could write about their fundamentalist societies, they had to transcend them. Until the literalist reading of the Gospels gives way again to a more playful detachment, the new revivalism is hardly likely to produce fictional transfigurations of greater aesthetic significance than the earliest efforts of the Christian socialists.

8. Rounding the Hermeneutic Circle

IN THE PRECEDING chapters we have considered some twenty fictional transfigurations that have appeared since the publication of *The True History of Joshua Davidson* in 1872. Although this survey does not pretend to be exhaustive, it can probably be regarded as reasonably representative, including as it does works from eight different literatures and from every decade since the nineties (see Appendix). We might note at this point that seven of the transfigurations appeared before the publication of *Ulysses* in 1922, and there is evidence that Joyce was familiar with at least two of them: *The Saint* and *Emanuel Quint*. This fact does not necessarily imply that the fictional transfiguration had any direct impact on the postfigurative technique so brilliantly employed by Joyce. But it proves, contrary to T. S. Eliot's view, that the use of "a continuous parallel between contemporaneity and antiquity" was quite common in the European novel long before the achievement of *Ulysses*, which should therefore be viewed as the perfection of an existing technique rather than as a radical structural innovation. At the same time, although the largest single category comprises the early Christian socialist works, half of the novels are concentrated in the past thirty years. This suggests that the fictional transfiguration was given a new impetus by the sophistication of postfigurative techniques at the hands of such novelists as Joyce and Thomas Mann in novels using other mythic bases.

In Chapters Three through Seven we saw that most of these novels fall easily into certain categories that are temporally fixed according to generation. We noted certain exceptions, of course: psychiatric and mythic transfigurations continued to be written long after the categories were established by Hauptmann and Hesse. In addition, there is a certain cumulative principle at work: later transfigurations, though they are inspired by one impulse, may be affected by techniques perfected for other types: e.g., Steinbeck exploited the mythic parallels although his orientation is essentially social. Yet many of the novels—notably the Christian socialist, the Marxist-oriented, and the Fifth Gospels—group themselves so naturally that the categories may be taken as historically valid and not simply as imposed willfully by the literary historian's compulsive desire for systematic tidiness.

In addition, we were able in many cases to document the authors' awareness of the view of Jesus that was current in their generation. It is important to remind ourselves again that this understanding does not necessarily reflect the prevailing theological thought of the age: the psychiatric interpretation was almost immediately rejected by biblical experts; the Marxist view existed concurrently with form criticism; and the Fifth Gospelists, regarding religion as largely irrelevant, were more interested in the process than in the substance of the New Testament scholarship that they parodied. Our categories, then, reflect a popular climate of opinion rather than any scholarly consensus. This makes sense, for these novelists were writing not for theologians but for a general audience, and it was reasonable for them to employ those associations and motifs that would arouse an immediate response in the reader's mind. By the same token, it is the more familiar stories of Jesus that underlie the fictional transfigurations. The authors of fictionalizing biographies—e.g., Robert Graves in *King Jesus*—may include and popularize recondite details and exotic incidents known only to New Testament scholars. But all of the novels we have examined have relied for their effects on episodes and figures that should be familiar to any reasonably attentive Sunday school pupil or, in an increasingly secular age, to any reader at home in the Western cultural tradition. Similarly, the verbal reverberations that echo in these works—e.g., "the grapes of wrath" or "the power and

the glory"—are generated by the culturally familiar texts—
the King James version or Luther's German translation—
rather than by more recent critical editions of the Bible.

At the same time, even though the general outlines are
clear, there is no need to force the twenty novels into any
rigid categories. *The True History of Joshua Davidson*
amounts to a Christian socialist tract cast in the form of a
"theoretical novel"; and John Barth's "Revised New Syllabus" is a palpably parodistic analogue to the New Testament. But between these two extremes of tract and parody,
which could be said to represent the beginning and end of
this particular literary form, we have encountered numerous shadings and overlappings. The Christian socialist
Nazarín anticipated the psychiatric interest that engaged
the next generation, while Hauptmann mixed a conspicious
portion of social criticism into his analysis of the paranoid
Quint. *A Fable*, though in many respects as conventional as
the earliest Christian socialist efforts, makes use of mythic
effects that were developed much later. Similarly *Demian*
and *Manuel the Mexican*, despite their central obsession
with myth, anticipate the techniques of the Fifth Gospels,
while the dominant social criticism of *The Grapes of Wrath*
is not in the least vitiated by the mythic framework into
which it is cast. It would be a mistake, in other words, to insist on hard and fast distinctions: the categories should be
regarded, rather, as general tendencies that help us to understand the basic impulse of each work—social criticism,
psychological understanding, analysis of myth, parody, and
so forth—and that enable us to identify the features that
unite or differentiate these novels among themselves. To put
it another way: these "ideal" categories simply provide us
with sets of questions that can be put to any transfiguration
in order to determine its aims and its general intellectual
provenance.

We should also remind ourselves that no generation or
category has a priority on successful novels. Each of the five
principal sections has provided, along with certain almost

grotesquely bad (though highly representative) novels, one or two works that belong on anybody's shelf of modern fiction. In fact, it is a matter of considerable significance that the typological pattern of Jesus should have consistently attracted an unusually great proportion of first-rate writers —far greater than the number of those who have written postfigurative novels about Ulysses or Faust, for instance. While it has not been our purpose to examine in any detail the motives that inspired writers to choose this form—that is a question that must be determined biographically in each case—our considerations would suggest that for many of them the thematic (religious) impulse has been no stronger than the aesthetic challenge of adapting this most familiar story to the exigencies of the generation. It is the quality of the fiction represented here that elevates a study of fictional transfigurations above those purely thematological catalogues of subject matter that the Germans call *Stoffgeschichte*. Presumably we should welcome any occasion that invites us to examine under a common rubric such writers as Galdós, Fogazzaro, Hauptmann, Silone, Kazantzakis, Faulkner, and others from our list. At this point, however, we should undertake a more systematic analysis of the material produced by our historical survey.

While the historical approach tended to highlight the differences among the various categories, we have repeatedly noted other features that, cutting across these divisions, unite the twenty novels into a group sharing the common label "fictional transfiguration." It is sobering to discover how few new tricks there are—an insight that should protect us against the overvaluation of "originality" in literary creation. Both Coccioli and Kazantzakis employ the device of a village Passion Play in order to instigate the action of their novels and to make plausible something as farfetched as a modern crucifixion. Surely no one would attribute to literary "influence" the fact that Günter Grass, more than twenty years after Graham Greene, came up with the same idea of disfiguring a drawing or photograph of the hero in such a way as to suggest the halo and thus to contribute to the effect of the transfiguration. Koestler and Harold Kampf alike, in novels notably divergent in quality, resort to the device of the interrogation—which, after all, represents the first high point of the Passion—as the framework for a narrative that proceeds largely by flashbacks. Silone shares with Fogazzaro and Galdós the rather quaint old Victorian triangle of the hero caught between two women representing, respectively, purity and passion. The list could go on and on, but we shall restrict ourselves to a recapitulation of the most frequent and characteristic devices.

If we scan our list of novels, it soon becomes apparent that the titles themselves follow certain fashions. (Only one of the titles, *Cat and Mouse*, reveals no discernible associations with Jesus or the New Testament.) The Christian socialist authors were prone to hint coyly at the exceptional nature of their narratives: *The True History of Joshua Davidson*, *A Singular Life*, or *The Stranger: A Parable*. This is the tradition that Faulkner followed when he called his novel *A Fable*: the old-fashioned title anticipates the tone and techniques of the entire novel, which is closer to the preachiness and heavy-handed allegory of *The Stranger: A Parable* than to the irony and parody of Silone and Barth. Galdós contrives to arouse associations with Jesus through the name of his title-hero *Nazarín*, while Fogazzaro contents himself with the more general religious allusiveness of *The Saint*. Curiously, the only three works that explicitly mention Jesus in their titles are those with a pronounced psychiatric slant: *The Fool in Christ Emanuel Quint*, *Jesus in the Bohemian Forest*, and *Christ Re-Crucified* (the literal translation of the Greek original and the title under which *The Greek Passion* was published in England). In all three last cases the title is descriptively precise, suggesting as it does the paranoid identification with Jesus that ultimately emerges as the central theme; and in at least the first two cases there is more than a hint of the irony that establishes the tone of the works. The novels featuring Comrade Jesus are perhaps most consistent in their use of titles: all four employ a clearly identifiable allusion to the New Testament. The phrase is not merely a precise anticipation of the theme; it also implies the inversion of meaning that, in turn, reflects the hero's ironic consciousness of his own similarity to Jesus. Thus "bread and wine" is not simply the central symbol around which the major scenes of Silone's novel are built; it also represents a total secularization of the traditional Christian sacrament into the mundane rites of human companionship. In the Fifth Gospels the titles are charged with parodistic meaning: Vidal's "Messiah" turns out to be the model of a false prophet; *Giles Goat-Boy or, The Revised New Syllabus* exploits the form of the New Testament to portray a savior whose goals are anything but Christian. And if the title *491* is not instantly intelligible, its inverted significance becomes apparent as soon as we turn the page and read the motto from the Gospel of Matthew. (All the authors but Görling avoid any sort of motto from the Gospels, and he required the motto only to clarify the title.) The development of titles from *The True History* through *Bread and Wine* to *The Revised New Syllabus* alerts us to a typical progression that we shall note in other connections: from tedious allegory through the understatement of technical sophistication to pure parody of the achieved form. It is primarily in such details I believe, that we can trace the rise and decline of a literary form.

After the title, it is the hero's name that most frequently signals the transfiguration. (Many of the titles, of course, include the name.) Variations on Emanuel seem to be the all-time favorite: from Emanuel Bayard and Emanuel Quint down to Kazantzakis' Manolios and Coccioli's Manuel. Both Jim Casy and John Cave have the initials of Jesus Christ; mad Marie in the Bohemian Forest actually christens her son Jesus; while Joshua Davidson, Nazarín, and Krister connote the person of Jesus in somewhat more allusive yet equally manifest ways. Hans von Kahlenberg,

Faulkner, and Graham Greene achieve a certain mysterious effect by leaving the hero nameless; but in each case the title has already warned us to be on the lookout for a "parable" or "fable" or a story with Christian dimensions. Hesse achieves a similar effect with the unusual name Demian, which suggests anything from the Greek *daimon* to a reshuffling of the German word *niemand* ("nobody"). In fact, of all the heroes we have considered, only N. S. Rubashov and Joachim Mahlke have names that do not contain an allusion to Jesus or, at least, some hint of mystery: Piero Maironi assumes the significant sobriquet Benedetto; Pietro Spina's name reminds us of the crown of thorns; Janek Lazar suggests a figure from the New Testament. We shall consider John Barth's onomastic play in another connection.

We see the movement from allegory toward parody in other elements used to characterize the hero. The earliest transfigured heroes were specifically designated as the sons of carpenters—Joshua Davidson, Emanuel Bayard, "the stranger," Emanuel Quint—whereas Lars Görling's Krister, the son of middle-class parents, is as clumsy at his amateur carpentry as he is at everything else (the fiberboard is too thin; the lock works badly; the shelf is flimsy). Similarly, Nazarín is the descendant of Moorish shepherds; Manolios is himself a shepherd; but George Giles has been raised among goats—"Enos Enoch with balls." Another common feature is the mystery of birth or parentage. Emanuel Bayard, Piero Maironi, Pietro Spina, and Manolios have explicitly been orphans since childhood; and it is stressed that Demian, Krister, and Mahlke have no fathers (while each celebrates a curious cult of the mother). Emanuel Quint, the Bohemian Jesus, Faulkner's corporal, and the Mexican Manuel are illegitimate, an ironically rationalistic analogue to the virgin birth. George Giles, in the ultimate parody of the legend of virgin birth, was sired by a computer from a mother named "Virginia" who has never "gone all the way" with a boy. Emanuel Bayard, like the Mexican Manuel, has parents named Mary and Joseph; the Bohemian Jesus' mother is called Marie, but his father has the more allegorical name Christian.

Many authors have also adapted the transfiguration along with its iconographic symbol, the halo, as a salient characteristic of the Jesus figure. In the oldest works, like *A Singular Life*, the narrator may simply dwell upon the "extraordinary" personal beauty of the hero. Piero Maironi is repeatedly described, by those who know him, as "transfigured." The strange "brightness" that illumines Demian's forehead is at the same time a nimbus and a sign of his intellectual and personal power. Jim Casy is called "that shiny bastard" by the men who club him to death, while Kazantzakis adapts a psychosomatic disorder from his own medical history to justify the transfiguration of Manolios after his face heals. (His friends notice "a strange brightness" about him: "in the darkness his face was dazzling.") In *The Power and the Glory* the effect has become ironic: the nimbus is reduced to a circle crudely penciled around the whiskey priest's head to distinguish him in a group photograph. John Cave is said to become "transfigured" whenever he steps in front of a television camera. And in *Cat and Mouse* the same element becomes wholly parodistic when a classmate, drawing a caricature of Mahlke on the blackboard, adds a halo to his "redeemer's countenance."

In many cases, finally, the hero's age is explicitly given as the age conventionally associated with Jesus: Faulkner's corporal is thirty-three years old when he is executed; George Giles is thirty-three and a third when he disappears from the campus for good; and the hero of *When He Shall Appear* is likewise said to be precisely thirty-three at the time of his trial. Both *A Singular Life* and *Messiah* begin when the hero is thirty and end with his death at thirty-three. In other works the age is not pinpointed so precisely, yet it is specifically stated that Nazarín, "the stranger," Piero Maironi, Pietro Spina are in their early thirties; Emanuel Quint is twenty-eight when he sets out on his year-and-a-half mission; and we have no difficulty in calculating that Jim Casy and Greene's whiskey priest are close to the age of Jesus during his years of ministry. In most novels, in other words, the transfigured hero is made for purposes of characterization roughly the same age as Jesus. In the few cases when this is not so, we can comprehend the reason. Either the author is interested in the process of psychogenesis, as in *Jesus in the Bohemian Forest* or *Manuel the Mexican*, or the transfiguration takes place solely in the consciousness of a narrator who attributes these characteristics retrospectively to teenage protagonists (Hesse, Günter Grass, Lars Görling).

Apart from the name of the title-hero there is surprisingly little onomastic play in these novels. Hauptmann, Hans von Kahlenberg, and Faulkner include women named Mary and Martha. Graham Greene achieves an unusual effect with the murderer James Calver, whose initials remind us of Jesus Christ and whose function and surname suggest Calvary. John Barth has created many connotative names through the same process of analogy by which he conceived his entire fiction: he does not resort to initials or variations of Emanuel, but his allusions are clear. Once we enter the spirit of the "Revised New Syllabus" we have no difficulty in identifying Enos Enoch, the Moishians, the Founder, the Dean o' Flunks, and the other figures from Barth's inverted New Testament. Generally speaking, however, authors depend upon function rather than name to identify the supporting characters in their transfigurations.

The Gospels provide novelists with relatively few clear-cut characters. Most of the disciples are leveled down to a faceless choral function from which only Peter and Judas emerge in any sharp detail. As a result, we find in these novels primarily those few figures who are clearly defined by their function in the New Testament. The disciple Peter is distinguished by two traits: the denial of Jesus and the attempt to defend him in Gethsemane. Tom Joad denies Jim Casy while roosters crow in the distance; Pierre Bouc at first denies that he belongs to the group surrounding Faulkner's corporal; the porter Wassilij signs the resolution against Rubashov even while Jesus' words about the cock's crowing run through his memory; and Padre José, the married priest, denies his friendship and refuses to administer the last rites to Greene's whiskey priest. In *491* and *Manuel the Mexican*, in contrast, "Peter" is identified by the hotheaded violence with which he attacks those who have come to arrest Krister and Manuel. In *Nazarín*, Andara fulfills this same function when the three itinerants are arrested by the local authorities.

Equally popular is the figure of John the Baptist, who is sometimes represented as an evangelical figure (Franz Kuhlemann in *The Stranger*, Brother Nathanael in *Emanuel Quint*, Uncle Joad in *The Grapes of Wrath*) and sometimes more soberly as the teacher or tutor of the transfigured hero (Giovanni Selva in *The Saint*; the *cristero* Guadalupe in *Manuel the Mexican*; Don Benedetto in *Bread and Wine*; Max Spielmann in *Giles Goat-Boy*). In several cases this figure experiences the fate of John the Baptist by being executed (*The Stranger, Bread and Wine, Giles Goat-Boy*). And in almost every case he stands at the beginning of the novel to prepare the way for the coming of the transfigured Jesus: either seriously as in the Christian socialist works— e.g., Giovanni Selva as the theoretician behind Piero Maironi's reforms—or parodistically as in *Giles Goat-Boy*.

In another group of novels the figure of Pontius Pilate plays an important functional role: the *alcalde* in *Nazarín*, the judge in *The Stranger* and *When He Shall Appear*, the ironic Minister of Interior in *The Saint*, the agha in *The Greek Passion*, and Ivanov in *Darkness at Noon*. In still other works there are clear echoes of Pilate: Pietro Spina's former schoolmate, Nunzio, wishes to "wash his hands" of all responsibility for Spina's safety; and in *A Fable*, the supreme commander in one of his hypostases offers to free the corporal and turn Polchek, like Barabbas, over to the firing squad. The parodistic inversion of this figure arrives in *Giles Goat-Boy*, where the Chancellor's "fastidious official neutrality" becomes the absolute trivialization of the agonizing question: "What is truth?"

Even the repentant thief on the cross shows up in several novels, for though he has no name in the Gospels, he has a clearly identifiable role in them. In *Nazarín* it is the thief Sacrilege who aids Nazarín on the trip to Madrid and who is in fact redeemed in Nazarín's hallucinatory vision of heaven; in *The Power and the Glory* it is the outlaw James Calver, whom the priest urges to repent—"like the thief." In *A Fable* it is the apelike Casse-tête, who keeps whimpering for Paris and whom the corporal consoles as they stand ready to be shot. In *Demian*, finally, the story of the repentant thief is inverted by transvaluation: Demian argues that it would be preferable to have as a friend a man of strong character like the unrepentant thief rather than the man who at the last moment forsakes all his principles for an empty promise of deliverance.

Mary Magdalene, a popular because readily identifiable role, undergoes certain transformations with the changing historical circumstances. The early Christian socialists, crusading against prostitution, routinely included the fallen woman who is rescued by the transfigured hero: Mary Prinsep in *Joshua Davidson*, Lena in *A Singular Life*, Andara in *Nazarín*, an unnamed streetwalker in *The Stranger*, and Elise Schuhbrich in *Emanuel Quint*. In *The Saint* and, by derivation, in *Bread and Wine* the prostitute is promoted to become the woman of passion whose advances the hero must ward off: Jeanne Dessalle and Bianchina. Both Kazantzakis and Faulkner revert to the original pattern: the widow Katerina, the village harlot, subsequently sacrifices her life to save Manolios; and Faulkner's corporal is reportedly married to a Marseilles streetwalker, though she plays no role in the novel. The inevitable inversion of this figure arrives with the last two parodies: the transfigured hero of *491* finds himself thrust, unwittingly, into the role of pimp to an already depraved prostitute; and in *Giles Goat-Boy* the great moment of revelation arrives when George Giles beds down with Anastasia, the epitome of the whore with a heart of gold, in the belly of the computer WESCAC.

The inevitable complement to Jesus is Judas, without whom the Passion cannot come to pass. But again we note the same adaptation of role and function to the exigencies of the times. In *A Singular Life*, with its campaign against alcoholism, the Judas who turns the citizens against Emanuel Bayard and kills him with a stone is the owner of a seamen's grog shop, while in *Nazarín* it is strongly implied that Beatriz' jealous lover, El Pinto, has reported the three refugees to his cousin the *alcalde*. Emanuel Quint's betrayer is a former follower who, having murdered a young girl, tries to cast the blame on Quint, while the Judas in *Bread and Wine* turns out to be a priest who has sold himself to the regime.

The Power and the Glory and *The Greek Passion* raise the Judas-figure from the relatively minor function of catalytic agent to a major one. Greene's whiskey priest is so totally obsessed with the notion of betrayal that he ultimately pursues his own Judas, the fanged mestizo, and follows him knowingly into a trap. And Kazantzakis is fascinated by the emotional process through which Panayotaros eventually comes to accept the Judas-role that has been alloted to him against his wishes. The role of Judas in *A Fable* reveals again how old-fashioned Faulkner's transfiguration really is: it is included purely in order to satisfy the pattern. Since Polchek has betrayed the mutiny to the generals before the story even begins, we get no insight into his character and sense no psychological necessity for his act, but only a mythic compulsion. In *Manuel the Mexican* there is the tantalizing implication, widespread in many recent lives of Jesus, that Manuel has conspired to be betrayed in order to fulfill his pre-ordained role: the same Darío who arranges for Manuel to play the part of Jesus in the village pageant subsequently accuses him of rape so that he may be crucified in reality; and the two men constantly exchange significant looks and smiles.

With Günter Grass and Lars Görling we reach the parodistic inversion: Judas has so emphatically replaced Jesus as a model for the fiction that those two works can appropriately be designated as *Evangelia Judae*. In the one case Pilenz is pursued by his own "gloomy conscience" for some fifteen years after his "betrayal" of Mahlke; in the other Nils Nisseman sets out systematically to commit the legendary four hundred and ninety-first offense that will cause Krister to discard his well-meaning liberalism, which has proved to be wholly unsuitable for the harsh reality of modern society. In both cases Judas takes precedence over Jesus: the hero—Mahlke and Krister—is transfigured by the narrator's retrospective imagination only in response to his own consciousness of himself as a betrayer. Jesus is defined by Judas.

In only a few cases does the modern Judas come to the same end as his New Testament counterpart: Dr. Whipple in *When He Shall Appear* dies of a seizure when he realizes the implications of his betrayal; in *Emanuel Quint* Bohemian Joe hangs himself in the legendary Judas-gesture of despair; at the end of *A Fable* Polchek is hanged symbolically if not in actuality; and in *The Greek Passion* Panayotaros indicates his intention to kill himself as soon as he has gratified his overwhelming urge to destroy Manolios.

The figure of the Virgin Mary is singularly colorless in the Gospels and offers little material for the writer. In Pasolini's film, which adheres scrupulously to the text of Matthew's Gospel, Mary does not utter a single line of dialogue; for the most part she is nothing but a mute witness of the action. It was not until medieval times that the emerging Marian cults gradually endowed the Virgin Mother with the characteristics subsequently popularized in art and legend. As a result, the transfigurations that follow the Gospels most closely do least with this figure: in *Nazarín* and *The Saint* there is no mother; in *A Singular*

Life she dies after fulfilling the basic function of bearing Emanuel Bayard, and in *Joshua Davidson* she is not mentioned after the first few pages; only *The Stranger*, almost arbitrarily, introduces the mother as a witness in the court proceedings near the end so that the transfigured hero can deny her and thus re-enact one of the few action-scenes involving the Virgin Mary. The Virgin, in short, is an awkward figure to deal with. If she is present in a modern transfiguration, then realism will not permit her to be a virgin; but if she is not a virgin, then she is no longer the venerated object of cultic adoration. It is much simpler to ignore her: in the Marxist-oriented novels there is no mother-figure at all. Her fictional significance varies, it might be suggested, in inverse proportion with the degree of reverence. When the figure assumes a role of any significance, she is almost always the mother of an illegitimate child (*Emanuel Quint*), demented (*Jesus in the Bohemian Forest*), or a grand syncretic amalgam (*Demian*).

The first half of *Manuel the Mexican*, to be sure, is devoted to José and María, but the plot is almost wholly fictional and has virtually no prefigurative basis in the Bible; once Manuel is born and occupies the center of action, the mother disappears from the scene. Paradoxically, it is the parodistic transfigurations that make the most of this figure: both Krister and Mahlke celebrate weird cults of the Virgin. The conscious anachronism according to which Jesus adores the Virgin contributes to the parodistic effect of the story and heightens our sense of detachment from the material. The central tenet of the Marian cult achieves its complete inversion in *Giles Goat-Boy* when the story of Virginia Hector's violation by the computer is recounted in sensuous detail.

Since the transfigured hero is usually in his thirties at the time of the action, the circumstances of his birth and parentage contribute to characterization rather than to plot and are relegated, for the most part, to flashbacks. This makes sense because the "plot" of Jesus' life is confined almost wholly to the years of ministry and the Passion. The fictionalizing biographer—like Robert Graves in *King Jesus* or Kazantzakis in *The Last Temptation*—may be interested in inventing incidents or drawing upon apocryphal legend to fill in the so-called Silent Years. But the author of a fictional transfiguration is heavily dependent upon easily recognizable episodes: more recondite details might not be perceived through the fictional transformation. And the familiar episodes fall almost wholly into the years between the baptism at thirty and the crucifixion at thirty-three.

The novelists we have considered make use of surprisingly few specific episodes from the years of ministry. Many of the novels begin with a proclamation by John the Baptist; similarly, the conversion of Mary Magdalene is an incident tied to these years. A few works employ other details from time to time. Brother Nathanael sees doves hovering above when he baptizes Emanuel Quint. Faulkner's corporal performs a good deed that reminds us of the wedding at Cana. Hans von Kahlenberg includes an episode patterned after the raising of Lazarus. But such specific parallels to incidents from the years of public ministry are isolated and rare. Generally speaking, three distinctive features or motifs are used with consistent frequency to suggest the period preceding the Passion: "miracles," a mission, and a temptation.

Almost every transfigured hero is reputed to perform "miracles" of some sort. In the earliest novels the miracles are rationalized in the spirit of the liberal lives: Emanuel Bayard swims through a stormy sea to rescue a shipwrecked sailor; Nazarín devotes himself selflessly to the victims of a smallpox epidemic; and quite a few of the heroes—e.g., in *When He Shall Appear* and *The Saint*—perform acts of faith-healing. In all of these cases—including also *The Stranger, Emanuel Quint, Jesus in the Bohemian Forest, Bread and Wine*—the more credulous people surrounding the hero, believing that these acts are in fact miracles, take them as a sign of the hero's oneness with Jesus: Bianchina believes that Pietro Spina is Jesus until she notices that he has no stigmata on his hands. In some of the later novels the therapeutic wonders become psychological "miracles"—e.g., Demian's ability to manipulate classmates and teachers alike, the corporal's success in soliciting money from the soldiers for a good cause (an eye operation), or John Cave's hypnotic gaze that fascinates every viewer and subsequently makes him a sensation on television. In the last novels this thaumaturgic ability is also parodied: Mahlke performs "miracles" of masturbating. And it is the sardonic point of *491* that Krister is unable to perform any miracles at all and thus to help the boys in his care.

A second principal characteristic of the years of public ministry is the mission; the appeal of the fictional transfiguration for many writers stems precisely from the fact that the form evokes associations with the "minister" par excellence. In the novels the mission tends to fall into one of two categories, which might be called the fraternal and the quixotic. In most cases the hero's mission is fraternal or "organizational" in the broadest sense: this is evident in the Christian socialist novels with their Endeavor Societies and Leagues of Catholic Laymen. But it applies just as clearly to the Marxist-oriented writers: Jim Casy is a labor organizer; Rubashov sacrifices himself for the good of the Party; and Pietro Spina celebrates the brotherhood of all men with the sacrament of bread and wine. Max Demian assembles— "organizes" would be too plebeian an expression for his élitist activities—a group of followers devoted to his Nietzschean kingdom of the spirit. Faulkner's corporal organizes an entire regiment of three thousand men into a pacifist mutiny. Manuel also has a public mission: to unite his countrymen in a new unity of Mexican time, which will liberate them from the acedia in which they have been caught for centuries. The ironic extreme of this tendency shows up in

Vidal's *Messiah*, where John Cave's message is "sold" by the super-missionary Paul Himmell, who manipulates all the techniques of modern public relations. The inevitable *reductio ad absurdum* of this fraternal mission shows up in *491*: Krister does not have to win disciples; they are turned over to him by a solicitous welfare state. Yet they remain so contemptuous of his liberal "mission" that he is unable to unite them in any meaningful way; his behavior, in fact, contributes more to the dispersal than to the fraternal unification of the boys.

In other cases the years of ministry are characterized not so much by this fraternal impulse as by a feature that is often regarded as equally typical of Jesus: the quixotic insistence on pursuing one's own goals in opposition to the Establishment. (It is no accident that Miguel de Unamuno has repeatedly and explicitly stressed the essential identity of Don Quixote and Christ.) Among the Christian socialist novels *Nazarín* is unique in that the hero makes no attempt to organize others but goes his own way, oblivious of ecclesiastical admonishments. The psychiatric impulse motivating Hauptmann and Kazantzakis produces heroes who are more quixotic than fraternal: their paranoid identification with Jesus compels them to act out their own Passion even in the face of the strongest opposition and even when, as in Quint's case, his disciples ultimately desert him. For altogether different reasons Greene's whiskey priest belongs to the quixotic type. Political circumstance in Tabasco make any sort of organization impossible; and when the priest finally has a chance to escape and to operate within the official Church in a free state, he refuses. He is obsessed wholly by the—in the loftiest sense—quixotic ambition of being the sole representative of the Church in an otherwise godless state. Mahlke's escalating series of feats turns out ultimately to be a pursuit of the Knight's Cross with only incidental fraternal value; this adolescent with the quixotic dream of becoming a clown is as much of a loner as George Giles,

who has the mission of descending into the belly of
WESCAC in order to reprogram the computer—the ultimate inversion of the mission theme.

Perhaps not quite so common as the miracles and the mission, but related to them, is a third motif of the years of
ministry: very often the transfigured hero is tempted to betray his calling. Sometimes there is an explicit parallel.
When Emanuel Bayard is trying to decide whether to
marry Helen Carruth or to continue with his work in the
seaside slums, the narrator reminds us: "So Emanuel
Bayard entered into his Wilderness. Therein he was
tempted like other men of God who renounced the greatest
joy of life for its grandest duty." Similarly, at the beginning
of *The Saint*, when Piero Maironi catches sight of Jean Dessalle for the first time in three years, he goes up into the
hills to struggle against his passion. But then he is afflicted
by an even more insidious temptation: he sees himself, in
a vision, proclaimed the reformer of the Church and the
true Vicar of Christ: "At that moment there flashed across
his mind the thought of Satan offering the kingdoms of the
world to Christ. . . . 'Jesus, Jesus, I am not worthy to be
tempted as Thou wast.'" And in *A Fable* a similar reminis-
cence of Jesus' temptation is slyly worked into the great dialogue between the corporal and his father, the supreme
commander. In *The Greek Passion* Manolios is afflicted by
a dual temptation: the sensual attraction of the widow
Katerina, which ultimately brings about his conversion and
transfiguration, and the temptation of pride which, as he
confesses to his friends, caused him to put himself on a level
with Christ: "'I set off for the mountain, for solitude, far
from temptations. "Up there," I said to myself, "where the
air's pure, I will consecrate myself to Christ." Well, at the
moment when I was going to take the path and was about
to be saved, lo and behold at Saint Basil's Well, just outside
the village, Satan was waiting for me.'" The temptation to
which Quint is subjected is a perfectly sound one: to remain

at Gurau in the company of intelligent and reasonable friends. When he rejects this "temptation" in order to return to the Valley Brethren, he is in fact returning from sanity to paranoia. Greene's whiskey priest is often tempted to give up and to flee to the safety of a neighboring state; but when he finally does so, he finds that he cannot avoid his own Passion, and so he willingly returns. And George Giles, finally, is tempted by promises of vast power in the university-world to give up his mission of liberating the campus.

Generally speaking, then, the action of the years of ministry is organized around certain miracles that the transfigured hero is reputed to perform and around his either fraternal or quixotic mission, from which he is often tempted to desist, either by lust or the lure of worldly power. If he perseveres, however, his ultimate reward is a Passion scene. A few of the earlier novels—notably *Joshua Davidson, Nazarín,* and *The Saint*—explicitly lead the hero from the provinces to the capital for his Passion; and in his delusion Emanuel Quint identifies the city of Breslau with Golgotha. The triumphal entry is treated ironically in *Quint*: as his disciples observe, nobody seems to notice that Quint has actually arrived. *A Fable* begins with a scene calculated to remind us of the triumphal entry: the corporal and his twelve men are brought into the city in a truck through streets lined with people. The whole motif is satirized in *Cat and Mouse*: when Mahlke returns from the war with his Knight's Cross, he is not allowed to speak to the students in his high school—the triumphal entry is inverted into a tragicomedy.

In general, the Passion is characterized primarily by two features: some combination of the Last Supper and Gethsemane, and a crucifixion scene. Possibly the Christian socialists were too devout to play aesthetically with an event as sacred as the Last Supper. In any case, only *Nazarín* includes a clear imitation of that episode when the quixotic priest shares his final meal with Beatriz and

Andara, speaking words of comfort to the two of them before the authorities arrive to arrest him. In Hauptmann's
novel the parallels are worked out in considerable detail—
down to the washing of feet and quotations lifted from the
Gospels—since Quint in his total derangement realizes that
he requires some dramatic gesture in order to hold his disciples together. One might almost say that *Bread and Wine*
is written in such a way as to culminate in a totally secularized Last Supper before Pietro Spina, betrayed, flees into
the mountains. In *The Power and the Glory* Greene's whiskey priest, who has no disciples, re-enacts the agonies of
Gethsemane rather than the Last Supper. *A Fable* reduces
the Last Supper to a crassly naturalistic scene; but it includes the telling detail of the Judas, who goes out to betray
the corporal, and it is followed by the Gethsemane-like
scene above the city in which the corporal is momentarily
tempted to let the cup pass from him. In *Manuel the Mexican* the Last Supper is transformed into a big party given
in Manuel's honor by the village notables; on Holy Thursday he is strolling in the garden-like court of the church
when he is seized by the villagers and accused of rape:
"Alone in this silence, the Boy has to face the breath of
fear." In *491* there is no Last Supper; but when the police
come to arrest Krister, we see an unmistakable motif from
Gethsemane when Genghis leaps on the policeman standing
beside Krister and almost bites his ear off: like Peter, Genghis then succeeds in escaping. Similarly, in *Cat and Mouse*
we detect analogies to Gethsemane in the Thursday evening
scene in which Mahlke—inverting the biblical event—actually attacks his Pharisaic persecutor, Dr. Klohse. The next
day's mass contains clear allusions to the Last Supper, but
immediately afterwards the entire effect is travestied when
Mahlke gets a stomach ache from making his own last meal
of unripe gooseberries.

The hero's death is the almost inevitable result of every
fictional transfiguration: only *Nazarín* and the hero of

When He Shall Appear do not die at the end. And yet the death presents a challenging fictional problem because, as the *alcalde* reminds Nazarín, crucifixion is no longer fashionable. Two authors do contrive to have their heroes die on the cross: in *The Stranger* the crucifixion is carried out in a madhouse, where it is almost wholly unmotivated and yet not altogether implausible, and in *Manuel the Mexican* the hero is crucified at the height of the village Passion Play. Although he does not die, Nazarín experiences in his hallucinations what amounts to a *via dolorosa* and crucifixion. In many of the other novels the hero suffers a violent death that constitutes a satisfactory modern equivalent to the violence of the crucifixion: Joshua Davidson is trampled by a mob; Emanuel Bayard is killed by a stone; Jim Casy is clubbed to death; and Manolios is stabbed. John Cave and Koestler's Rubashov are shot; Greene's priest and Faulkner's corporal are executed by firing squads; and the Bohemian Jesus is thrown into a raging fire. Piero Maironi simply dies, apparently of typhus, but the circumstances resemble those of the crucifixion: he has been threatened by the secular authorities; the people mutter that he has been murdered; and the sky turns dark at midday. Quint likewise dies, presumably freezing to death in an Alpine storm, but his death is an ironic inversion of the Passion because we know how monomaniacally he had sought to be "crucified" in an act of self-sacrifice. Pietro Spina escapes death at the end of *Bread and Wine*; but four months later, in the sequel, he surrenders to the police and is led away to be executed. Demian dies on the battlefield, where he is fighting for the birth of a new humanity. Mahlke and Krister both die by suicide, Mahlke by drowning and Krister by hurling himself out of a kitchen window. And George Giles simply disappears from the campus at the age of thirty-three and a third, relieved of his "tenure" by the university authorities. In almost every case the death has symbolic significance as an act of redemption or self-sacrifice in service of the hero's mission.

We have already had occasion to note (in Chapter One) that the resurrection belongs to the realm of the kerygmatic Christ and not of the historical Jesus. Most of the fictional transfigurations, accordingly, contain no hint of anything resembling this item of Christian faith. But since the expectation of a resurrection is so strongly inherent in the story of Jesus Christ, a few writers have managed to incorporate even this detail. In several novels (*Demian, The Greek Passion, The Grapes of Wrath*) a mystical transferral of mission occurs at the end, suggesting that the hero's idea endures even without anything as supernatural as a resurrection. But in at least three novels we find an allusion to physical resurrection. *A Fable* accomplishes this by implying that the corporal's body is chosen to occupy the tomb of the Unknown Soldier in Paris. Similarly, when the new priest appears at the end of *The Power and the Glory*, the boy Juan at first mistakes him for the whiskey priest, who has just been executed, and thus intimates a mystical identity. George Giles returns "clandestinely" to the campus after his dismissal—in analogy to Jesus, who appeared to his disciples on several occasions after the crucifixion. Finally, we find what amounts to a parodistic inversion of the resurrection in *Cat and Mouse*: for Pilenz' anguish stems almost entirely from the fact that Mahlke did *not* ascend from the sunken ship; he is condemned to spend his days waiting vainly for the resurrection that does not take place.

Most of the novels retain the general temporal sequence of the Gospels, beginning with the baptism by John and moving through the years of mission to the "crucifixion" (e.g., *A Singular Life, The Saint, The Stranger, Emanuel Quint, Bread and Wine, The Grapes of Wrath, The Greek Passion, Messiah, Giles Goat-Boy*). A few others open with the birth and childhood of the hero (*Joshua Davidson, Jesus in the Bohemian Forest*). Several novels, however, achieve a different effect by temporal inversion. Both *Darkness at Noon* and *When He Shall Appear* concentrate the action into the framework of the trial, presenting the exposition in-

directly through flashbacks. Faulkner uses a similar flashback device, but he expands the framework to begin with
the "triumphal entry" and to end with the "resurrection."
Coccioli begins with the crucifixion and then adds a chronological account of the birth, childhood, calling, and years
of ministry in order to justify this otherwise irrational
happening.

In a few cases, finally, we encounter an ironic inversion
of the normal sequence from Christmas to Easter. This is
made most explicit in *Bread and Wine*, which begins with
Pietro Spina's return to Italy around Easter time. He refers
to his hiding place, from which he emerges "reborn" as
Paolo Spada, as a crèche; his disappearance shortly before
Christmas is underlined by the discussion regarding the
nine months that it requires to make a loaf of bread, a glass
of wine, or a man. This same inversion is used quite effectively in the two major psychiatric novels. It is at Easter
that Manolios is appointed to play the role of Christ and
that Quint, after his eight months at Gurau, ultimately succumbs to the blandishments of his followers. *The Greek
Passion*, which begins with Manolios' spiritual rebirth at
Easter, ends when he is murdered at Christmas. Similarly,
Quint sets out at Eastertime to pursue his own Passion. But
because reality will not immediately adapt itself to his hallucination, time drags along for months, and it is not until
Christmas that he finally disappears for good and perishes
in the snow storm.

In summary we might stress two points. First, every work
of the type that we have chosen to call "fictional transfiguration" contains in varying configurations a number of formal
signals that, regardless of theme or content, alert us to the
Gospel parallel: title, characterization of the hero, function
of the secondary figures, organization of the plot, imagery,
and so forth. Our awareness of the parallel, in turn, arouses
certain expectations in our imagination. Our enjoyment of
the form depends in large measure upon the manner in
which these expectations are fulfilled. If the fulfillment is

too obvious, too mechanically "allegorical," then our pleasure is proportionately decreased. But if the author contrives to satisfy our expectations in an unexpected way, our appreciation is enhanced. In other words, a twofold process of continuity and discontinuity takes place in every fictional transfiguration: the author must stress the literary tradition sufficiently to make us aware of the form within which he is working, yet he must achieve a certain originality within that self-imposed framework in order to sustain our interest.

Second, the history of fictional transfigurations over the past century reveals in almost paradigmatic clarity the growth of a literary form. Again and again in countless details, we noted that the form initially came into existence as a rather tedious and clumsy allegory in order to serve a specific social purpose. It grew through increased psychological insight, ironic understatement, and technical sophistication to become a pliable means of fictional expression. Having attained this formal perfection, which is displayed in several of the major works, it was inverted—perhaps inevitably—into self-parody. Needless to say, this process of literary growth can be observed in many other genres as well.

We now turn to a final question: How does an author persuade us to accept this greatest of implausibilities—that the story of Jesus has repeated itself in modern times? Almost all the novels, as we have seen, use essentially the same basic techniques of transfiguration. If the authors have varying degrees of success in persuading us to suspend our disbelief, therefore, their achievement lies not so much in the technique used as in the filtering consciousness through which the parallels are presented.

Very few of these novels, it turns out, expect us to accept the transfiguration at face value: *The True History of Joshua Davidson, A Singular Life, The Stranger, When He Shall Appear,* and *A Fable.* With the possible exception of

Faulkner's novel, no one would be tempted to argue that these works, in which the author or narrator proposes with a straight face that history is repeating itself, represent any peak of fictional art. In all of these novels the parallel is so obtrusive that it shatters all of our illusions, and we read the work as an allegorical tract rather than as fiction.

In almost every other case, however, and notably in the works that we feel to be most successful, some other consciousness interposes itself as a mediating agent between the credulity of the reader and the implausibility of the events, making the transfiguration somehow more acceptable. In novels with an impersonal narrator we are inclined to credit the fictional transfiguration when it is presented as residing in the consciousness of the characters themselves, rather than as being imposed by the author. We have seen two possibilities. First, in the psychiatric novels the author clearly does not believe in the transfiguration: the fiction is credible because the hero himself, in a delusion that is made psychologically plausible, identifies himself with Jesus and actively seeks out his own Passion. It is, so to speak, the hero and not the author who is organizing the action according to the Gospel (*Emanuel Quint, Jesus in the Bohemian Forest, The Greek Passion*). In other third-person narratives we accept the transfiguration when it resides in the hero's ironic consciousness. The author does not invite us to suspend our disbelief totally—as, for instance, the author of *A Singular Life* asks us to do—but merely to savor along with the hero the ironic awareness that circumstances have thrust him into a role sharing certain points in common with that of Jesus. The hero knows that he is not Jesus; the author knows that he is not; and so do we, the readers. But we are all sophisticated enough to enter into a three-way conspiracy of irony (*The Saint, Bread and Wine, Grapes of Wrath, The Power and the Glory*, and *Darkness at Noon*). Since no one seriously maintains that the Gospel is being mystically re-enacted, the parallels do not need to be so obtrusive as they are in the psychiatric novels, where the hero actively pursues his own Passion, or in the naïvely allegorical works, where the transfiguration is thrust upon us as a mystical fact.

To the extent that it is a psychological study, *Nazarín* belongs to the first group: we accept the transfiguration because it exists largely in the hero's own deluded mind. But to the extent that the novel, notably in its first section, has a personal narrator rather than an objective author, it belongs in another category. The first-person narrator of *Joshua Davidson* thrusts the miracle of transfiguration upon us in all seriousness; but most of the first-person narrators have a far more problematic attitude toward their material. The narrator of *Nazarín* is troubled because he is unsure, in retrospect, to what extent the priest is "a true and real personality" and to what extent he is merely a figure "constructed from materials extracted from my own ideas." Here, as well as in *Demian* and the two Gospels of Judas (*Cat and Mouse, 491*) we must face the likelihood that many of the transfigurational elements have been imposed on the hero retrospectively by a narrator who has some interest in making a Jesus-figure of his hero: Emil Sinclair found it desirable in order to lend special significance to everything that he had learned from Max Demian; in the cases of Pilenz and Nisse, the narrator's consciousness of being a betrayer, a Judas, was so overpowering that it summoned forth a Jesus-figure as an adequate counterweight.

The narrator of *Manuel the Mexican* is not a Judas-figure, but he has a highly ambivalent attitude toward his material: sitting in Florence and writing about his Mexican experiences, he repeatedly worries about the seeming absurdity of his story, and these reflections, combined with his mythic interpretation of the hero, paradoxically make the entire fiction more acceptable. The narrator of *Messiah* does not impose the transfiguration retrospectively on his past experiences; alone among the characters of the story he has the historical sophistication necessary to glimpse the parallels between the life of Jesus and that of John Cave at the time that he is witnessing them; but his sense of irony never permits him, even for a moment, to take them seriously. *Giles Goat-Boy*, finally, is so ironic an allegory that there is no pretense at suspension of disbelief. The fun of the novel lies in our recognition of its absurdity.

In sum, none of the major transfigurations except *A Fable* seriously urges upon us the totally irrational implication that the life of Jesus is being re-enacted in modern times. The parallels are almost always thrust into the fiction itself—that is, into the consciousness of the hero or narrator —and thereby become psychologically plausible. We are willing to accept the transfiguration as parody; we accept it when it is a delusion in the mind of a paranoid hero or an ironic comment in the consciousness of a sophisticated hero; we accept it when it is imposed retrospectively by the narrator out of some emotional need of his own; and we are willing to suspend our disbelief, at least tentatively, when the narrator admits that even he finds his story somewhat difficult to believe. Among modern writers only Faulkner makes the old-fashioned demand that we credit a fictional transfiguration that is imposed from without, by the author, and not motivated from within.

The consistency with which the basic characteristics have survived through so many modifications as a vehicle for so many meanings—from the earnest pamphleteering of the Christian socialists through the humanism of the Marxists to the parodies of the Fifth Gospelists—seems to verify the hypothesis with which we began: that we can speak of a literary category known as "fictional transfigurations of Jesus" and that this category can be recognized and defined wholly on the basis of its form and fictional characteristics —and explicitly not on the basis of its meaning or contents. Our investigation has also provided answers to the questions that were initially generated by the example of Mynheer Peeperkorn. We have seen that the category does indeed have a definable history: it arose in the latter part of the nineteenth century in response to a unique and specific set of historical circumstances, and it has undergone various transformations in the course of the years in an effort to adapt itself to the exigencies of the times. Yet in the face of these changes its techniques and identifying features have remained remarkably constant.

Our awareness of the category not only enhances our historical understanding; it can also contribute to our critical evaluation of the texts. It enables us to locate novels of a certain type within a meaningful framework: we recognize that fictional transfigurations have aims and techniques that differ perceptibly from those, say, of the "pseudonyms of Christ" and other superficially similar forms. Structurally, it makes more sense to compare *Emanuel Quint*, for instance, to such a postfigurative novel as *Ulysses* than to *The Idiot*, although thematically Hauptmann's work may have more in common with Dostoevsky's novel. Further, the history of the category reminds us that literary works represent an aesthetic response to urgent impulses of the times—social, psychological, political, mythic, parodistic, and so forth. Our interpretation of the work must therefore be grounded in an understanding of the society that produces it, including explicitly our own, since the value and meaning of the common denominator "Jesus" can shift so radically. Finally, the systematic analysis of the category helps us to keep in mind the formal limitations within which the author has chosen to work and thus to evaluate more precisely the skill and originality with which he employs the various techniques inherent in the category.

The form, to be sure, seems to labor under at least two handicaps. We have noted a recurring tendency toward preachy prolixity that enters with *The True History of Joshua Davidson* and continues right down to *A Fable* and *Manuel the Mexican*. This is paralleled by a tendency toward over-explicit allegory, which is evident as early as *A Singular Life* and which finally weighs down *Giles Goat-Boy*. Both of these predispositions, it might be argued, are inherent in the Gospels themselves. The finest novels, however, have avoided these shortcomings by exploiting the detachment afforded by psychology and irony. The ironic temper is rarely inclined to preach, and shrewd psychological insight is not content with the vague generalities of allegorical or mythic motivation.

At the beginning of *The Quest of the Historical Jesus* Albert Schweitzer stated the seeming paradox that the greatest lives of Jesus were written with "hate," that hate that strips away the supernatural nimbus in which the figure of Jesus is all too often falsely and facilely shrouded. Our own investigations lead us to believe, by way of analogy, that the finest fictional transfigurations have also been inspired by a kind of "hate," an aesthetic detachment that sharpens psychological insight, heightens irony, and receives its fullest gratification from the play with pure form that transcends all meaning. As we look back over the list of novels from *Joshua Davidson* to *Giles Goat-Boy*, we detect in fact a logical progression of increasing alienation, from the still intact faith of the Christian socialists to the complete indifference of the Fifth Gospelists. If we now introduce our own activity into the survey as symptomatic of many recent studies—the inversion of the observing subject into the observed object is a procedure that can be justified fashionably by relativity theory or, less pretentiously, by romantic irony—we might conclude that the seventies find the figure of Jesus as fascinating as ever. But this very willingness to contemplate Jesus in any and all of his transfigurations, this substitution of mere interest for the commitment of love or hate, suggests that we have attained a new peak of alienation. Proceeding from the flesh-and-blood Jesus of social criticism and psychiatry, we have moved beyond the attenuated *figura* of myth and parody to arrive at a bland construct twice-removed from its Gospel source: the scholar-critic's Jesus. And that, as Faith might concede to Skepticism, is perhaps the only Jesus we deserve.

APPENDIX

Chronological List of Fictional Transfigurations
(by first edition)

[Elizabeth Lynn Linton.] *The True History of Joshua Davidson.*
London: Strahan, 1872.

Elizabeth Stuart Phelps [Ward]. *A Singular Life.* Boston and New
York: Houghton, Mifflin, 1895 [c1894].

Benito Pérez Galdós. *Nazarín.* Madrid: La Guirnalda, 1895.

Hans von Kahlenberg. *Der Fremde: Ein Gleichniss.* Dresden und
Leipzig: Carl Reissner, 1901.

Antonio Fogazzaro. *Il Santo.* Milano: Baldini e Castoldi, 1905.

Gerhart Hauptmann. *Der Narr in Christo Emanuel Quint.* Berlin:
S. Fischer, 1910.

[Hermann Hesse.] *Demian: Die Geschichte einer Jugend von Emil
Sinclair.* Berlin: S. Fischer, 1919.

Robert Michel. *Jesus im Böhmerwald.* Wien: Speidel, 1927.

Ignazio Silone. *Bread and Wine.* Trans. Gwenda David and Eric
Mosbacher. London: Methuen, 1936.

————. *Pane e vino.* Nuove ed. di Capolago, Lugano, 1937; rev. ed.
(*Vino e pane*), Milano: Mondadori, 1955.

John Steinbeck. *The Grapes of Wrath.* New York: Viking, 1939.

Graham Greene. *The Power and the Glory.* London: Heinemann,
1940.

Arthur Koestler. *Darkness at Noon.* Trans. Daphne Hardy. London:
Cape, 1940.

Nikos Kazantzakis. *Den eviga vandringen uppåt.* Trans. Börje Knös.
Stockholm: Ljus, 1950.

————. *Ho Christos xanastauronetai.* Athens: Diphros, 1954.

Harold Kampf. *When He Shall Appear.* Boston: Little, Brown, 1953.

William Faulkner. *A Fable.* New York: Random House, 1954.

Gore Vidal. *Messiah.* New York: E. P. Dutton, 1954; rev. ed., New
York: Little, Brown, 1965.

Carlo Coccioli. *Manuel le Mexicain.* Paris: Librairie Plon, 1956.

Günter Grass. *Katz und Maus.* Neuwied und Berlin: Luchterhand,
1961.

Lars Görling. *491.* Stockholm: Bonniers, 1962.

John Barth. *Giles Goat-Boy or, The Revised New Syllabus.* Garden
City, N. Y.: Doubleday, 1966.

SELECTED BIBLIOGRAPHY

THE FOLLOWING BIBLIOGRAPHY does not repeat information supplied elsewhere in the book. The Appendix lists the twenty fictional transfigurations by first edition; notes specify the editions and translations to which I have referred. All secondary works consulted by me have already been cited fully in the notes. It would be an exercise in pedantry to furnish complete bibliographical data for the scholarly lives of Jesus adduced as examples of various trends; that information is available in the cited works by Schweitzer, Drews, and others. This bibliography, therefore, includes only those literary treatments of Jesus mentioned in the text but not listed in the Appendix. The editions and translations are the ones that I actually consulted; the date of original publication is given in the text.

Asch, Shalom. *The Nazarene*. Trans. Maurice Samuel. New York: Putnam, 1939.

Balzac, Honoré de. "Jésus-Christ en Flandre." *Œuvres complètes*. Vol. xv (Paris: Lévy, 1879), pp. 243-59.

Bishop, Jim. *The Day Christ Died*. New York: Harper, 1957.

Blok, Alexander. "The Twelve." *A Treasury of Russian Literature*. Ed. Bernard Guilbert Guerney. New York: Vanguard, 1943. Pp. 1012-24.

Caldwell, Taylor. *Great Lion of God*. Garden City, N. Y.: Doubleday, 1970.

Clark, Glenn. *What Would Jesus Do? Wherein a new generation undertakes to walk in His Steps*. St. Paul, Minn.: Macalester Park, 1950.

Constant, Alphonse Louis. *The Last Incarnation*. 3rd American ed. With a Preface by Charles H. Kohlmann. Boston: Gorham, 1914.

Dostoevsky, Fyodor. *The Brothers Karamazov*. Trans. Constance Garnett. New York: Macmillan, 1912.

———. *The Idiot*. Trans. David Magarshack. Baltimore: Penguin, 1955.

Douglas, Lloyd C. *The Big Fisherman*. Boston: Houghton, Mifflin, 1948.

[Dowling, Levi H.] *The Aquarian Gospel of Jesus the Christ: the philosophic and practical basis of the Religion of the Aquarian Age of the World and of the Church Universal, transcribed from the Book of God's Remembrances, Known as the Akashic Records, by Levi*. With Introduction by Henry A. Coffeen. London: Cazenove, 1908.

Erskine, John. *The Human Life of Jesus*. New York: Morrow, 1945.

Frenssen, Gustav. *Hilligenlei*. Berlin: Grote, 1905.

Goethe, Johann Wolfgang von. *Die Leiden des jungen Werther*. In *Werke*. Ed. Erich Trunz. 3rd ed., Hamburg: Christian Wagner, 1958. Vol. vi, pp. 7-124.

———. *The Sorrows of Young Werther*. Trans. Catherine Hutter. With a Foreword by Hermann J. Weigand. New York: New American Library-Signet, 1962.

Graves, Robert. *King Jesus*. New York: Minerva Press, n.d.

Hale, Edward Everett. *If Jesus Came to Boston*. Boston: Lamson and Wolffe, 1895.

Hauptmann, Gerhart. *Der Apostel. Bahnwärter Thiel: Novellistische Studien*. Berlin: S. Fischer, 1892.

———. *Hannele: Traumdichtung in zwei Teilen*. Berlin: S. Fischer, 1894.

Herburger, Günter. *Jesus in Osaka: Zukunftsroman*. Neuwied: Luchterhand, 1970.

Hollaender, Felix. *Jesus und Judas*. Berlin: S. Fischer, 1891.

Jerome, Jerome K. *The Passing of the Third Floor Back: An Idle Fancy in a Prologue, a Play, and an Epilogue*. New York: Dodd, Mead, 1921.

Kazantzakis, Nikos. *The Last Temptation of Christ*. Trans. Peter A. Bien. New York: Simon and Schuster, 1960.

Kesey, Ken. *One Flew Over the Cuckoo's Nest*. New York: Viking, 1962.

Kretzer, Max. *Das Gesicht Christi: Roman aus dem Ende des Jahrhunderts*. Dresden: E. Pierson, 1897.

Lagerkvist, Pär. *Barabbas*. Trans. Alan Blair. With a Preface by Lucien Maury and a Letter by André Gide. New York: Random House-Modern Library, 1951.

Langguth, A. J. *Jesus Christs*. New York: Harper and Row, 1968.

Le Fort, Gertrud von. *Die Frau des Pilatus*. Wiesbaden: Insel, 1955.

Ludwig, Emil. *Der Menschensohn: Geschichte eines Propheten*. Berlin: Rowohlt, 1928.

[McCowan, Archibald.] *Christ, the Socialist*. By the author of Philip Meyer's Scheme. Boston: Arena, 1894.

Mann, Thomas. *Gesammelte Werke in zwölf Bänden*. Frankfurt am Main: S. Fischer, 1960. Vol. iii: *Der Zauberberg*. Vol. vi: *Das Leben des deutschen Tonsetzers Adrian Leverkühn erzählt von einem Freunde*.

———. *The Magic Mountain*. Trans. Helen T. Lowe-Porter. New York: Modern Library, 1955.

———. *Doctor Faustus: The Life of the German Composer Adrian Leverkühn as Told by a Friend*. Trans. Helen T. Lowe-Porter. New York: Knopf, 1948.

Melville, Hermann. *Melville's Billy Budd*. Ed. F. Barron Freeman. The Complete Text of the Novel and of the Unpublished Short Story. Cambridge, Mass.: Harvard Univ. Press, 1948.

301

Moore, George. *The Brook Kerith: A Syrian Story.* New York: Macmillan, 1916.

Nathanson, E. M. *The Latecomers.* Garden City, N. Y.: Doubleday, 1970.

Notovitch, Nicolas. *The Unknown Life of Christ.* Trans. F. Marion Crawford. New York and London: Macmillan, 1894.

Papini, Giovanni. *Storia di Cristo.* Terza edizione, corretta. Firenze: Vallecchi, 1922.

Payne, Robert. *The Shepherd.* New York: Horizon, 1959.

Pesin, Harry. *Why Is A Crooked Letter.* New York: Perspective Publications, 1969.

Planitz, Ernst von der, ed. *Der Benan-Brief.* Berlin, 1910.

Rilke, Rainer Maria. *Visions of Christ.* A Posthumous Cycle of Poems. Ed. with an Introduction by Siegfried Mandel. Trans. Aaron Kramer. Boulder: Univ. of Colorado Press, 1967.

Sheldon, Charles M. *The Heart of the World: A Story of Christian Socialism.* New York and London: Fleming H. Revell, 1905.

―――. *In His Steps: What Would Jesus Do?* New York: Grosset and Dunlap, 1935.

Silone, Ignazio. *The Seed Beneath the Snow.* Trans. Harvey Fergusson. New York: Atheneum, 1965.

Sinclair, Upton. *They Call Me Carpenter: A Tale of the Second Coming.* New York: Boni and Liveright, 1922.

Slaughter, Frank G. *The Crown and the Cross.* Cleveland and New York: World, 1959.

Stead, William T. *If Christ Came to Chicago.* Chicago: Laird and Lee, 1894.

Stendhal [Henri Beyle]. *Le rouge et le noir.* Ed. Louis Landré. With an Introduction by Paul Hazard. New York: Scribner, 1931.

Voss, Richard. *Die Erlösung: Die wundersame Geschichte eines wundersamen Menschen aus jüngster grosser Zeit.* Stuttgart: Engelhorn [1920].

Wallace, Lew. *Ben-Hur: A Tale of the Christ.* New York: Harper, 1880.

Ward, Mary Augusta [Arnold]. *Robert Elsmere, by Mrs. Humphry Ward.* Ed. with an Introduction by Clyde de L. Ryals. Lincoln, Neb.: Univ. of Nebraska Press, 1967.

Winter, Betty. *Unser Heiland ist arm geblieben.* München: Georg Müller, 1911.

Index

Christianity, 46, 48; "Celebri-
tät," 46
Goeze, Johann Melchior, 32
Goguel, Maurice, *Life of Jesus,*
31n, 38
Goodspeed, Edgar J., *Modern
Apocrypha,* 13n
Görling, Lars, 234, 234n
    491: as *Evangelium Judae,*
    232-33, 234, 238; hero as
    Jesus, 235; meaning of title,
    236-38; sardonic inversion of
    Jesus-figure, 238; compared
    with *Cat and Mouse,* 238-39;
    mentioned 226, 241, 250, 255,
    266; analysis of techniques,
    270-98 *passim*
Grant, Richard B., "The Death
of Julian Sorel," 44n
Grapes of Wrath, The, see
Steinbeck, John
Grass, Günter
    general: his religious indif-
    ference, 228, 245; *The Tin
    Drum,* 231, 239; *Local
    Anesthetic,* 248
    Cat and Mouse: 8, 226; as
    Evangelium Judae, 232-33;
    compared with *491,* 238-39;
    function of narrator, 239-42;
    Mahlke as Jesus figure, 242-45;
    myth of regeneration, 245-47;
    Pilenz as Judas, 247-50;
    255; analysis of techniques,
    270-98 *passim*
Graves, Robert, *King Jesus,* 16,
17, 33, 271, 284
Greek Passion, The, see
Kazantzakis, Nikos
Green, T. H., 40
Greene, Graham
    general: influence on Coc-
    cioli, 161; intellectual back-
    ground, 214, 226; *The Lawless
    Roads,* 161, 216; trip to
    Mexico, 216
    The Power and the Glory:
    12n, 161; compared with
    Bread and Wine and *Darkness*

at Noon, 214-15; analogical
thinking of author, 215-16;
historical background, 216-17;
"abandoned" world of, 217-18;
three encounters between
protagonists, 218-19; New
Testament parallels, 219-21;
symbolic resurrection, 222;
mentioned 242; analysis of
techniques, 270-98 *passim*
Grenzmann, Wilhelm, "Christus-
Thematik in der heutigen
Literatur," 29n
Grosz, Georg, 21
Gundert, Hermann, 151
Guthke, Karl S., *Gerhart Hauptmann,* 106n
Guttzeit, Johannes, 107

Hale, Edward Everett, *If Jesus
Came to Boston,* 20
Hall, G. Stanley, *Jesus, the
Christ, in the Light of Psy-
chology,* 29n, 102-103
Hall, Robert A., "Fogazzaro's
Maironi Tetralogy," 92n
Hamilton, Neill Q., *Jesus for a
No-God World,* 226n
harmonies of Gospels, 31
Hartlaub, Geno, interview with
Günter Grass, 228n
Hassan, Ihab, "The Existential
Novel," 228
Hauptmann, Gerhart
    general: caricatured in *The
    Magic Mountain,* 4; early
    socialist tendencies, 99-100;
    youthful religious crisis, 105-
    106; Jesus studies, 106-107;
    The Assumption of Hannele,
    19, 107; *Lonely Lives,* 55, 107,
    228; "The Apostle," 107-110,
    113, 117; autobiographical
    elements in *Emanuel Quint,*
    113; compared to Kazantzakis,
    125, 126, 128; mentioned
    94, 227, 267, 269
    *The Fool in Christ Emanuel
    Quint:* ix, 8; Christian socialist